Controlling the Weapons of War

Controlling the Weapons of War: Politics, Persuasion and the Prohibition of Inhumanity examines the ethical and intellectual issues and dilemmas associated with attempts to establish humanitarian limits on weaponry. It considers how governments, non-governmental organizations, political commentators and others have responded to the predicaments associated with imposing classifications about the relative acceptability of force. Existing texts about arms control focus on documenting prohibitions, assessing the reasons for their agreement, and appraising their prospects. While this volume examines such topics, its main preoccupation is with asking the more fundamental question of what is involved in attempts to devise and impose classifications that can serve as the basis for assessing the relative acceptability of the use of force. In taking this step back from most analyses it reinterprets many of the conventional approaches to studying arms control. It develops these issues through combining multi-disciplinary theoretical analysis with varied cases of prohibitions on 'conventional' and 'unconventional' weapons (e.g. biological weapons, landmines, nuclear weapons) through customary and statutory law, multilateral treaties, UN resolutions and national legislation.

This book will appeal to students of security studies, military technology, peace studies, international relations and discourse theory.

Brian Rappert is a Reader in the Department of Sociology at the University of Exeter, UK. He has produced numerous articles about the management of controversial technologies and is the author of *Non-Lethal Weapons as Legitimizing Forces?* and co-editor of *Contested Futures*.

Contemporary Security Studies

Controlling the Weapons of War

Politics, Persuasion and the Prohibition of Inhumanity

Brian Rappert

Routledge
Taylor & Francis Group

LONDON AND NEW YORK

First published 2006
by Routledge
4 Park Square, Milton Park, Abingdon, Oxon OX14 4RN
605 Third Avenue, New York, NY 10017

First issued in paperback 2013

Routledge is an imprint of the Taylor & Francis Group, an informa business

British Library Cataloguing in Publication Data
A catalogue record for this book is available
from the British Library

Library of Congress Cataloging in Publication Data
Rappert, Brian.
      Controlling the weapons of war : politics, persuasion, and
   the prohibition of inhumanity / Brian Rappert. – 1st ed.
         p. cm. – (Contemporary security studies)
      Includes bibliographical references and index.
      1. Arms control. 2. Military weapons. I. Title. II. Cass
contemporary security studies series

   JZ5625.R37 2005
   327.1'74–dc22   2005020200

ISBN 13: 978-0-415-38667-8 (hbk)
ISBN 13: 978-0-415-64701-4 (pbk)

Contents

Illustrations

Boxes

Tables

Acknowledgements

This book was only made possible by the generous assistance of many individuals and organizations. In particular, for their comments, criticisms and encouragement I would like to thank Brian Balmer, Barry Barnes, Malcolm Dando, Nick Lee, Les Levidow, Michael Lynch, Brian Martin, Richard Moyes, Birgitte Munch, Graham Pearson, Nigel Pleasants, Steve Woolgar and not least Steve Wright who has played no small part in encouraging me down my current research path. Stuart Croft, Jeanne Guillemin and an anonymous referee provided many helpful comments on the first draft of this manuscript. Presentations based on themes in the book were presented at the University of Amsterdam, the University of Barcelona, the University of Nottingham, The University of Exeter and the University of Oxford.

Several groups and organizations stand out for mention. Current and former colleagues at the Department of Sociology at the University of Exeter provided a productive intellectual space for writing. I am indebted to the members of the Amnesty International (UK) Working Group on the Arms and Security Trade who were willing to allow me to enter as a novice into the group so many years ago. Through this membership I was able to meet and learn from many others concerned with the darker aspects of human behaviour addressed in this book, not least those in the Omega Foundation. Their continuing work in exposing state hypocrisy has always been a source of inspiration. Likewise my more recent exchanges with those in the Cluster Munition Coalition have enriched my thinking in many ways. Parts of this book have been reprinted by permission of Sage Publications Ltd from Brian Rappert. 2005. 'Prohibitions, Weapons, and Controversy', *Social Studies of Science*, 35(2): 211–40 (© Sage publications, 2005). The research undertaken in the course of writing this book was funded, in part, by the UK Economic and Social Research Council (ESRC) New Security Challenges Program (RES-223-25-0053).

Abbreviations

AI	Amnesty International
APM	Anti-Personnel Mines
BAe	British Aerospace System
BTWC	Biological and Toxin Weapons Convention
BW	Biological Warfare
CCW	Certain Conventional Weapons Convention
CW	Chemical Warfare
CWC	Chemical Weapons Convention
DIA	Defense Intelligence Agency
DoD	Department of Defense (US)
ERW	Explosive Remnants of War
EU	European Union
HRW	Human Rights Watch
HUD	Head Up Display
ICJ	International Court of Justice
ICRC	International Committee of the Red Cross
IDF	Israeli Defense Agency
IHL	International Humanitarian Law
ISG	Iraqi Survey Group
JNLW	Joint Non-Lethal Weapons (Program or Directorate)
MAC	Mines Action Canada
MoD	Ministry of Defence (UK)
MP	Member of Parliament
NATO	North Atlantic Treaty Organization
NGO	Non-governmental Organization
NPT	Treaty on the Non-proliferation of Nuclear Weapons
R&D	Research and Development
UK	United Kingdom
UN	United Nations

UNMOVIC	United Nations Monitoring, Verification and Inspection Commission
US	United States of America
UXO	Unexploded Ordnance
WMD	Weapons of Mass Destruction

Part I

This happening world

Chapter 1

The chains that bind?

Throughout history, technology has been instrumental in the undertaking of violent acts. Perhaps as with no other area of technical development, weaponry makes explicit the potential for innovations to serve destructive ends. With the development of new destructive capabilities have come attempts to establish and enforce agreements that certain acts are wholly inappropriate – that is, they lay outside the realm of the necessary, just or civil. Establishing such accords entails surveying across the landscape of injuries and deaths inflicted in conflict in order to offer some general account of what is acceptable and what is not.

With varying degrees of success, in the past attempts have been made to signal out crossbows, firearms and poisons as deplorable options.[1] At the start of the twenty-first century, through their actions and statements, many governments have reinforced long standing claims made by a wide range of social groups that chemical and biological weapons are abhorrent and unacceptable. That some might use, proliferate, possess or be suspected of possessing such indiscriminate and deadly 'weapons of mass destruction' (WMD) can, at least on some occasions, lead to a significant response in the international community of states.

Although typically topics of less high profile media coverage, in recent years non-governmental organizations (NGOs) have led efforts to halt or curtail the spread of landmines, small arms, cluster bombs and other weaponry. A plethora of sometimes complementary, sometimes conflicting formal and informal means – international treaties, humanitarian law, customary law, rules of engagement, codes of conduct – have been employed to delineate the rights and wrongs with force. Government officials deciding on the suitability of arms exports, NGOs campaigning for the end to state practices or diplomats formulating international arms control treaties do so through making determinations about the relative acceptability of the development, deployment or use of weaponry.

Existing international and national prohibitions identify various topics for concern: the types of weapons developed, their purpose, who uses them and in what circumstances, who suffers from them or other consequences of their use. Alternative determinations of what is the primary source of concern justify alternative assessments of what needs to be done. In practice, agreement on the 'it' or 'its' that should be the centre of attention often proves elusive. Many may agree on the need to control 'WMD', but what that should mean by way of specifics does not follow on in some straightforward fashion. Despite the often expressed condemnation of this category of weaponry in political debate, there is arguably little interest today among nuclear nations in abolishing all such weapons, specifically the nuclear ones. In addition, while limiting who possesses chemical, biological or nuclear weapons is a matter of focused international attention; attempts to establish prohibitions are confounded by disagreement about what 'having' these weapons means in the first place. Should the desire to control only require action in addressing the actual possession of weapons, the believed intention of acquiring them or the potential capability to do so? As well, the recurring interest in countries such as the US and the Russian Federation into developing 'tactical' (low yield) nuclear weapons and incapacitating biochemical agents indicate the potential importance of circumstantial and consequential considerations in determinations of the rights and wrongs of chemical, biological and nuclear weapons.

This book examines attempts to limit, regulate and outlaw the development and use of weaponry in relation to humanitarian concerns; or just how it is possible to set the 'limits at which the necessities of war ought to yield to the requirements of humanity' to quote from the ground breaking 1868 Declaration of St. Petersburg. It considers the challenges of cutting through complex and often contested situations in order to offer appraisals of what prohibitions are prudent and workable. It asks what is at stake in how determinations are made about what constitutes 'appropriate' or 'inappropriate' technologies of violence. On what basis then, do individuals identify particular forms of inflicting death and injury as unacceptable whereas others are deemed permissible or at least tolerable? Determinations of the acceptability of force and thus the need for prohibitions are not commonly conceived across the globe or invariant over time, but rather topics of dispute and reappraisal.

Stated in somewhat different terms, this book searches for meaning about the acceptability of force and technology – how problems are identified and how evaluations are negotiated. It considers how classifications are marshalled to impose an understanding on controversial events so as to suggest what should be done and when enough has been done. Just how determinations are made of what is really taking place and why are matters of some importance that arguably raise highly problematic empirical and ethical questions. As contended here, discussions about the merits of force and the prohibition of weapons are characterized by a complex inter-play between moments of treating the world as fixed, determinate, and known and alternatively treating it as fluid, indeterminate and unknown. While attempts to capture some definitive understanding of what is taking place and why that might underpin control measures are ever elusive, attempts to devise prohibitions necessitate trying to do just that.

As argued, the fundamental and (in many respects) inescapable disagreements and controversies associated with specifying the acceptability of weaponry should serve to alert us to the pervasive problems associated with the very analysis of this topic. So, as this book considers contentions with devising and enforcing prohibitions, it seeks to work out something the problems of associated with analysing the acceptability of force. In doing so, it scrutinizes how descriptions, evidence and arguments are employed to justify conclusions about the appropriateness of weaponry and equipment.

Overall, this book seeks to bring the study of arms control up to date theoretically and empirically. In doing so it addresses varied substantive, conceptual and practical issues associated with establishing and policing ethical limits on technology.

The meaning of metal

As a starting point into the wide ranging analysis that follows, the remainder of this chapter considers disputes about the humanitarian acceptability of so-called 'leg-irons'. As will be elaborated in later chapters, debates about the appropriateness of the development or employment of certain weapons often involves weighing complicated evidential claims in circumstances where uncertainties are rife. As opposed to the complexity of modern high-tech weapons, restraint technology such as handcuffs and leg cuffs consist of little more than the cuff 'bracelets' themselves and linking devices. Used by incarceration centres, police agencies, military forces and paramilitary organizations across the world for centuries, the case of physical restraint equipment would seem to be a straightforward area for devising and implementing controls. Briefly considering why this is not the case and why the very analysis of debates about restraint technologies should not be taken as straightforward will indicate something of the themes elaborated in later chapters.

Shortly after coming into political office, as part of its promise to bring an ethical dimension to the UK's foreign policy, in July 1997 the British Labour Government announced that it 'would take the necessary measures to prevent the export or transhipment from the UK' of various equipment designed primarily for torture and cruel, inhuman or degrading treatment; this including 'leg-irons, gang-chains, shackles – excluding normal handcuffs – and electric-shock belts designed for the restraint of a human being'. The statement set out an official classification of what various forms of leg restraints were primarily for (i.e. torture or other forms of cruel treatment) and thus their offensiveness. Since that time the UK has publicly supported a similar classification be adopted by European Union (EU) under its Code of Conduct on Arms Exports.

Concern about the need for prohibitions on the export of leg-irons (sometimes called leg cuffs) did not begin or end with the 1997 statement. In a 1992 publication entitled *Repression Trade (UK): How the UK Makes Torture and Death its Business*,[2] the human rights group Amnesty International (AI) provided an account of its previous encounters with restraint controls. As told therein, in 1983 two reporters from the newspaper the *Daily Mirror* were offered a supply of leg-irons from the company Hiatts based in Birmingham, England. Citing evidence regarding abuses committed with leg-irons and their medical effects, AI led a campaign against their export. In March 1984, the then Conservative government announced that 'Licences will not be issued for the export to any destination of leg-irons, shackles and gang-chains for the restraint of prisoners.'[3]

Just what the phrase 'leg-irons, shackles and gang-chains' meant came under question in 1991 when undercover human rights workers attending the Covert and Operational Procurement Exhibition (London) obtained a brochure for leg cuffs through a US company called Hiatt Thompson. Hiatt Thompson was formed in 1985 through a joint venture by Hiatts of England and the US Thompson Corporation. The brochure indicated the materials had been manufactured in Birmingham, England.

In an attempt to explain how British manufactured components were still appearing in prohibited leg cuffs, on 17 October 1991 the Secretary of State for Trade and Industry Tim Sainsbury announced: 'The export of leg irons, shackles – excluding handcuffs – and gang chains is subject to control under the Export of Goods (Control) Order 1989 and requires an export licence from my Department.' The Secretary explained that while no export licences had been granted for 'leg-irons' in recent years, licences had been 'issued for "oversized handcuffs" and linking chains'.[4] The potential for evading export controls for 'leg cuffs' through shipping their individual component parts (labelled as 'oversized handcuffs') lead to an official redefinition of the term 'handcuff'. Secretary Sainsbury declared that in the future, for the purposes of export controls, handcuffs would be defined as restraints where 'the maximum length of two cuffs and connecting chain [is] 240 mm. This standard would bring "oversized handcuffs" under control. The only United Kingdom exporter is being advised.'

AI later reported the spirit of the export regulations were violated in 1995 when journalists bought Hiatt leg cuffs in the US. In this case, 'It would seem that Hiatts had been exporting oversized handcuffs to a US company called Hiatt Thompson, where longer chains were added to turn them into leg cuffs, whose sale and export is still legal in the United States.'[5]

Just as what separates a 'leg cuff' from a 'handcuff' has been a topic of disagreement, so too has the desirability of prohibiting the former. Both the 1997 Labour government policy and AI's position condemning leg cuffs are bound up with their classification as tools for torture or cruel treatment. In 1992, for instance, AI called for a prohibition on the manufacture of equipment that can only be used 'for torture or other cruel, inhuman, or degrading treatment or punishment of prisoners', this including 'leg-irons and gang chains'.[6] Cited as part of the case for this, the organization argued, 'Leg-irons are designed to restrict severely the movement of prisoners. Their use is specifically prohibited by Rule 33 of the 1955 United Nations' Standard Minimum Rules for the Treatment of Prisoners.'[7] This rule states 'Instruments of restraint, such as handcuffs, chains, irons and strait-jackets, shall never be applied as a punishment. Furthermore, chains or irons shall not be used as restraints.'[8] AI's condemnation of leg cuffs was also supported by numerous accounts of how the equipment had been used and to what results. To cite just one account:

> Leg-irons are designed to severely restrict a prisoner's movement, making the wearer unstable and liable to overbalance, and often causing chafing of the skin. Welts and sores appear on the ankles of prisoners restrained in leg-irons after approximately 24 hours. They can also be used to facilitate torture.
> Patrick Foster witnessed fellow prisoners hung upside down by the leg-irons they were wearing and beaten [in Saudi Arabia]. Orton Chirwa [of Malawi] was handcuffed, leg-ironed and held in a squatting position by a metal bar behind his knees for two days and nights. Sipho Pityana, a former prisoner in South Africa described how leg-irons were used to torture him: *'They tied electric wires on the irons... so the iron was a contact between the flesh and the electric device.'* Sipho also described how his captors used the leg-irons to hold him upside down in the sea for long periods of time.[9]

That such practices should lead to categorical condemnations of leg cuffs has not been shared everywhere. In contrast to outlawing a whole class of technology, security agencies in countries such as the US have sought to adopt guidelines for how leg restraints ought to be used in order to minimize any potential for serious harm or misuse. The use of leg restraints on prisoners is fairly widespread in domestic incarnation settings and they have also figured into high profile military operations including the imprisonment of detainees in Camp X-Ray at Guantanamo Bay.[10] Such policies seek to make a legitimate place for leg-irons by shifting the focus from leg cuffs themselves to how they are used and by whom. Herein categorical condemnations misconstrue the source of any problems. How can a whole class of technology (so ubiquitous in the US) be ruled out?

The potential for legitimate practices with leg-irons is at least acknowledged in the 1955 United Nations' Standard Minimum Rules for the Treatment of Prisoners.[11] While (as noted by AI) Rule 33 specifies irons should not be used as restraints, all of the UN recommendations are prefaced with the qualification that:

> the rules cover a field in which thought is constantly developing. They are not intended to preclude experiment and practices, provided these are in harmony with the principles and seek to further the purposes which derive from the text of the rules as a whole. It will always be justifiable for the central prison administration to authorize departures from the rules in this spirit.

Just what counts as 'in harmony' with the principles expressed in the rules 'as a whole' is a key question.

Returning to the 1997 Labour government policy announcement, disputes similar to those surrounding the meaning of leg cuffs that preceded the announcement subsequently followed it. In November 1999, the newspaper *The Independent* reported that two of its journalists purchased Hiatt Thompson leg-irons in the US with 'Made in England' engraved on the cuffs and the Birmingham-based Hiatt's address printed on the box.[12] Chuck Thompson of Hiatt Thompson reportedly said such restraints were needed for criminals and others in the US because 'Their guys are big animals. They do more kicking now because they watch all this Bruce Lee fist fighting'. When asked to explain how such UK-made products were still available for sale, Mr Thompson said the cuffs for the leg-irons 'must have been old stock from the early 1980s'. This contention was challenged by the British Member of Parliament (MP) David Chidgey during a House of Commons meeting when he stated the leg cuffs and chains in question 'were bright, shiny and seemingly new'. Furthermore, added Chidgey:

> When Hiatt-Thompson, of the United States, was challenged on the manacles and chains, it claimed that they were made at its own premises, which turn out to be a warehouse that is barely the size of the average high-street shop. Thus a British company seems to be manufacturing components of banned instruments and implements of torture – oversized cuffs and separate chains – which, subsequently, are assembled overseas. Moreover, the practice is perfectly legal under current legislation. Customs and Excise officers have seen components in packing cases, but are powerless to intervene in their export.[13]

On 11 February 2000 the government Minister Peter Hain gave a Parliamentary statement maintaining that:

> During the course of our investigations into the allegations in *The Independent* newspaper on 16 November that UK-made leg-irons were on sale in the US, we... found no evidence that there had been a breach of the ban on the export of leg-irons.[14]

Echoing Hiatt Thompson's contention, Minister Hain said it appeared 'likely' the leg-irons were produced from old stock. He went on to say:

> We are also satisfied that the leg-irons mentioned in *The Independent* articles were not manufactured using oversized individual cuffs exported without a licence from the UK. Although we have no evidence to suggest that such single cuffs have ever been exported, there is a hypothetical loophole and amending legislation to extend controls to cover large individual cuffs is in preparation.

In July 2000 the UK government announced that all cuffs with an internal diameter greater than 52 mm would require a licence.

Related allegations about of the failure of British arms export policies were made in September 2000 when the newspaper *The Guardian* reported that a British company was willing to supply 'barbaric torture equipment' such as leg-irons to Rwanda where this equipment had been used in the past by military officers in acts of torture.[15] In this case, the export controls were reportedly to be evaded through brokering the equipment to Rwanda by the Spanish firm Larrañaga y Elorza.[16]

Attention returned to Hiatts of England again in late 2002 when the Birmingham newspaper the *Sunday Mercury* printed a story with the head caption 'Exporters of Torture'.[17] A journalist from the *Sunday Mercury* bought a pair of leg cuffs from the US, compared them to over-sized 'Big Brutus' handcuffs made in England and concluded the cuffs were identical, with only the length of link chain separating the handcuffs from the leg cuffs. A spokesperson from AI was quoted as saying:

> There are serious concerns that loopholes in the licensing system are allowing companies in Britain to export equipment that, once assembled overseas, can be used as leg-cuffs, manacles and other restraint devices frequently used by unscrupulous governments to inflict suffering. This type of medieval metalwork would not be allowed for export from the UK. Why is it apparently permissible for a British company to supply the key components of the products to its US distributor?

In 2003 as part of the hearings of the House of Commons Committees on Strategic Export Controls – a body set up by the Labour government to provide parliamentary oversight of its export decisions – some of the questions surrounding over-sized handcuffs and leg cuffs were put to government officials. In an exchange that evokes images of an export system simultaneously transparent and non-transparent as well as functioning and dysfunctional, David Chidgey MP and Tim Dowse (Head of the Non-Proliferation Department of the UK Foreign and Commonwealth Office) debated the merits of licences to various countries which the government asked to be unidentified in the public record:

DAVID CHIDGEY: ...in a further memorandum to the Committee the Government says that 'Handcuffs were licensed for export to reputable organisations akin to' our own UK Prison Service, for example, in Canada, New Zealand, Australia and America. They were 'for use either in escorting or transporting prisoners. There was no clear risk of use for internal repression in any of these cases. Handcuffs licensed to the *** were also for use in escorting prisoners'. I want to ask you...was there a clear risk of use for internal repression in the case of the handcuffs permitted for export to ***?

TIM DOWSE: I think that in terms of the licences that you are referring to – and we approved one and I think refused two – the cases involved different types of handcuffs in each case. To run through them, in the case of licence 28374, which we approved, the goods involved were normal over-sized handcuffs. We did not believe that there was a clear risk that the *** would use them in any way other than as over-sized handcuffs. In the case of licence 17084, ***.

We have no particular grounds for concern that the *** would misuse the equipment, but we did nevertheless judge that there was a clear risk that it could clearly easily be disassembled and reassembled in the form of leg-irons and therefore was covered by the scope of our export ban. A similar consideration was applied in the case of licence 21003. So I think it is an example, if you like, of the really rather detailed care that we do give in assessing individual licences case by case.

DAVID CHIDGEY: I will shorten this, but I would just make the point that the concern that we have is that the export licence that was granted was granted to escort handcuffs that in fact could be converted to shackles or leg-irons by virtue of a steel chain. I just make the point, rather than ask for an answer. There is a further point, if I may very quickly. This again refers to a specified end-use of a licence issued for the export of over-sized *** handcuffs which were the same mark and model as you have just referred to from ***. This was to ***. According to their own directives, leg-irons must be used for all inmates deemed to be a security risk and so on, but in this specification at their own direction they are saying that '*** cuffs shall be used'. The end-user of the over-sized handcuffs licensed for export to *** requires the use of leg-irons whenever a prisoner is deemed a security risk. My concern, and the Committee's concern, is that in this case, where they prescribed that this should be used, they are actually specifying that they should use *** cuffs with 'minimum one arm and one leg cuffed to secured bed or examining table'. So what we are really seeking is, what assurances has the Government received that the *** cuffs licensed for export to the *** will not be used as shackles or leg-irons? How can we have any confidence about that, when they are actually specifying how they should be used?

TIM DOWSE: The short answer is that we did not seek assurances. When the assessment of the risk was made, we judged that we had no end-user concerns. We will obviously be interested in any information you can pass to us.

While the Committees on Strategic Export Controls noted in its report following the hearing that they 'would not expect oversized handcuffs to be the Government's top priority among military exports of potential concern'[18] they criticized a number of 'administrative failures', including the handcuff cases alluded to in the previous quote. Nevertheless, the Committees concluded that overall the

> export control system usually – eventually – produces the right results... The Government deserves praise for the transparency that it has brought to its operation of strategic export controls and to the policy refinements it has introduced. But a little information can be more frustrating than none at all.

The preceding text indicates something of dispute about the rights and wrongs of restraint technologies and what should be done about them. Various sources of concern have been singled out – the entire class of leg cuff technology, the rules in place for their use, the 'big animals' they are used on and the potential for restraints to be disassembled and reassembled. The repeated introduction of controls for leg cuffs has been followed by questions about whether these measures are prudent or being adhered to. At this early stage in the book, let me suggest a few preliminary observations regarding what the case of leg restraints might suggest about prohibitions.

First, the idea that concerns about the rigor of export controls will be resolved through the next tightening up of export controls is questionable. Categories and rules about even the simplest of technologies are not merely applied, but interpreted and negotiated. What differentiates leg cuffs from handcuffs, handcuffs from oversized cuffs and even 'normal over-sized handcuffs' from presumably un-normal over-sized cuffs has not been something spelled at one time for all times. Rather, for the purposes of export controls such distinctions have been remoulded and reconfigured in response to criticisms of practices. With further events or technical developments, the existing understanding of categories will again be re-worked.

Along these lines, for instance, following various controversies about the role of its Member States' exports in human rights abuses, the European Parliament has called for the European Community to both place a '*ban* on the promotion, trade and export of police and security equipment whose use is inherently cruel, inhuman or degrading, including *leg-irons*, electroshock stun-belts and inherently painful devices such as serrated thumb cuffs' and '*suspend* the transfer of equipment where its use in practice has revealed a substantial risk of abuse or unwarranted injury, such as *leg-cuffs*, shackle boards, restraint chairs and pepper gas weapons' (emphases added).[19] This parliamentary 'resolution' aims to make a division between leg-irons which are deemed intolerable outright and leg cuffs whose acceptability depends on how they are used. In doing so it challenges the British government totalizing categorization that all leg restraints are primarily for torture and cruel, inhuman or degrading treatment. With the European Parliament's distinction, current or future plastic or Velcro-based leg restraints, for instance, might count as 'cuffs' rather than 'irons'. Yet, on just what basis leg-irons should be distinguished from leg cuffs is not specified in the resolution. The distinction has played no part in the implementation of British controls. Should such a division be made though, there seems enough historical precedent for safely assuming its meaning would be matter of imaginative argumentation.

As a second observation, discussions about the adequacy of prohibitions cannot be separated from questions about who is able to comment about such measures. Not every thing – classification, export decision, use of force, etc. – that is contestable is contested in practice. As suggested earlier, despite repeated claims by governmental representatives that certain exports are prevented, holes in legislation are being plugged, and that proper licensing decisions are being made, through campaigning and investigative activities, outsiders to the corridors of power have challenged such optimistic appraisals. Had it not been for such efforts it seems doubtful that successive British governments would have revised exports control classifications in the manner they did. While the text here would suggest that intense and wide ranging media scrutiny has been cast on British exports, this is an artefact of the specific argument made. All of the newspaper stories cited, at least in large part, derive from the behind the scenes primary investigative work of one small and precariously funded research organization based in England. This situation would suggest some caution in speaking about the adequacies and inadequacies of prohibitions. What is known, what is debated, what is considered to be the state of world is a function of who is in a position to know and say.

Third and related to this, whether the failures of export controls suggested earlier should be taken as justifying a sceptical or cynical orientation to official statements is a topic of some importance. Yet, any assessment of this will no doubt depend on evaluations made of a range of other issues. For instance, the proposed continuing deficiencies associated with regulating restraints could be taken as indicating an inability or unwillingness of governments to act in a manner consistent with their stated principles. To the proposal that the granting of questioned licences proves the UK exports system is in 'shambles', government officials would likely respond as UK Foreign Secretary Jack Straw did respond when this was put to him:

> Hang on... I do not accept that for a second. There may be discrepancies sometimes, but this is a very carefully administered system, all right, and I do not think that kind of description is at all justified. It is a complex system, complex because Parliament, quite properly, required that it should be thorough.[20]

Rather than being contingent matters of priority and purpose, however regrettable, dubious export licences are presented as inevitable lapses due to the complications of the matters at hand. Whether or not such licences should be understood as unavoidable or not depends on assessments of the practical ability of officials to scrutinize export applications.

Likewise, assessments of whether the continuing deficiencies of export policy in relation to restraint exports reflect some unwillingness of governmental officials to act in a manner consistent with their stated principles can depend on what is taken as a relevant context for making judgements. It is in relation to some sense of context that particular decisions are given their meaning. So while noting various 'discrepancies' or 'administrative failures' of exports controls, the Committees on Strategic Export Controls nevertheless gave the Labour government an overall positive evaluation citing the initiatives it had undertaken to improve decision making transparency – not least the establishment of the Committees on Strategic Export Controls. As noted earlier, that the Committees did not think leg restraints would be 'the Government's top priority among military exports' is another way of minimizing the relevancy of certain dubious transfers. Instead of focusing on these procedural changes, those that doubt the sincerity of government policy in the area of leg restraints have done so by situating it to a string of other questionable past transfers.[21] Instead of praising the Labour government for making improvements in export transparency (save for a discussion of *** country and ***cuffs as illustrated earlier), it could be criticized for failing to take other steps such as prohibiting the manufacture (rather than merely the export) of cuffs that are incorporated into leg cuffs. The set of contested relevance forwarded is central to alternative justifications for what has happened and why, and thereby what if anything is required in terms of further action.

Restricting a discussion of the difficulties associated with giving meaning to decisions about exports as done in the last few paragraphs arguably provides a fairly limited analysis. If a 'little information can be more frustrating than none at all' for committees scrutinizing export decisions then the same could be said for those reading case studies of prohibitions. The analysis presented in this chapter can be questioned in the same way accounts given by human rights groups or Parliamentary committees were questioned earlier. Nothing like a full and comprehensive historical analysis has (or indeed could) been given of prohibitions for leg restraints in the UK; not least because what should be taken as relevant to such a discussion is itself debated and part of justifying what appraisal should be given of the situation. This condition poses significant questions for the import and purpose of analysis, issues that deserve considered attention.

Chapter 2

Striving for order

One should not understand this compulsion to construct concepts, species, forms, purposes, laws... as if they enabled us to fix the real world; but as a compulsion to arrange a world for ourselves in which our existence is made possible... The world seems logical to us because we have made it logical.

(Friedrich Nietzsche[1])

The example of physical restraints in Chapter 1 illustrates something of the negotiation over the meaning and import of national legislation and international agreements regarding the permissibility of technology. In these negotiations a sense of the core problem (if there was any) with such equipment was identified in order to suggest what needed to be done and when enough had been done. In a similar fashion, other prohibitions attempt to locate the source of the problem with weaponry and force in order to justify a particular course of action. Agreements limiting the means of conflict such as the 1868 Declaration of St. Petersburg, the 1925 Protocol for the Prohibition of Asphyxiating, Poisonous or Other Gases, and of Bacteriological Methods of Warfare, the four Geneva Conventions, the 1972 Biological and Toxin Weapons Convention (BTWC), or the UN Convention on Certain Conventional Weapons (CCW) similarly attempt to secure agreement about the principal aspect of concern associated with an area of weaponry or equipment – whether that be their effects, how many there are, how they are used, in what situations, etc.

Such agreements offer a way of classifying equipment and practices so as to justify a particular course of action. Stated differently, the search for prohibitions is an effort to make sense of the world, to impose a sense of order on it. In an abstract and initial form, we can treat humanitarian prohibitions as taking the structure of the proposition 'X should Y because Z', wherein for leg restraints the

Xs, Ys and Zs filled in might include:

X	Y	Z
Leg restraints	Stop being exported	They are technologies of torture
Leg-irons	Stop being manufactured	They are widely misused by
Leg cuffs	Be used according	unscrupulous security forces
(Normal) over-sized	to strict guidelines	Manufacturers keep subverting the
handcuffs	Be actively promoted	spirit of government legislation
Handcuffs		They are valuable tools in the
		fight against...

While not all the combinations of the its, whats and whys listed here might make sense together, a number can be found in present debates about restraints. To forward a particular combination is to seek to include and exclude certain practices and technologies in and from evaluation. Imposing order – fixing the world – through boxing it up along distinctions by identifying an X, Y and Z enables individuals to 'know how to go on'.[2] The world becomes divided into distinct categories (e.g. leg-cuffs, over-sized handcuffs) and individual items are assigned to these categories (e.g. this model is a normal over-sized handcuffs whereas that is not) which then enables some evaluation (e.g. all factors considered this licence for mere restraints should be approved whereas this one for torture technology should not).

As suggested in Chapter 1, even for the seemingly simplest piece of equipment, box classifications often fail to provide a solid or lasting foundation for dividing and defining the issues at stake. Order must be imposed, not found. In practice, just what is meant by the term 'leg-iron' is not as self-evident as it may appear at first glance and just what needs to be done does not follow in any straightforward way from the reading of government declarations. The boundaries, lines, stipulations and definitions set out in prohibitions are never foolproof, but constantly open to re-interpretation. What, if anything, distinguishes defensive from offensive activities, primary from secondary effects, components from whole technologies, anti-personnel from anti-materiel weapons, intended from unintended consequences as well as research from development are in potential, if not in practice, matters of dispute, but also central to the functioning of current international prohibitions.

Moreover, classification schemes are often explicitly recognized as qualified and conditional and in need of being made relevant. As mentioned before, the UN Standard Minimum Rules for the Treatment of Prisoners states that 'irons' should not be used as restraints. This statement – like all the others rules of the UN Standard Minimum Rules – however, is itself qualified by the stipulation that the limits set are not meant to 'preclude experiment and practices' that might depart from individual rules. As will be argued in this book, the inclusion of such qualifications is a pervasive feature of formal limits on the means on force. Commenting on the general ability of weapons to lead to unacceptable outcomes requires abstracting beyond particular instances by grouping identified 'objects' or 'events' together in order to grasp what is common between them. Attempts to do so are open to question by pointing out the diversity of things brought together. Thus prohibition suggestions often take the form of the proposition that 'X should Y because Z, unless 1, 2 or 3, minding a, b and c and for cases i and ii'.

To cite a rather different example from that of leg restraints, on 8 July 1996 the International Court of Justice (ICJ) issued an Advisory Opinion regarding the legality of the threat and use of nuclear weapons. The ruling represented the first time such a major tribunal directly addressed the dangers and thereby the legality of nuclear weapons. While stating the threat or use of nuclear weapons 'would generally be contrary to the rule of international law' because such instruments would result in unnecessary suffering by combatants and indiscriminate harm to civilians, in the end the conclusion arrived at was that 'the Court is led to observe that it cannot reach a definitive conclusion as to the legality or illegality of the use of nuclear weapons by a State in an extreme circumstance of self-defence, in which its very survival would be at stake.'[3] Countries such as the UK argued against the contention that nuclear weapons *per se* could never be compatible with the principles of humanitarian law in suggesting:

> The reality ... is that nuclear weapons might be used in a wide variety of circumstances with very different results in terms of likely civilian casualties. In some cases, such as the use of a low yield nuclear weapon against war-ships on the High Seas or troops in sparsely populated areas, it is possible to envisage a nuclear attack which caused comparatively few civilian casualties. It is by no means the case that every use of nuclear weapons against a military objective would inevitably cause very great collateral civilian casualties.[4]

As expressed here, not all nuclear weapons or uses of them should be tarred with the same brush. Thus the UK government takes the rather curious position of cat-egorically condemning leg-irons whereas the acceptability of nuclear weapons depends on a weighing of circumstantial and consequential considerations. The decision by the ICJ is considered in more detail in Chapter 7. For now let me remark that the Court ruling, in significant respects, is a decision not to decide. As with other areas, general and sweeping classifications and evaluations of weapons (e.g. nuclear weapons are indiscriminate, leg-irons are torture technolo-gies, chemical weapons are abhorrent) can and are actively challenged by citing various 'ifs' and 'buts'.

In *Modernity and Ambivalence* the sociologist Zygmunt Bauman examined the ethical and intellectual problems of naming and classifying phenomenon.[5] As he argues, the desire to impose classifications on the world is pervasive in contemporary political and intellectual life. We regularly seek an ordered understanding of events. Yet, the quest for some final order is ever elusive. Our language and concepts repeatedly fail to capture a lasting way of understanding what is going on. They are too rigid, too limited, too sanitized to keep up with a messy world. Bauman argues, invariably the

> operation of inclusion/exclusion [in classifications] is an act of violence perpetrated upon the world, and requires the support of a certain amount of coercion. It can hold as long as the volume of the applied coercion remains adequate to the task of outbalancing the extent of created discrepancy.[6]

The failure of classifications creates a reaction of ambivalence, one that leads to a restless and ceaseless desire to find ever more precise and exacting ways of naming and classifying which will likewise prove inadequate and then spark a search for further ways of naming and classifying, etc. in a never ending search for final meaning.

In this book my central concern is how classifications are imposed on the world with the aim of suggesting what need to be done by way of arms prohibitions. In other words, it takes as its focus the imposition of certain forms of symbolic coercion to prevent certain acts of physical coercion. It seeks to understand how necessarily selective and particular characterizations are offered and by who as well as how they are challenged and by who. Establishing credible characterizations of the acceptability of weaponry is often bound up with specifying essences, that is, settling just what a technology really is, what it is for and what it does.[7] As will be elaborated, how this is done is always in principle open to question. Yet, whatever the widely acknowledged fragility and contestability of particular determinations of the acceptability of weaponry, attempts to establish prohibitions entail efforts to do just that.

In contrast with Bauman, however, this book does not suggest that the ambivalences of naming and classifying are always treated by individuals as problems needing to be resolved. Rather, it considers how in offering prohibitions, individuals and organizations manage the difficulties associated with specifying what must be done, this by both embracing and distancing themselves from the problems associated with classification. A focus runs throughout this book on the highly significant movement back and forth between the ordered and disordered, the named and nameless as well as the established and unknown.

Hesitations, actions, doubts and convictions

> This trying to say what's an acceptable way to kill people, it's nonsense.
> (Remark to the author by veteran campaigner against
> anti-personnel mines at conference entitled *Cluster
> Bombs: Effective Tools or Humanitarian Foe?* (2003))

The previous argument suggested something of the difficulty of specifying the acceptability of weaponry for the purpose of devising prohibitions. Barring a pacifist rejection of the importance of the issue, trying to establish clear rationales for what weapons might be more or less acceptable is not straightforward. What makes killing and maiming by one method any worse than another? Why, for instance, should chemical weapons be labelled as weapons of mass destruction (WMD) and deemed abhorrent when conventional explosives under certain conditions may cause much greater harm? At a basic level, is not there something slightly perverse about analyses that try and establish what means of killing and maiming are more acceptable than others anyway? That the British government condemns the export of leg-irons to any destination while at the same time makes a space for the appropriateness of the use of nuclear weapons indicates something of the peculiar moral calculus at work in arms controls.

We can further develop an initial sense of the precariousness of the classifications and definitions set out in formal agreements in considering some of the ethical issues identified with them. Yves Sandoz, writing as Director for Principles, Law and Relations at the International Committee of the Red Cross (ICRC), identified one major problem in proposing 'humanitarian standards applicable to armed conflict: the stumbling-block of public incomprehension. Why seek to humanize war rather than work for its prohibition?'[8] As an organization that has been a key guardian of international humanitarian law, throughout its history the ICRC has had to counter claims that it gives war a greater legitimacy by 'humanizing' it.[9] As argued by Sandoz, while it is important to seek a world in which there is no place for war,

> building this new world will take time and that the need for it will not prevent the proliferation of particularly disastrous conflicts. It is therefore essential to pursue this goal while at the same time continuing to seek ways of limiting suffering caused by war, to develop humanitarian standards applicable to armed conflict, and, above all, to make these standards known, accepted, and respected.[10]

While debates about weapon prohibitions involve a complex balance between 'humanitarian' and 'military' requirements, he argues it is necessary to struggle for the development of standards. This is not a matter ' "set apart" from more fundamental issues, but has potentially a considerable impact on the humanitarian situation in the short and medium term, saving innumerable lives and preventing an immense amount of suffering'.[11]

While agreeing that prohibitions may reduce suffering, this book seeks to hold a question mark over claims about the likelihood that establishing standards will necessarily meet such an objective. For instance, critics of the current state of international arms control ask whether the present set of agreements inappropriately give greater legitimacy to some forms of suffering over others (so, those caused by high-tech versus low-tech weaponry; 'conventional' weapons versus 'unconventional' forms), whether the search for rules of conduct in war distracts attention away from others issues such as the justification for going to war, and whether by excluding certain groups from their reach (e.g. terrorists) prohibitions misconstrue the key contemporary security problems.[12] By keeping an eye on certain things rather than others, we are always producing a particular understanding of what is going on; marginalizing certain issues by paying attention to others. A question is whether the understanding formed is appropriate. The establishment of standards of acceptable conduct depends on being able to comprehend and rationally analyse – that is to identify, differentiate, separate, compare, contrast – the character of violent acts so as to both understand their origins and how they might be prevented. A danger herein is that of over-intellectualizing questions about nature of violence.

Of course, questions about the wisdom of seeking prohibitions are not just asked in general, but also in relation to specific debates and weapons. By considering such cases it is possible to develop a sense of the situated problems associated with classifications and definitions. Consider the quote at the start of this section. Particularly because of the deaths and injuries caused to civilians post-conflict from cluster munitions that do not explode on initial impact (see Chapter 9), a number of non-governmental organizations (NGOs) joined together under the Cluster Munition Coalition in 2003 to call for an end to the use and production of such weapons until their humanitarian problems are resolved.

As part of the first Coalition conference[13] its members considered what basis in international law existed for this moratorium. The remark made to the author at the start of this chapter followed that session. Central to the legal discussion was the concept of proportionality under international law. Protocol I to the Geneva Conventions stipulates attacks should not be 'expected to cause incidental loss of civilian life, injury to civilians [or] damage to civilian objectives... which would be excessive in relation to the concrete and direct military advantage anticipated'. Determining whether certain attacks with cluster munitions fall foul of the notion of proportionality requires some notion what would constitute a 'reasonable' (as opposed to 'excessive') expectation for harm and thereby what subsequent civilian casualties would be proportionate and permissible. In relation to long term civilian injuries, while cluster munitions might sometimes fail to explode as intended, much the same could be said of other weapons such as artillery shells, mortars and grenades. Presuming some inevitable 'dud rate', in 2001 the US Secretary of Defense proposed to reduce the failure rate of its new cluster munitions to below 1 per cent by 2005.[14] For those in peace, human rights and disarmament groups, assessing the desirability of such a policy has not been easy. While 1 per cent might be relatively low rate of failure for ordnance, because individual cluster devices consist of multiple bomblets (up to several hundred) their use could still result in significant post-conflict casualties. Moreover, while decreasing the dud rate might be beneficial in the short term in reducing deaths to civilians, if this leads to an increasing willingness to employ 'new and improved' cluster bombs or less care in the way they are handled,[15] any initial reductions in casualties could be lost or reversed. In addition, those outside of armed conflict are largely reliant on belligerents for assessments of dud rates, military advantage and even civilian casualties. It is perhaps understandable then, that some of those campaigning for an end to the use and production of such weapons until their humanitarian problems are resolved may regard trying to formulate a formal legal basis for this position as entailing a bit of 'nonsense'.

Consider a related issue for a different type of weaponry. In recent wars conducted by the US and other technologically sophisticated countries, much emphasis has been placed on the ability of precision-guided munitions to minimize 'collateral damage' to both individuals and infrastructure. The large scale and effective use of such weapons was central to US government claims that the 2003 Iraq war was one of the most humane in history.[16] Indeed, the NGO Human Rights Watch (HRW) (a member of the Cluster Munition Coalition) recommended precision-guided munitions should be used wherever possible as substitutes for 'dumb bombs'; a recommendation that stands in sharp contrast to that made for cluster munitions.[17] A vivid example of a capability deemed highly desirable from one perspective might not be so from another was given in the US *Air Force Magazine* which reported:

> Many Russian military theorists believe nuclear weapons provide the best answer to the challenge posed by conventionally armed precision guided munitions, which have become such an important part of Western military strategies. Russian generals fear that, in a general war, Western nations could employ such 'smart munitions' to degrade Russian strategic forces, without ever having to go nuclear themselves. Consequently, said General Volkov, Russia 'should enjoy the right to consider the first [enemy] use of precision weapons as the beginning of unrestricted nuclear war against it'.[18]

While statements such as those by General Volkov might be taken as mere posturing exercises, the quote does indicate a potential for a radical re-think in the assessments of the consequences of technology.

Just as the desirability of certain capabilities or future controls might be revised when seen in some wider context, so too can existing prohibitions. Along these lines, Richard Falk suggests the appropriateness of limits on weaponry need to be approached with considerable caution. The 1972 BTWC, for instance, forbids states from acquiring or developing weapons employing biological agents or toxins for hostile purposes. While often hailed for codifying a norm against the weaponization of disease, Falk's analysis of this Convention situates the threat from bioweapons in relation to the growing importance attached to them by the US government in the 1990s. The most credible line of explanation for this focus is presented as that of diverting public attention from US nuclear capabilities. Whereas Washington's approach across successive administrations has emphasized the non-proliferation of nuclear capabilities and a selective focus on the unacceptability of chemical and biological weapons, an abolitionist approach as championed by Falk calls for the elimination of *all* WMD. It is against this understanding of how weapon prohibitions are being selectively (mis)appropriated that he asks whether

> the ongoing process that supports CW [chemical warfare] and BW [biological warfare] regimes, as well as the nuclear non-proliferation treaty regimes, [should] be reevaluated and possibly rejected? From the perspective of the equality of states, a fundamental norm in international law, are these regimes embodiments of the hegemonic structure of world politics that controls and deforms diplomatic practice?[19]

The initial points made in this section suggest something of the uneasiness and disputability of determinations about the acceptability of force and the need for prohibitions. Alternative assessments of the proper context for considering weapons or the subtext of declarations support alternative assessments of what controls are about and whether they are desirable. In many assessments, the argument rarely far from being explicitly stated is that 'While commentators have hitherto assumed controls have served X and Y purposes, it is now possible to see it is really about Z because of 1, 2, and 3.' In each direction there is potential danger in specifying what is desirable, achievable, effective, etc. Those proffering evaluations of what controls are really about and really doing hazard appear naïve or misguided with the passage of time.

The difficulties that affect officials, policy makers and others in trying to comprehend and rationally analyse the world also affect those wishing to study their policies. As proposed at the end of Chapter 1, those scrutinizing how determinations are made about the acceptability of force are not somehow immune from needing to scrutinize the assumptions and characterizations given in their analysis. While it is possible to employ taken-for-granted categories (e.g. this is a leg-iron, that is an indiscriminate weapon), it is also prudent to question how categories emerged in the first place. As well, concerns about the nature of power and interests are not just central to assessing the effectiveness and purpose of prohibitions in reducing some identified wrong, but central for those analysts wishing to explain the reasons for restrictions. Falk's analysis raises the prospect that the machinations of political power (in the final analysis) give place and purpose to (seemingly desirable) prohibitions. Restrictions ostensibly justified on some reasoned basis (e.g. biological weapons must be banned because they are abhorrent, a perversion of medical knowledge, etc.) can, in fact, act to serve purposes quite different to those publicly stated. The 'power politics' involved need not be concealed. In contrast to other regulatory domains (such as the approval of pharmaceuticals or the regulation of pesticides), power and national interests are routinely attributed a pivotal role in negotiations about arms controls. However, as matters in need of decoding, the nature of power and interests are topics of much debate in the study of international security. Scholars might routinely draw on these concepts to give motivation to actions in complicated and contested world, but they do in different ways with different conceptions of the issues at stake.[20] Just who can speak for the 'real' meaning of power is itself, of course, a matter of much debate.

Thus, what can be said of the limitations and contingencies of the representations of violence made by those under study here applies to this analysis. This argument is not somehow above or beyond the problems of specifying the acceptability of force. Analysts of technology and warfare face major problems experienced by others in drawing on notions of motive, context and history to give a sense of meaning to the actions studied. Choices must be made about what is said, how it is said, when and what is left out. The problems for 'analysts' are particularly acute because they often draw on the interpretations of others 'closer' to events in questions – military commanders, diplomats, soldiers, etc. – who are themselves engaged in analysing the world.

As maintained here, it is ethically dangerous and intellectually questionable for those assuming the role of analyst to scrutinize the contingencies of categorizations, the open-endedness of what constitutes the 'proper context' for consideration, and the indeterminacies associated with the others' descriptions while not acknowledging and assessing the implications of such matters for their own arguments. This reflexive turning back is not a trivial possibility or a mere distraction to be swept under a theoretical rug at the first discrete opportunity. Instead it is central to asking how the acceptability of weapons is approached and how as part of that history, facts and language are marshalled to propose what is at stake. The selective practice of making problematic certain assumptions and arguments but not considering the implications of these for one's own analysis (what Woolgar and Pawluch called 'ontological gerry-mandering'[21]) might ostensibly shore up the face objectivity of analysis by avoiding inconvenient issues, but this practice is of doubtful merit.

These issues raised in this section are problems to confront and work with, not matters to be posed and then simply done away with. What knowledge is required is not a question with a simple or singular answer. Intellectualizing, analysing and theorizing might be indispensable aspects of how we come to understand the world, but they are also questionable in terms of what understanding they enable. Our constructs never prove adequate for capturing the full nature of history or action, perhaps especially in depicting the horrors of violence. As Nietzsche counsels, the unity and order presented in analysis is given at the end of it, rather than being a property of the world that pre-exists. Throughout the following argument, questions are posed of how to go on, the implications of certain ways of going on, what and how to make sense of what is taking place in discussions about the appropriateness of force.

The prohibition of weapons: managing the unmanageable

This book is an analysis of varied national and international attempts to constrain the development and employment of weaponry, principally in relation to humanitarian concerns. I approach efforts to establish prohibition systems as attempts to sort through disorderly and diverse practices so as to identify the source of concern that can justify a particular course of action. Such efforts are bedevilled by problems of specifying just what is important in evaluating the use of force. A goal is to understand how contrasting claims about the acceptability of weapons are shorn up to support an interpretation of what should be done.

As such the book is not an attempt to resolve disputes or propose some iron-clad control measures. Instead, it is concerned with how concerns about the acceptability of weapons are practically managed – with how individuals attempt to cut through the world to characterize what is really going on despite the fragility, disputability and contestability of doing so. If attempts to 'name' the problem associated with the employment of weaponry are always potentially open to challenge, then the processes by which determinations are made are of some importance. A consideration of the difficulties of setting out fixed and stable lines will be used to prompt consideration of how lines are drawn in the first place. In the subsequent argument I suggest determinations of the acceptability of weaponry should be situated between various problematic distinctions including those of:

Topic/resource	Similarity/difference
Apparent/hidden	Order/disorder
Part/whole	Determinacy/indeterminacy
Adherence/deviation	Social/technical
General/specific	Knower/known

As argued, debates about prohibitions are characterized by a movement between the terms of these binaries. Agreements about what is considered as following or deviating from a policy, how general rules can be related to specific instances, what counts as a social or technical matter, and just what is a part (rather than a whole) of a weapon are contingent achievements. The following chapters examine how determinations of the acceptability of weaponry and the need for prohibitions switch between contrasting ways of understanding the issues at stake. By asking how meaning is attributed to concepts and terms such as apparent/hidden, part/whole, adherence/deviation, and order/disorder are advanced, contested and otherwise managed, I hope to raise issues and connections that might otherwise not be made and evoke a sense of the issues at stake in prohibitions.

As an analysis that seeks to provide convincing general commentary about the nature of debates about weapon controls that is responsive to particular cases, the argument has and will exemplify the various tensions associated with managing the generalizations, characterizations and contexts it examines. In considering disputes about weaponry, I will specify some context for understanding actions, employ certain categorizations while scrutinizing others and attempt to offer a general analysis that is grounded through specific cases. In other words, the analysis exemplifies the dynamics it attributes elsewhere (rather than only 'describing' or 'explaining' them).[22] So in asking what is at stake in discussions about the prohibitions of weapons – paralleling Bonner's general suggestion for social theory[23] – this book seeks to work out something of the problem of approaching this topic. It does so by moving back and forth in a somewhat circuitous manner between a concern about the substantive issues regarding conflict and controls and theoretical discussions regarding the analysis of technology. By doing so the attempt is being made to question what counts as reasonable, persuasive and credible accounts of the world.

The structuring of the argument

The remainder of the chapter briefly outlines the argument that follows. I wish to foreshadow some of the troubles to be examined in attempts to set limits on what constitutes an acceptable way of killing. Before doing so it is worth establishing the bounds on this book by stating what it is not. Unlike many works concerned with arms control, this book does not adopt as its primary task judging the effectiveness of prohibitions, establishing the 'real' motivations behind their formation, or assessing the prospects for uni-, bi- or multi-lateral agreements in the future security environment. Rather, it is an examination of what takes place in accounts for what is 'appropriate' by way of weaponry and force. As an effort to ask what is troubling in this, the argument that follows does not follow a well-defined path, but rather branches off into numerous avenues in order to develop an appreciation of the issues at stake. Much effort is spent working towards a sense of the problem with prohibitions, rather than presuming such an understanding could be simply stated at the outset.

By way of furthering the initial remarks made so far and setting the ground for later chapters, Chapter 3 considers something of the disagreements associated with the use of force. It does so through attending to the use of language. The basic starting point for this book is the open-endedness of descriptions. There is more than one way to describe (defend, discuss, decry) the state of the world and just which is most apt is disputable. Following from this, this chapter approaches accounts of the world as forms of action. Language does not merely provide a way of representing what is; rather the specific characterizations and arguments are highly consequential in constituting an understanding of what is taking place and why. Whether prohibitions are violated, what they mean, whether they are even relevant for a given case depends on how acts or technologies are defined in particular situations. In making these points, this chapter establishes the importance and problems of orientating to accounts of the world as both as 'representations' and 'discourse'.

Part II moves on to issues associated with specifying and evaluating technology. Chapter 4 offers some initial observations of the alternative ways in which weapons are thought to be implicated in action and the dilemmas faced in appraising their appropriateness. The remaining three chapters of Part II examine disputes about what weapons are, what they do and what they are for. The cases examined include prominent historical and contemporary attempts to devise and implement prohibitions on 'conventional' and 'unconventional' weapons through customary and statutory laws, multilateral treaties, UN resolutions, administrative regulations and national legislation. In this attention is given to those formal arrangements which, following Croft's typology of arms control, are designed to 'create norms of behaviour' through limiting the development or use of weaponry.[24] The cases examined are aligned with the different ways of theorizing 'the problem with technology' discussed in Chapter 4: the intrinsic effects of weapons, the purposes they serve and the intentions of users. The broad range of cases covered is intended to illustrate the pervasiveness of the problems of analytically attempting to cut up socio-technical assemblages so as to justify specific prohibitions.

Chapter 5 argues that how technologies and acts of force are defined should be thought of as contingent matters readily open for reassessment. Debates about what counts as an instance of a napalm bomb and a component part are examined to illustrate the problems associated with offering definitive categorizations of what weapons are. To label or categorize objects or acts together demands establishing what is similar between them, but the search for definitive relations of similarity is elusive. With particular emphasis on recent controversies about what counts as evidence for the existence of chemical and biological weapons, Chapter 6 considers how attributions of purpose are ascribed to 'weapons-related activities' *vis-à-vis* controls. Attributions are implicated in concerns about the motivations of individuals and determinations of what counts as the proper context. As elaborated, the relevant 'context' is as problematic as it is a widespread aid in making determinations about the purpose of acts and objects. To allude to Scranton's distinction,[25] context here is not treated as a merely some theatric backdrop on which actions are played out nor as a structural set of barriers out there that determine events. Instead, attention here is with the processes by which instances and contexts are given meaning in relation to each other.

Chapter 7 examines attempts to specify what weapons do. While establishing the effects of weapons might seem a relatively straightforward undertaking, in relation to determining what needs to be done by way of establishing workable prohibitions, this is often far from so. It is maintained that the complications and contestations of establishing effects can be usefully conceived of as a problem of generalization. Attempts to adjudicate the effects of nuclear weapons are examined to illustrate the scope for dispute about what weapons do and thereby what should be done with them.

In offering this argument, Part II forwards an orientation that runs throughout the book: a sceptical approach to rules as determiners of what future action is permissible. Following the legal scholar Hart, the 'proper' interpretation of rule is approached as a matter that must be argued for rather than found by uncovering the essential meaning of the rule.[26] In contentious debates about the acceptability of weaponry, the arguments can (but do not always) go on for quite some time without a sense of finality. This orientation is offered to raise the matter of what is sought from rules.

Part III directly addresses attempts at establishing prohibitions. Chapter 8 summarizes many of the persistent and intractable ethical and intellectual challenges discussed in Part II regarding the acceptability of weaponry: cutting through complex socio-technical systems to identify some principal source of concern; making categorizations which necessarily entail particularizations; specifying the basis for attributions of similarity and dissimilarity between acts and object; situating these 'in context'; and making generalizations responsive to some specific instance. It is suggested that the predicaments about the acceptability of weapons can be usefully conceived in terms of three inter-related questions: 'What and where is the problem?', 'What is like what?', and 'So what?'. Yet whatever the impossibilities of resolving these questions once and for all, attempts to devise prohibitions necessarily entail posing them. In making these points, Chapter 8 poses the question of what analytical responses would usefully follow. Rather than attempting to devise ever more precisely crafted rules or explain the motivations for certain prohibitions, the case is made for the importance of attending to what is being accomplished through particular accounts offered of the acceptability of weaponry and the desirability of prohibitions.[27] This chapter contends that doing so can offer helpful insights in understanding what is troubling in characterizing the acceptability of weaponry. Chapter 9 examines wide ranging and tension ridden debates about the prohibition of cluster munitions through an analysis structured along the themes of Chapter 8.

Chapter 10 considers in some detail what is accomplished through accounts of force. It does so by reconsidering and re-describing many of the disputes analysed up to that point through attending to how the problems associated with establishing formal rules on the acceptability of violence are managed. It will be suggested that when faced with fundamental difficulties and dilemmas associated with offering determinations of where unacceptability rests, individuals and organizations engage in various strategies to deny, defer, deter and deflect making specifications about the issues at stake. Alternative characterizations and definitions often involve alternative ways of shifting the burden of proof for resolving the difficulties of substantiating claims about the acceptability of weaponry. Chapter 11 concludes with further reflections on these issues through considering practical interventions by the author into attempts to limit the development and use of cluster munitions.

Chapter 3

Forceful arguments

[F]or America, there will be no going back to the era before 11 September 2001, to false comfort in a dangerous world. We have learned that terrorist attacks are not caused by the use of strength. They are invited by the perception of weakness. And the surest way to avoid attacks on our own people is to engage the enemy where he lives and plans.

(US President George W. Bush 7 September 2003)

The application of military force is often a matter of controversy. What one individual deems a just exertion of force, another labels as unwarranted violence. While self-defence is widely recognized as one justification for resorting to violence (as alluded to in the quote by George W. Bush) in many conflicts – from international wars to public house brawls – all those involved invoke this as a justification for their action. While doctrines such as the 'Just War' propose criteria for judging whether force is justified, whether the criteria have been met or whether they are even relevant in particular circumstances are readily contested. In terms of what kind of force can be used, varied national and international laws require organizations with official authority – such as the police and the military – to exert force proportional to the threat faced. What such general prescriptions mean for particular cases though, must be worked out in each case.

This chapter examines how the use of force is alternatively characterized, in particular through examining debates about the 2003 Iraq War. In doing so I want to ask what is at stake in the descriptions offered. As maintained, in examining disagreements about the justifications for conflict, consideration should be given to how the meaning of acts and things are constituted. Rather than just treating accounts of the world as representations that are more or less accurate, this chapter stresses the importance of approaching them as forms of *situated action* that attribute motive, interests and responsibility in sometimes subtle but often highly consequential ways. The importance of treating accounts as situated action will be extended in later chapters as debates about the merits of weaponry and the need for prohibitions are considered.

Controversy in conflict

The acceptability of the use of force is profoundly questionable. Just how the life and death consequences associated with it can be assessed or even 'reasonably' discussed are matters that generate substantial dispute. Many people would accept in the abstract that it is both sometimes necessary to employ force and regrettable to have to do so. What should be done in specific cases then is often contentious. If nothing else, the recurring disagreements about the wisdom of some people setting about to inflict harm on others should signal the importance of considering the basis for diverging assessments in some detail.

In addition, descriptions of force are thoroughly questionable. Characterizations of an event as a disturbance, a riot, an insurgence, a breakdown of order or a political protest evoke contrasting appraisals of what has taken place, why, and what responsive action should be taken. To describe that 'response' as the exercise of force against a crowd or the beating of citizens by security forces again provides alternative ways of orientating to understanding what went on.[1] 'Use of force' is itself (in contrast to phrases such as 'inflicting violence') a relatively sanitized expression. Nothing like exact, literal, exhaustive, neutral, 'just-so' labels exist for characterizing acts of violence. Instead the terms we use and how we use them are directly or indirectly implicated in evaluations.

Consider the following extract from George W. Bush's first national televised address since declaring the end of major military operations in Iraq, given on 7 September 2003. The speech discussed various details about and justifications for military operations by the US and others in Iraq and elsewhere:

> Good evening. I have asked for this time to keep you informed of America's actions in the war on terror.
>
> Nearly two years ago, following deadly attacks on our country, we began a systematic campaign against terrorism. These months have been a time of new responsibilities, and sacrifice, and national resolve, and great progress.
>
> America and a broad coalition acted first in Afghanistan by destroying the training camps of terror and removing the regime that harboured al-Qaeda. In a series of raids and actions around the world, nearly two-thirds of al-Qaeda's known leaders have been captured or killed, and we continue on al-Qaeda's trail.
>
> We have exposed terrorist front groups, seized terrorist accounts, taken new measures to protect our homeland and uncovered sleeper cells inside the United States.
>
> And we acted in Iraq, where the former regime sponsored terror, possessed and used weapons of mass destruction, and for 12 years defied the clear demands of the United Nations Security Council. Our coalition enforced these international demands in one of the swiftest and most humane military campaigns in history.
>
> For a generation leading up to 11 September 2001, terrorists and their radical allies attacked innocent people in the Middle East and beyond,

without facing a sustained and serious response. The terrorists became convinced that free nations were decadent and weak. And they grew bolder, believing that history was on their side.

Since America put out the fires of 11 September and mourned our dead, and went to war, history has taken a different turn. We have carried the fight to the enemy. We are rolling back the terrorist threat to civilization, not on the fringes of its influence, but at the heart of its power.

This work continues. In Iraq, we are helping the long-suffering people of that country to build a decent and democratic society at the center of the Middle East. Together we are transforming a place of torture chambers and mass graves into a nation of laws and free institutions. This undertaking is difficult and costly, yet worthy of our country and critical to our security.

The Middle East will either become a place of progress and peace, or it will be an exporter of violence and terror that takes more lives in America and in other free nations. The triumph of democracy and tolerance in Iraq, in Afghanistan and beyond would be a grave setback for international terrorism.

The terrorists thrive on the support of tyrants and the resentments of oppressed peoples. When tyrants fall and resentment gives way to hope, men and women in every culture reject the ideologies of terror and turn to the pursuits of peace. Everywhere that freedom takes hold, terror will retreat.

In this speech the effort is made to identify just what various 'actions', military and otherwise, were about. So, those into Afghanistan and Iraq were part of a *common* endeavour: the war on terror. In response to the past events of 9–11 and any future threats against the US, its government along with a broad coalition has taken action. This included one of the most humane wars of all time in Iraq, where demands were enforced on a regime that has continuously and clearly defied the just will of the international community. The systematic action being taken stands in contrast the failure to engage in sustained and serious efforts in the past to combat a long time, though admittedly poorly recognized, threat. Thus, as Bush tells it, because of the harsh lessons of 9–11 the US government is finally breaking from its past practice of passive fire fighting and doing what it must. Least anyone be complacent or plead for some hiatus to war and sacrifice, it is repeatedly stressed that much more still needs doing.

The argument elaborates a series of contrasts and dichotomies about what is going on and what should be done, including distinctions between the lawful and lawless; the civilized and uncivilized; decisive and weak action; democracy and tyranny; pre- and post-11 September 2001; progress and chaos; and sources of peace and those of terror. It is through these distinctions that the world is ordered and the path ahead is justified. These contrasts and others are further drawn on as Bush later goes on to state:

> I recognize that not all our friends agreed with our decision to enforce the Security Council resolutions and remove Saddam Hussein from power, yet we cannot let past differences interfere with present duties.

Terrorists in Iraq have attacked representatives of the civilized world and opposing them must be the cause of the civilized world. Members of the United Nations now have an opportunity, and the responsibility, to assume a broader role in assuring that Iraq becomes a free and democratic nation . . . .

[W]e are encouraging the orderly transfer of sovereignty and authority to the Iraqi people. Our coalition came to Iraq as liberators and we will depart as liberators. Right now Iraq has its own governing council, comprised of 25 leaders representing Iraq's diverse people. The governing council recently appointed cabinet ministers to run government departments.

Already more than 90 per cent of towns and cities have functioning local governments which are restoring basic services. We are helping to train civil defense forces to keep order and an Iraqi police service to enforce the law, a facilities protection service, Iraqi border guards to help secure the borders and a new Iraqi army.

In all these roles, there are now some 60,000 Iraqi citizens under arms, defending the security of their own country. And we are accelerating the training of more.

Iraq is ready to take the next steps toward self-government. The Security Council resolution we introduce will encourage Iraq's governing council to submit a plan and a timetable for the drafting of a constitution and for free elections.

Through drawing on particular descriptions of actions, mobilizing a certain sense of history and making reference to particular outcomes, speeches such as this forward a sense of what is happening, the identity and intentions of those involved, and the next necessary steps. Through the repeated use of contrast pairs, Bush asks the other nations of the world to decide which side they are on and leaves no doubt where any right standing nation would side.

What further needs to be done is also clear: states that failed to agree on the appropriateness of enforcing what had to be enforced and ousting Saddam Hussein (the said defining characteristics of the Iraq war and goals that at an abstract level are not likely to be refuted by the vast majority of the listening audience) must now do the right thing. In contrast to the proactive accomplishment of the US (and its coalition partners), members of the United Nations (UN) must merely assume responsibility for what they are responsible for: building free and democratic Iraq; again a goal in the abstract terms of undeniable worth. In an embryonic form that Iraq is said to be present already in the shape of the governing council, local governments and various security measures, the detailed listing of which in the speech indicates things are happening and progress is being made.

As formulated, contributing to the rebuilding of Iraq then is not about endorsing US actions, as that might prove controversial given prior debates about the war, but helping those finally beginning to help themselves. As liberators, US forces are merely enabling the Iraqis to do what they want to do. Representatives of the US government made the decision to go war because it had to uphold its duties and responsibilities. This stands in contrast to others who had turned away from theirs and certainly differs from any suggestion that the war was motivated by oil or geostrategic interests.

For those that might offer a contrasting appraisal of what the Iraq war was really about, the speech was perhaps most interesting for what it did not address: the limited evidence of weapons of mass destruction (WMD) found in Iraq at the time, the troubled state of the peace process between Israelis and Palestinians, how many civilians died directly or indirectly from the fighting, whether it might have spawned support for terrorism, etc. Making such linkages would support an alternative assessment of the use of force by offering an alternative sense of what is relevant to making evaluations.

Consider, for instance, a 2003 cover story article for the journal *New Statesman* by long-time critic of US foreign policy Noam Chomsky. Here a rather different understanding is offered regarding just what the war was about:

> High on the global agenda by autumn 2002 was the declared intention of the most powerful state in history to maintain its hegemony through the threat or use of military force, the dimension of power in which it reigns supreme. In the official rhetoric of the National Security Strategy, released in September 2002: 'Our forces will be strong enough to dissuade potential adversaries from pursuing a military build-up in hopes of surpassing, or equalling, the power of the United States.'
>
> One well-known international affairs specialist, John Ikenberry, has described the declaration as a 'grand strategy [that] begins with a fundamental commitment to maintaining a unipolar world in which the United States has no peer competitor', a condition that is to be 'permanent [so] that no state or coalition could ever challenge [the US] as global leader, protector and enforcer' ....
>
> The imperial grand strategy asserts the right of the US to undertake 'preventive war' at will. Preventive, please note, not pre-emptive. Pre-emptive war might fall within the framework of international law. Thus if the US had detected Russian bombers approaching from Grenada in 1983, with the clear intent to bomb, then, under a reasonable interpretation of the UN Charter, a pre-emptive attack destroying the planes and perhaps their Grenadian base would have been justifiable. (Cuba, Nicaragua and many others could have exercised the same right for many years while under attack from the US, though the weak would need to be insane to implement their rights.) But the justifications for pre-emptive war do not hold for preventive war, particularly as that idea is interpreted by its current enthusiasts: the use of military force to eliminate an imagined or invented threat, so that even the term preventive is too charitable.

This extract offers a rather different identification of the war aims and the proper context for understanding it than that given by President Bush. Instead of Iraq representing a clear and present danger, the imperative to go to war was a contingent priority that reflected the long time and officially acknowledged US desire for world political hegemony. Rather than upholding international laws and agreements, the rule of international law was undermined by the war; subservient as the law is to the whims and aspirations of its political masters. That the US certainly did not detect Russian bombers approaching from Grenada prior to its 1983 invasion of the island also indicates that US doctrine of 'preventive' war is not new to some post 9–11 context.

While Bush speaks to various facts on the ground in Iraq to justify his assessment, Chomsky draws on quoted experts and historical events to derive a highly sceptical evaluation; one, for instance, which later evokes a comparison of the US practice of anticipatory self-defence with that of the Japanese in the Second World War:

> As Arthur Schlesinger, the former adviser to President Kennedy, observed, George W Bush's 'policy of "anticipatory self-defence" [against Iraq] is alarmingly similar to the policy that imperial Japan employed at Pearl Harbor, on a date which, as an earlier American president said it would, lives in infamy . . . today, it is we Americans who live in infamy'. Schlesinger added that even in friendly countries the public regards Bush 'as a greater threat to peace than Saddam Hussein' . . . .[2]

By quoting credible commentators or official documents, Chomsky implicitly refutes potential criticisms that the claims made are 'merely' those of someone who has been a long time ardent critic of US foreign policy. Least anyone think this is a partisan analysis, he further goes on to argue that this 'strategy is not new, nor is it solely a Republican construct'. Rather, if one looks closely at the statements made and the practices of previous administrations, it is possible to find ample evidence of the view that the US cannot be bound by inconvenient facets of international law in its quest of global power. As such, the specific motives of Bush, Vice-President Cheney or Secretary of Defense Rumsfeld or others are not particularly relevant. Indeed, if the examples discussed up to one point in the article were not convincing:

> We can go back further. The fundamental assumption that lies behind the imperial grand strategy is the guiding principle of Woodrow Wilson's idealism: we are good, even noble. Hence our interventions are necessarily righteous in intent, if occasionally clumsy in execution. In the words of President Wilson, we have 'elevated ideals' and are dedicated to 'stability and righteousness', and it is natural, as he wrote of the conquest of the Philippines, that 'our interest must march forward, altruists though we are; other nations must see to it that they stand off, and do not seek to stay us'.

Thus, the essence of the foreign policies of successive US governments is said to be much the same and what rationale lies behind official statements is known and dubious. This essence enables Chomsky to pose wide ranging concerns about the merits of interventions. Rather than locating the prime impetus behind US foreign policy in the recent events of 9–11 as Bush does, Chomsky sets the actions in Iraq against a longer historical context. The said conflation of Iraq and 9–11 terrorism is further questioned later:

> The brilliant success of public diplomacy on the domestic front was revealed once again when the president, at the end of the war in Iraq in May 2003, stood on the deck of the aircraft carrier *Abraham Lincoln*. He was free to declare that he had won a 'victory in a war on terror' by having 'removed an ally of al-Qaeda'. It was immaterial that the alleged link between Saddam Hussein and Osama Bin Laden (his bitter enemy, in fact) was based on no credible evidence. Also immaterial was the only known connection between the Iraq invasion and the threat of terror: that the invasion enhanced the threat, as had been widely predicted, by sharply increasing al-Qaeda recruitment.

Bush and Chomsky present highly contrasting accounts of both the wisdom of what happened in Iraq and just what happened. Being only two sets of extracts from two commentaries about the war from two individuals, the given statements are not offered here as representing definitive or even exemplar pro- and anti-war stances. They do, however, illustrate how contrasting appraisals of force are supported.

Both Bush and Chomsky deal with the issue of how to give a sense of meaning to what happened in Iraq. In doing so the accounts attribute motives, emphasize certain events instead of others, and demark a sense of what counts as the germane background to situate contemporary events. Just what is presented as relevant to the story is part and parcel of the evaluations made. Yet, what should count as the relevant context or issue for assessing what the Iraq war was about are much disputed. In reading the accounts here many readers will no doubt have drawn on other contexts, evidence, motives, points of view or events to suggest an alternative appraisal. Any description of what the war was about could be extended and elaborated. In theory, if not in practice, there is no end to the questioning of what is relevant.

Following from this, what counts as relevant for assessing force is itself something a case must be made for. That disagreement exists about the proper characterization is hardly surprising. For instance, the import and crediblity of each claim marshalled earlier (e.g. the said previous lack of US resolve, the US invasion of Grenada) in supporting an evaluation is contestable. As well, even if it was agreed by many that the war resulted in a certain outcome and that it was relevant for assessing the war – such as al-Qaeda members and Saddam loyalists joining together in a common cause post-war – just what this should imply is debated. For instance, proponents for the war could and have argued that these historically antagonist groups would have collaborated sooner or later if it had not been for the 2003 intervention – probably with devastating consequences because of the (future) WMD capability of Iraq.

Moreover as part of the open-endedness of accounts, specific acts can and are characterized in multiple ways. No one particular depiction is the only one that is reasonable or possible. Descriptions of the Iraq war as an invasion, intervention or liberation as well as one of the swiftest and most humane military campaigns in history versus a bloody act of killing and maiming are not necessarily mutually exclusive. Yet, the particular characterizations given are significant in supporting some evaluation. This could-be-otherwise quality of accounts suggests the need for caution in just what is said. The descriptions presented are contingent and highly consequential for the framing of issues rather than being mere reflections of the world as it is.

Two approaches to language

This book takes the open-endedness of description as a key starting point for analysis. To say that description is open-ended or that there is no one single way of characterizing actions and events is not to imply that all depictions should be treated as equally credible or plausible. Rather it suggests the necessity of attending to what is done through certain accounts and how arguments are fashioned. This section begins this by outlining an alternative way of conceiving of the functioning of language other than that of simply representing the world. As argued, thinking about the performative and action-oriented consequences of language poses a number of challenges for assessing and even discussing the acceptability of the employment of weapons.

Derek Edwards contrasts two views of language: one as *representation* and the other as *discourse*.[3] To view language as *representation* is to portray it as a means of describing the world that enables individuals to cognitively comprehend and then communicate about what is taking place. Language operates as a device for standing for actions and objects and thus enables thoughts and concepts to be connected with an independent reality. The implicit metaphor here is one of mapping. Language enables the world to be surveyed and known through the classifications and labels employed. Names provide categories for building mutual agreement about the nature of a given state of affairs. Particular representations can be scrutinized as to whether they accurately and clearly depict what is taking place.

As Kitching suggests, holding such a view of language, a key aim for language is to devise 'the right nouns for the right objects – that is, as choosing the right labels to "stick" propositionally on the right "things" in the world' and focus is given to

> the definitional task, to the job of 'cutting out' the labels as carefully and exactly as possible in order to ensure that the boundaries of the label exactly match those of the object upon which it is to be stuck.[4]

Certainly much effort in formulating formal prohibitions adopts this goal of representational precision; exactly defining and classifying the nature of objects and individuals (e.g. what is a leg cuff, who is a responsible user, etc.) is taken to provide a solid foundation for establishing effective proscriptions and prescriptions. Likewise many analyses of international arms controls seek to offer precisely defined theories and concepts – such as those involving interests, rational choice or norms – to suggest what is really taking place in certain negotiations.

In contrast, approaching language as *discourse* entails treating it as a form of social action.[5] In other words, it is necessary to attend to how 'to *say* something is to *do* something'.[6] Herein the specific details of accounts are not of secondary interest to the real phenomenon (reality) under question. Instead the particular descriptions given are central to constituting an understanding of what is under discussion, be they motives, identities, objects or actions. Descriptions of the world do not simply represent the output of some underlying reasoning process that reports on the nature of reality; they are instead managed descriptions given in a particular interactional setting and have their specific meaning within that setting. If descriptions could be otherwise then just what description is given is significant. In treating language as discourse 'the analytical task is to see how those accounts are constructed, how and when they are produced as explanations, how they are designed and positioned with regard to alternative accounts, and in what interaction sequences they are produced'.[7] In other words, just what and how descriptions are given is treated as a topic of analysis in itself.

Accounts of acts of violence or anything else can be thought of as stories that are 'rhetorically organized, construct the nature of the events, assemble description and narrative, and make attributional inferences available'.[8] In doing so, they do not just speak about those issues explicitly mentioned, but also to possible alternative counter characterizations.[9] For instance, in the Bush quotes in the earlier section, the relatively detailed listing of rebuilding activities taking place in Iraq by Iraqis can be treated as not just a description of what was going on that was more or less accurate, but an implicit refutation of the accusations being voiced at the time that the US government was really running the affairs of the country and thus acting as conquerors. Initiatives being undertaken by the US were done in the spirit of liberation, since it was the Iraqi people themselves that were in charge.

Following a discursive approach, for instance, McKenzie has examined official accounts given in interviews of the motives for countries' participation in the 1990–91 Persian Gulf War.[10] In a representational view of language, statements given by officials for the reason for war would be taken as (more or less believable) accounts that analysts could use as a resource for then building arguments regarding what the war was really about. Rather than taking motivations as something definite and given that could be marshalled in this manner, McKenzie was concerned with how depictions of motivation were assembled through the accounts given. As he argued, many officials actively problematized attempts to establish heads of states' motives by suggesting various equally plausible interpretations that meant just what the real motive was could not be resolved.

Consider the following simplified and abridged version of exchange between a social scientist and a junior-level American ambassador discussing the motivations of those partaking in the 1991 Persian Gulf War:

AMDIP: There, uh, I personally – there's a whole range of interests.

INT: Yeah.

AMDIP: And if you focus on one set you are missing the whole picture. I think a good deal of... for instance some people say one of the reasons the Egyptians ended taking up the position they did here was because... right before the war... Saddam Hussein had told [Egyptian President] Mubarak that he wasn't going to invade then he turned around and he did. Y'know and the fact that he lied to another leader y'know and embarrassed him publicly... some would say that was one of the major reasons why they ended up sending troops. Y'know not because Egyptian... economic interests. I mean there were all sort of other things there but it's just the real offense, the insult was enough to motive some real action. And that's the way a lot of people work. I think. George Bush, some would say, operates in very much the same way. There's a lot of personal involvement in politics and if he feels betrayed or he feels that, y'know, we've been betrayed or people have been made to look like idiots he'll be inclined to act where another president might not have. Another president's not as sensitive to that might have, people have... you know people [would] say Carter, a lot would say, had some real moral interests... worldwide and pursued an agenda that was based in a large part on you know a moral vision of the world. Others said that was just cynical politics. What he was really pursuing, you know, economic interests but with a moral veneer sort of on the top. But who knows. You know if uh, if the participants themselves don't really understand their motives fully, I don't think anyone outside can.

INT: So you are saying that President Bush and Carter may not understand their own motivations. Is that right?

AMDIP: Well I dunno if anyone really does. I mean I think there is just too much going on... I may take an action that I consider to be purely rational or based on good cold motives and somebody will say 'Oh, well you're just responding emotionally because when you were four years old your father did this and that to you and so now you see', y'know, 'Saddam as a father' ....

In the setting of an interview where the nature of motives are debated, this official and others ironized both the range of justifications given for the Gulf War by proponents and detractors as well as attempts to analytically explain those through recourse to concepts such as economic interests. Indeed, as told, the particular accounts given by leaders for their action might not even matter. In addressing the motivations in this way, the diplomat has questioned his own ability to comment on the issues addressed. This stepping back by officials from their own formulations, this 'produced undecidability',[11] meant appraisals of Allied action and the possibility of accurately representing them had to be suspended because knowing the true motives for war was rendered problematic. This problematizing of Allied leaders stands in contrast to Saddam Hussein's motivations which were taken as unproblematically available. McKenzie's analysis illustrates how questions about motivations and intent for war can be, in at least some cases, treated as practical problems for those involved. Determinations of motivation are negotiated accomplishments, enacted in certain settings.

Consider another example of the discursive and highly performative dimensions of language. On 21 February 2003 in Rome the Prime Ministers Tony Blair and Silvio Berlusconi hosted a joint press conference outlining the situation in Iraq. At that conference the following exchange took place:

REPORTER: As a practicing Christian, when you see the Pontiff tomorrow, is not there inevitably going to be a collision views on this because he is implacably opposed to this crisis ending in war?

TONY BLAIR: We do not want war. No one wants war. I understand exactly why people feel so strongly and I certainly don't in any shape or form think I have all the answers to questions. But in the end I have to make a decision, and that is the difference between leadership and commentary. Are we just going to hope somehow that Saddam is going to have a change of heart and become a kind and decent man after 25 years of brutal and bloody oppression [shrugs].

But there is a moral dimension to this question too. If we fail to disarm Saddam peacefully then where does that leave the authority of the United Nations? And if we leave Saddam in charge of Iraq with his weapons of mass destruction, where does that leave the Iraqi people who are the victims of Saddam?[12]

The response refutes the suggestion that there is an inevitable collision of views between the Pope and Tony Blair. Neither wants war, this is clear. Blair presents himself as just like everyone else; there are no substantial differences with regard for the desire to avoid war. What is different is that unlike journalists, protesters or others that might pose awkward questions about the possible implications of Blair and Berlusconi's policies, these leaders must make unpleasant decisions. The need to make a decision about war is not something they sought; rather events have forced it on them. By way of pre-empting possible future queries about what will happen should war commence, Blair readily admits that he does not have all the answers – yet the need to act remains. The statement implicitly refutes arguments by would-be critics that the Prime Ministers are warmongers searching out a fight for some economic or political advantage. Personalizing the situation in terms of the past 25 years of Saddam Hussein's rule and the possibility of what he might do with his WMD (i.e. his readily known motives and likely actions), there can be little doubt about the need to consider war. Indeed, war, with or without the further UN resolution being negotiated at the time, might well be the only way to maintain the authority of the UN.

A discursive approach along the lines suggested earlier would treat such responses and other statements as topics of analysis where the focus is on analysing what is done though accounts (e.g. how an understanding agency or motivations are forwarded or problems defined) rather than considering the validity of what is said. This would require a detailed analysis of the sequence of claims made. Extracting accounts out of their interactional context to marshal them in general arguments about what individuals really think relies on a simplified and artificial view of language, one that passes over their particular formulation as well as how they have implications for and on the particular setting in which they are made.[13]

Representation, discourse and persuasion in prohibitions

The representational and discursive concepts of language suggest alternative ways of orientating to the competing contentions about the acceptability of force. In simplified terms the distinction is between treating accounts of the world as resources for making arguments about what is really taking place that can then inform evaluations of actions or instead of taking accounts themselves as a topic of study to consider the performative aspects of their particular formulation. As another way of stating that contrast, one can assess the persuasiveness of claims or assess how claims are fashioned so as to make them persuasive. Both approaches can inform a discussion about the dynamics of disputes regarding the appropriateness of force, yet they entail contrasting strategies for doing so.

The problems of how to approach disagreements about force and the acceptability of weaponry are more entrenched than stated earlier because the comments made previously about the discursive, action-orientated aspects of language apply to the given analysis. In asking how contingent and contested characterizations are made in an effort to advance or undermine certain evaluations and prohibitions, this book utilizes categories and claims in an attempt to give a certain interpretation of the issues examined.

The comparison given of the statements by Bush and Chomksy, for instance, could be scrutinized in terms of how through its specific and selective telling it assembled a sense of the nature of the speeches under question. Considering other extracts about the Iraq war, other parts of the commentaries made, or other conflicts might well have suggested a different set of issues. Examining 'on-the ground' accounts amid the screams, blood, fear of war rather than abstracted political commentary, for example, would highlight a different set of issues about the way accounts of force function as actions. Moreover, any such scrutinization of the accounts could itself then be scrutinized in terms of its discursive features, the way it assembled an understanding of context, and so on. Where this could or should end is less than clear, but the standing back from and questioning of all accounts can never be fully carried out.

This book is not primarily an exploration of the nature of argumentation and language; rather it is an examination of what is at stake in attempts to establish prohibitions on weapons and equipment. As argued in this chapter though there are significant issues in offering accounts about the acceptability of force related to how language is conceived and employed as part of that analysis. Instead of being mere reports of the world, descriptions of the issues associated with the use of force are open-ended, partial and consequential in framing a sense of the issues at stake.

Just how 'we' respond to this is a crucial issue. That might mean seeking ever more precise wording to describe events and objects or turning our attention to how things are done through accounts. While both are reasonable lines of pursuit, they are also restrictive. The opened-ness of descriptions of the world means the search for ever more precise labels to characterize objects and actions is limited in its ability to provide a lasting bedrock for agreement. Whether prohibitions are violated, what they mean, whether they are even relevant for a given case very much depend on how particular acts or technologies are described for some purpose and as part of some action. The hope that incontrovertible, general, once-and-for-all definitive characterizations can be given to events and objects that might ground prohibitions is futile. A focus on depictions themselves as phenomenon for study though threatens to become preoccupied with the study of language rather than the socio-political affairs that they are purported to be about.

As contended earlier, this book seeks to work through rather than resolve the problems of specifying the acceptability of weaponry. In doing so, it seeks to both evoke a sense of what is at stake in the claims made about weapons and what is taking place in depictions. Chapter 2 argued classifications of weaponry are situated between a host of difficulties regarding what we know and how we know it. Justifying prohibitions can depend on imposing a sense of order on the world and yet this should be approached as a contingent achievement. From the argument stated, much the same ambiguity exists in relation to language. Undoubtedly our descriptions of force fail to capture a full or even reasonably adequate account of what is going on. Language is as problematic as indispensable.

Reiterating a point made in Chapter 2, I want to suggest that in enforcing prohibitions or 'merely' describing the state of the world are acts that always involve suspending asking questions about what might well be questioned in order to say what is going on. Designating certain weapons or employments of them as 'benign', 'indiscriminate' or 'abhorrent' entails equating actions or objects in a manner that will be contestable. Why and how certain comparisons are made, contexts cited or time-frames offered can always be questioned, though they may not be in practice.

In this book attention is given to how individuals ('analysts' and 'non-analysts' alike) address the problems associated with specifying the acceptability of force options and the necessity of prohibitions – this might mean specifying what is really going on despite the contestability of any determinations or leaving the issues involved unspecified despite the importance of elaboration. In considering this, accounts of the world are treated both as resources and as topics of analysis. In moving between orientations, the aim is not just to alternate between at one time examining the accuracy of representations of 'the world' and at other times investigating the functioning of 'words' in accounts. Rather the aim is to consider how movement is conducted and what is entailed in doing so. In working in terms of both resource and topic, the aim is not to resolve theoretical disputes about the nature of language, but acknowledge and evoke a sense of the contested ground associated with discussing the acceptability of weaponry.[14] As such, I do not seek to avoid the discursive argumentation, but to engage in it and through doing so pose and explore a sense of what is at stake in making arguments. Part II begins this by considering how the status of weaponry is established: that is, what weapons are, what they are for and what they do.

PART II

Weaponry

Chapter 4

The technologies of conflict and the conflicts about technology

Part I made an initial case for why attempts to establish humanitarian inspired prohibitions for weaponry are fraught with difficulties. Controls are situated at the intersection of various problematic moral and technical distinctions which evade any easy resolution. Prohibitions seek to cut through a complex and a disputable world to specify what measures need to be taken. How this can and should be done is open for questioning.

Part II furthers this argument by considering how place and purpose is given to weaponry in evaluations of force. Just how technologies are understood as implicated in the use of force is highly significant in justifying determinations about what, if any, prohibitions might be required. Whether, for instance, particular types of weapons are portrayed as inherently abhorrent or conditionally acceptable is of some significance for what kinds of controls are forwarded and how they are justified. Through general commentary and case studies, Part II elaborates something of the negotiations and contingencies associated with the questions of what weapons are, what they are for and what they do.[1] Part III then shifts emphasis to concentrate on how prohibition regimes attempt to manage the difficulties outlined in Parts I and II.

As with previous chapters, the following ones ask what is at stake in attempts to specify the acceptability of force. In contrast to those who seek to lay claim to a definite understanding of technology, settling effects or purposes is not the aim of the chapters that follow.[2] The analysis presented will suggest that much scope exists for disputing what technologies are, what they are for and what they do when attention is turned to devising control measures. In making this case, I do not wish to simply note there is disagreement about weaponry. Rather a central concern is with how individuals move back and forth in debates about prohibitions between treating the purposes of weapons as open-ended and fixed, between considering specific instances of their use and general claims about how they are used, as well as between identifying their 'social' and the 'technical' aspects.

This chapter begins by examining alternative ways in which weapons are presented as implicated in action and some of the related difficulties of appraising their rights and wrongs. It is sometimes suggested that a number of weapons (for instance, biological ones) by their very nature are abhorrent and should be banned. The slogan 'Guns don't kill people, people do' suggests a rather different way of making sense of where any problem might rest and thus what controls should be contemplated. Depending on how technology is conceived as implicated in action, an undesired outcome might be alternatively characterized as the result of conscious and calculated decisions, the likely but unfortunate consequence of acting in a confusing situation, or the inevitable effect of an inherently unacceptable weapon. These alternative conceptions are central in suggesting what deserves condemnation: overall types of weapons, who uses them, how and in what circumstances, or the consequences of their use. A preliminary consideration of such contrasting ways of conceiving of weaponry in this chapter will set the stage for the more detailed cases given in the remainder of Part II.

Neutral tools, unpredictable systems and abhorrent weaponry

When security personnel don protective 'riot control' equipment to 'maintain order', when populations subject to international peacekeeping operations routinely carry machetes for 'self-protection', or when one nation decides to invest billions of dollars into an inter-continental missile 'defence' system, the wisdom of these acts are readily contested. Different appraisals often derive from alternative assessments of the purpose of these actions. Standards of acceptable practice depend on assessments of available options. If the means exist to selectively destroy certain targets with precision-guided munitions, then the failure to employ such options – as alleged in the 1999 NATO air attacks with cluster munitions near populated areas in the Federal Republic of Yugoslavia[3] or in 2003 air strikes in Iraq[4] – brings condemnation. Underlying such 'moral' debates are pragmatic 'technical' assessments regarding the possibility of avoiding what is referred to euphemistically as 'collateral damage' as well as political assessments about the necessity of employing force in the first place.

The role of technology in contributing to or facilitating inappropriate acts is multiply conceived. Perhaps the most common framing is in terms of the use of neutral tools. The knife that allows for preparing food or the opening of letters might, in the wrong hands, end up being used to stab someone. To characterize technology in a tool-like manner provides a certain understanding of what is going on – one that gives a central role to the aims of users and the consequences of actions. After suffering from the effects of cluster bombs during the Vietnam War, a North Vietnamese official reportedly argued against an international ban on them stating 'A weapon used by the imperialist is an imperialist weapon... In the hands of a liberation fighter, it is a sacred tool'.[5] In 'tool' conceptualizations, to the extent that unfortunate or unexpected consequences arise, they result from certain individuals crossing permissible boundaries of conduct.

Considerable criticisms have been levelled at the portrayal of the abuse of technology in terms of the (mis-) application of tools. For one, uncertainty, unpredictability and uncontrollability are all long-standing conditions of conflict.[6]

Abstract calls to clearly demarcate use from abuse and refrain from the latter give little indication of the difficulties of achieving this in practice. The military strategist Clausewitz referred to the 'friction' of warfare – the complications associated with coordinating 'men and machines' – as stifling the best-laid plans. Abuse with 'tools' (weapons) might indeed take place, but a singular effort to differentiate intended versus unintended consequences neglects the crucial deployment choices made prior to instances of application, the conditions required for technology to function as advertised and intangible and cumulative implications of action.[7]

Whereas in the 'tool model' responsibility follows from intent, the possibility of tracing outcomes back to someone's intent in the case of complex technology systems, in particular, is deemed quite limited by some. Langdon Winner argued that perhaps nowhere is this more apparent than in the case of modern weapon systems. Herein those close to instances of employment are often said to be just following orders, while authority figures are presented as too distant to be held responsible for actions on the ground. Thus:

> [b]oth proximity and distance count as excuses. The closer you are, the more innocent; the farther you are, the more innocent. It is a magnificent arrangement in which everyone is safe except the victims. In [modern complex technical systems] the very notion of 'deed' seems to evaporate. The concept of responsibility becomes as slippery as a squid in a fish market bin.[8]

Just how uncertainty and unpredictability ought to enter into characterizations of specific outcomes is contestable. Unfortunate outcomes of action involving technology might be deemed due to accident, mechanical failure, intentional purposes or inadvertent mishap.[9]

The relevance of such points is not limited to highly complex technical systems. For instance, beginning in the late 1980s the Israeli Defense Force (IDF) deployed rubber kinetic munitions in street clashes with Palestinians. Despite being introduced as a less lethal alternative to firearms, many deaths and hundreds of serious injuries were attributed to these munitions.[10] Israeli Defense Force spokespersons denied allegations that widespread violations were taking place of the guidelines regarding the minimum firing distance and target placement. Various justifications and excuses were offered by the Office of the Military Advocate to explain casualties: the unpredictability of 'riot' situations, the difficulty of aiming with the precision required and the 'considerable difficulty in estimating distance'. In other words, save for a few isolated cases, the weapons were not being abused. Deaths to Palestinians in these situations were regrettable, but unavoidable. While acknowledging some level of unpredictability, critics argued that the sheer number of severe injuries and the failure to reprimand officers suspected of violating the guidelines suggested something much more systematic was at work than a said 'combination of chance and unanticipated circumstances'.[11]

Following from the arguments of Chapter 3, in disputes such as this, just how the deaths and injuries are described and contextualized is of fundamental importance in constituting a sense of the problem. Episodes in which casualties were inflicted can be compared to cases where they did not for the purposes of trying to suggest what went wrong. Israeli spokespersons suggested that various circumstance-specific factors led to the deaths: a soldier's aim erred slightly; a child appeared suddenly in the line of fire from a 'dead space' between a solider and rioters; etc. Since such matters are unavoidable in street conflicts, citing them acts to minimize condemnation and close legal investigations. Rather than focusing on the particularities of events in context, critics of the IDF contrasted it to other security forces and point to the failure of leadership to monitor soldiers' action, prosecute their wrongdoings or furnish them with less lethal munitions. Responsibility rests with leaders of the defence force who were entrusted to act appropriately. Which account holds sway is crucial, as those 'who are most effective in establishing causal background may be able to control public assessment of blame'.[12]

In contrast to treating weapons as simple means to ends or complex means to disputed ends, often the case has been made that certain weapons have a definite moral standing. In assessing implications of precision-guided munitions, George and Meredith Friedman commented:

> The accuracy of [precision-guided munitions] *promises to give us a very different age, perhaps a more humane one.* It is odd to speak favorably about the *moral character of a weapon*, but the image of a Tomahawk missile slamming precisely into its target when contrasted with the strategic bombardments of World War II does in fact contain a deep moral message and meaning. War may well be a ubiquitous part of the human condition, but war's permanence does not necessarily mean that the slaughters of the 20th century are permanent.[13]

More typically, however, when some moral standing is attributed to weapons it is that they are abhorrent and inhumane. Chemical, biological and nuclear weapons – what are often lumped together under the abbreviation of weapons of mass destruction (WMD) – are likely often categorically condemned. Herein, no particular motives or justifications for use need be offered to substantiate condemnation.[14] For example, that the Iraqi military employed chemical weapons to kill over 5000 Iraqi Kurds in Halabja and elsewhere during 1988 was widely cited in 2002–03 by some Western political leaders and commentators in the build up to war as an indicator the treachery of Saddam Hussein's regime. In contrast, the fact that thousands of Kurds perished through conventional weapon attacks with bombs and bullets in countries such as Iraq and Turkey in recent decades[15] was not so widely cited preceding the war as an indicator of the barbarity of these governments. For whatever reasons, chemical weapons were placed in an especially repugnant moral category.[16]

As suggested in the split between chemical (a sub-category of 'unconventional' weapons) and conventional weapons, sweeping condemnations of one type of weaponry requires distinguishing it from others. Of all weaponry, perhaps no other category has been singled out so much as nuclear weapons. Writing at the height of Cold War tensions in the 1980s, for example, Malcolmson[17] maintained nuclear weapons were qualitatively unlike any others because:

- they made possible the entire annihilation of a state and its people;
- a comprehensive defence against them was 'virtually inconceivable';
- when more than one state had them, their use by any would be 'potentially suicidal';
- their large scale use would render the Earth for the most part uninhabitable.

Given such considerations, he concluded '[n]uclear weapons ... are means without any appropriate ends; and the use of these weapons has no credibility as an instrument of policy'.[18] As such there was no scope for tinkering around the edges to change the core facts. Moreover nuclear deterrence policies of the Great Powers based on assured retaliation were fundamentally misconceived. Similar appraisals that nuclear weapons are fundamental 'obstacles to, rather than ... facilitators of international security' continue to be made.[19]

Contrary evaluations of weaponry

> Every development of Science that makes warfare more universal and more scientific makes for permanent peace by making warfare more intolerable.
>
> (US Chemical Warfare Service (1921))[20]

> Every step change in science has opened up new and more terrifying methods of killing and incapacitating; and in turn made more urgent that these means be subject to internationally enforceable control.
>
> (UK Foreign and Commonwealth Office (2002))[21]

As argued in the previous section, numerous contentions often take place regarding the manner in which weapons are implicated in certain outcomes. Just how weapons' attributes, situational factors or the identity of those involved with their use contribute to outcomes deemed unacceptable. Appeals to pragmatics, politics and purposes are at play in such disputes. Consider a few opposing ways of thinking about technology.

- *Limits on the means of force reduce suffering. Limits on the means of force increase suffering.*

As the two given quotes indicate, contrasting assessments have been offered regarding the desirability of enhancing the destructiveness of weaponry. The former US Chemical Warfare Service motto expressed a long-standing contention that it is desirable to seek the most the severe means of force possible. While many today may dismiss the suggestion that this logic should justify the development of chemical weapons, a very similar logic underpinned the nuclear retaliation policy of 'mutually assured destruction'; that being that the availability of highly destructive options (combined with the will to use them) is the surest way of deterring conflict in the first place.[22]

Such sentiments have not been limited to 'WMD' or just averting the outbreak of conflict. In their time, the relative effectiveness of bows, artillery pieces and tanks were all said to be so effective that wars would come to a quick end.[23] The enthusiasm in contemporary US military circles for employing overwhelming force and promoting 'the revolution in military affairs' are justified, at least in part, as ways to avoid prolonged conflict which would increase human and financial costs.[24] Herein, if force is to be used, it should be as decisive as possible – a short, sharp, shock. The use of atomic bombs on Hiroshima and Nagasaki during the Second World War was one of the most extreme and well-known examples where the case for overwhelming force has been forwarded. The hundreds of thousands of deaths and unknowable suffering to civilian populations caused have been justified as averting even more causalities by achieving a swift Japanese surrender. While whether the dropping of the atomic bombs in these cases was necessary has been much debated since, arguably the general consequentialist argument that it might be acceptable to cause death and suffering to some (even civilian populations) to prevent a far greater amount (or even a future risk of a far greater amount) to others is less disputed.[25]

In contrast, the quote from the UK Foreign and Commonwealth Office report about biological weapons contends that the destructive potential of (at least some) weaponry demands a speedy response. Those advocating such a position might well point to the failure of past enthusiastic predictions about the supposed potential of advances in force capabilities to reduce suffering. So, in a wide ranging analysis of how military technological innovations can worsen security problems they were meant to resolve, US Air Force Colonel Dulap[26] quotes John Donne (1621) as stating:

> So by the benefit of this light of reason, they have found out artillery, by which wars come to a quicker end then heretofore, and the great expense of blood is avoided, for the number slain now, since the invention of artillery, are much less than before, when the sword was the executioner.

With the historical hindsight of the large-scale destructiveness of artillery in warfare since the early seventeenth century, it is difficult to see how this conclusion could be justified. Along similar lines, one counter to claims that nuclear weapons helped maintain relative peace between the Great Powers of the late twentieth century is that this 'is a pimple on the face of history. Can they work so for millenniums to come?'.[27, 28]

- *Weapons are instruments developed for a purpose. Weapons are instruments in search of purpose.*

Perhaps as with no other area of technical development, weapons are thought of in terms of their intended functions. *Webster's Dictionary* defines a weapon as 'an instrument of offensive of defensive combat; something to fight with; anything used, or designed to be used, in destroying, defeating or injuring an enemy, as a gun, a sword, etc'. Particular weapons accomplish the goals of destroying, defeating, or injuring an enemy through inflicting a specific type of damage, such as the kinetic energy imparted to individuals and objects from bullets and fragmentation bombs.

Various criticisms can be made of the suggestion that weapons should be understood as instruments developed to fulfil a given purpose. To start with, in the history of the development of weapons, much like that of technology in general, many examples can be found of how devices originally developed for one purpose ended up serving another.[29] Much of the impetus for the renewed interest in so-called non-lethal weapons in US military circles, for instance, dates back to the Cold War and the need to break the tempo of a possible Soviet invasion of Central Europe. Rather than seeking to minimize injury, some recent proponents of this class of weaponry stated the original agenda was increasing the ultimate destructiveness of force.[30]

Alterations made to the purposes of weapons can have substantial bearing on their assessment and thus subsequent determinations of what they should be used for. Collins and Pinch examined the controversies about the effectiveness of the Patriot missile system in the Persian Gulf War.[31] While the Patriot was originally designed for use against aircraft, particularly because of the firing of Scud missiles against Israel, it was extensively employed as part of an anti-missile defence system in the Gulf War. After the war estimates of the efficacy of the Patriots against the Scuds varied from almost 100 per cent to nearly 0 per cent. Although tests for the effectiveness of the missiles against aeroplanes might be somewhat straightforward, against other missiles heading for a ground target at high speed, establishing measures of success, let alone determining whether they were met, proved quite controversial. Criteria proposed for judging effectiveness included whether the Scuds were duded, damaged, diverted or intercepted. The criteria chosen had significant implication for determinations of efficacy. Moreover, Collins and Pinch argue that as the Patriots were deployed to help prevent Israel from retaliating against Iraq and undermining Arab states support for the war, in practice official suggestions about the ultimate criteria offered for assessing them went well beyond those associated with their technical performance. Criteria included whether they boosted civilian moral, the profitable sale of Patriot missiles or support for other anti-missile programmes such as the Strategic Defense Initiative.

Another type of criticism of thinking about weapons as instruments intended for some purpose centres on the highly complex and politicized systems for developing and acquiring modern weapons. In relation to the US, Farrell argued that acquisition systems often produce ill-conceived and unproven weapons that serve little in the way of strategic purposes.[32] The extended time frames that often characterizes weapons acquisition means that particular weapons can be developed over the course of many political administrations. As such, weapon programmes initiated for one reason, such as the B-2 stealth bomber's original role in nuclear strikes against the Soviet Union, are often subsequently justified for very different and arguably dubious purposes.[33]

As well, the terms 'low-cost decisions', 'reverse adaptation', 'functional shift' and 'technology drift' have been offered to refer to the manner in which a gradual transformation can take place in how force is used. A capability originally introduced as a last step measure in a narrow range of situations and designed to achieve some specific desirable end can, over time, become much more widely used. In this vein, for example, while CS gas was initially introduced into the Vietnam War by the US Army for limited riot control situations, it eventually became employed in a wide range of settings.[34] Likewise if an option such as precision-guided munitions allows for targeted damage with minimal (immediate) threats to users, this may encourage decision makers to lower the threshold[35] for using violence.[36] To portray certain consequences as 'unintended' or 'secondary' is itself questionable in that this presumes some definite and shared understanding of the intended purpose of a weapon.

Answering questions about whether weapons serve the purposes intended relies on some certain notion of intent, but often intent is the matter disputed. As in the case of the IDF's employment of rubber kinetic munitions, one person's unintended consequence is another's predictable outcome. Attributions made of intent can serve as a resource for judging situations. In a critical appraisal of policy responses to the 2001 anthrax attacks in the US, Barbara Hatch Rosenberg argued 'the perpetrator's motive was not to kill but rather to raise public fear and thereby spur Congress to increase spending on biodefence. In this, the attacks have been phenomenally successful'.[37] In these examples, claims about what is foreseeable, planned, unintended, etc. are highly bound up with determinations about the appropriateness of action and where culpability (if any exists) rests.

In short, weapons can be taken as objects which fulfil intended and straightforward aims of inflicting injury or damage, but such views can be questioned as to whether they offer a robust view of the range of functions weapons ultimately serve. As prohibitions on weapons are often established on the basis of future speculations about their function and rationale, these competing ways of making sense of purpose are significant.

- *The development and employment of weaponry helps resolve conflict situations. The development and employment of weaponry escalates conflict.*

When the use of force is considered, often one area of concern is whether such action will end the conflict in question or spawn yet further conflict by encouraging cycles of reaction and retaliation. So as in Chapter 3, Bush and Chomsky offered competing appraisals of whether the 2003 Iraq war had diminished or heightened the terrorist threat against the West. In relation to pre-emptive or preventive wars, questions about whether force will increase or decrease threats are central to the justifications given. Much of the same questioning takes place for the development of weaponry. So, for instance, programmes such as the Strategic Defense Initiative are justified as defending Western states against a missile attack. In contrast for those critical of it, however, the initiative threatens to destabilize international relations and undermine trust and thereby make such a strike more likely.

In a similar fashion, the Biological and Toxin Weapons Convention (BTWC) allows states to undertake activities intended to prevent and counter a bioattack (see Chapter 6). A major source of disagreement has been the matter of what, if anything, distinguishes the knowledge and techniques necessary for such protective steps and what is required for the production of biological weapons. In general terms, offensive and defensive programmes require similar knowledge about the mechanisms of pathogenic agents the response of the immune system to those agents and the means of dispersing them.[38] So research undertaken for otherwise legitimate medical and scientific goals might end up suggesting novel weapon possibilities.[39] Even those within biodefence establishments have spoken about the risk that the existence of biodefence programmes may inadvertently further ends such initiatives were designed to prevent.[40] So, the work undertaken to counter infectious disease might well end up suggesting new ways of furthering it. The wish by some countries to develop extensive protective measures for their troops and populations against bioweapons might be taken by others as a prelude to their use. When the US government earmarked $2.5 billion in 2003 for research and development into new 'biodefence' research,[41] whether or not this would ultimately help or hinder international attempts to limit the viability of bioweapons became a highly salient issue.[42]

These three opposing ways of making sense of weaponry and equipment suggest something of the difficulties associated with making appraisals. There are pressing and arguably historically recurring problems in how to adjudicate on the issues stated and therefore justify what action should be taken. The place of purpose in assessing technology depends on whether human action is understood as controllable and predictable or uncertain and unpredictable. Making determinations about how future suffering or conflict might be reduced *vis-à-vis* controls will necessary involve some degree of speculation and ethical uncertainty about how to weigh outcomes.

Simply to mention the contrary ways of thinking in the brief manner done here though only begins to hint at how they enter into specific debates about prohibitions. Instead of thinking about dilemmas as invariant conditions, attention instead needs to be directed to dilemmas-as-situated-events. For instance, while it seems reasonable to assume 'hawks' and 'doves' will hold predictable positions in debates about prohibitions, such typifications are of limited insight. In a historical analysis of the origins of the taboo against chemical weapons, for instance,

Price argues that individuals and organizations have taken opposing positions about the morality of such weapons over time because of changing local institutional and historical circumstances.[43] One major historical shift has been that as capabilities for producing chemical weapons have proliferated in recent decades, highly industrialized states have moved from a policy of downplaying their abhorrence and uniqueness to pressing for more and more stringent prohibitions of these 'WMD'. Whereas in the past the development of chemical weapons was cited by many as a sign of a progressive modern state (as indicated in the quote at the start of this section by the US Chemical Warfare Service), today refraining from the possession of such weapons is generally taken as a sign of what constitutes a civilized state. The reversals associated with appraisals of weapons over time would caution against the long-term viability of any particular evaluation made of them.

To say debates about controls involve dilemmas though is not only to contend there are competing ways of making sense of the issues at stake. Rather, as Billig and others have elaborated, stances taken on debates can contain the seeds of counter forms of argument.[44] In this regard, while many categorical claims are made against weapons, these are rarely as all-inclusive as they might seem at first. The suggestion that leg-irons are '*primarily* designed for torture and cruel, inhuman or degrading treatment', that defence against nuclear attack are '*virtually* inconceivable', or that the use of nuclear weapons where more than one state has them would be '*potentially* suicidal' might be offered as justifications for sweeping condemnations of leg-irons or nuclear weapons, but such claims leave open at least the possibility that some conditions might justify a re-think.

Following on from the points in Chapter 3 about the importance of description, it further can be noted that just what counts as an instance of a given weapon is often disputed. Even though 'chemical and biological weapons' are often condemned outright in international conventions and media presentations, there is much discussion about the desirability of such categorizations in security circles. Herein agents with selective, known and short term minor effects might offer far more humanitarian ways of resolving conflict. The US government is currently sponsoring 'research'[45] into employing peptides and cell signalling molecules to alter body temperature, mood and hormone release and through this function as incapacitants.[46] Indeed, it has long been argued that such agents might be far more acceptable alternatives than conventional weapons.[47] As the Chemical Weapons Convention (CWC) and the BTWC place significant restrictions of the development of chemical and biological weapons, just whether such 'non-lethal agents' are designated as 'chemical and biological weapons' or something else is of considerable significance in appraising their permissiblity. Predictably, attempts by weapon developers to occupy the moral high ground through the refinement of technology have generated significant scepticism and condemnation.[48] Rather than agreeing that some progressive or even preferential ends are embodied in incapacitating weapons, various critics have drawn attention to situational or user related factors that are supposed to undermine the possibility that this technology serves the ends (and only the ends) avowed by proponents.[49]

Part II

This chapter suggested something of the alternative ways in which weapons are said to be implicated in action and it made a number of initial points regarding the contrary ways of appraising their relative appropriateness. Attempts to justify prohibitions or argue against them entail forwarding some sort of characterization of what is going on with weaponry. Whether modifying who uses which weapon in what situation should change an evaluation of force or the desirability of prohibitions is contested.

The remainder of Part II now moves on from these preliminary points to make a more detailed consideration of attempts to specify what weapons are, what they are for and what they do. Understandings of these matters underpin many humanitarian-inspired prohibitions, yet as will be argued, determinations of the capabilities of technology can be readily unpacked. Even while many acknowledge problems with the categorizations, generalizations and contextualizations, prohibitions rely on such processes. In addition, the next three chapters reiterate and extend the importance of approaching questions about what technologies are, what they are for and what they do as matters:

> never transparently obvious and [that] necessarily requir[e] some form of interpretation; technology does not speak for itself but must be spoken for. Thus our apprehension of technical capacity is the upshot of our interpreting or being persuaded that the technology will do what [some individuals] say it will do.[50]

Part III then considers in further detail how prohibitions attempt to address or resolve the scope for disagreement about the properties, purposes and potential of weaponry.

Chapter 5

Weapons

What are they?

'I don't know what you mean by "glory",' Alice said.

Humpty Dumpty smiled contemptuously. 'Of course you don't – till I tell you. I meant "there's a nice knock-down argument for you!"'

'But "glory" doesn't mean "a nice knock-down argument",' Alice objected.

'When *I* use a word,' Humpty Dumpty said, in rather a scornful tone, 'it means just what I choose it to mean – neither more nor less.'

'The question is,' said Alice, 'whether you *can* make words mean so many different things.'

'The question is,' said Humpty Dumpty, 'which is to be master – that's all.'

In the fantasy world of Lewis Carroll's *Through the Looking Glass*, many of the conventions of everyday life are suspended or upturned. Instead of the meaning of words being a matter of social convention, Humpty Dumpty insists meaning is the exclusive province of those in a position of 'master'. As illustrated in the confused conversation between Alice and Humpty Dumpty, the attempt to follow through this tenet leads to bewilderment (at least for those not 'master'). While the suggestion that glory means 'there's a nice knock-down argument for you' would seem odd to most, just what is and is not meant by words is not always clear-cut.

This chapter examines disputes about the naming and categorization of technology; that is, disputes about what they are. In doing so, the main concern is with how objects and events are treated as similar or dissimilar to one another for the purpose of commenting on their acceptability in relation to prohibitions. It extends many of the initial points made in Part I regarding the contested meaning of names, concepts and rules by examining in detail two sets of controversies. In one set competing terms are offered as part of the evaluation of a particular type of incendiary bomb while in the other a new category of 'incorporation component parts' is forward to establish the appropriateness of exports. In doing so I want to illustrate the substantial scope for dispute about the meaning of terms and therefore how prohibitions are established and 'applied'.

Returning to the themes of Chapter 3, this one also considers the representational and discursive aspects of language. It elaborates the problems and performative aspects of establishing the meaning of terms. While there may be a constant desire to name the world so as to provide for a shared sense of what needs doing, the classifications made are often questioned. As argued here, once and for all determinations of what counts as the significant similarities and differences between events and objects is ever elusive but also ever pervasive. This has important implications for how terms and categories are debated and what it means to 'follow' rules for appropriate conduct. In considering the basis of dispute, this chapter highlights the importance of context as a descriptive and explanatory resource for seeking to close down disputes, a topic that will be further pursued in Chapter 6.

What is it, really?

On 5 August 2003, a report appeared in the *San Diego Union-Tribune* stating that US forces had employed firebombs earlier that year against Iraqi troops.[1] The report cited various US Marines Corps officers fighting in Iraq who said American helicopters and jets had dropped these incendiary bombs at approaches to the Saddam Canal and the Tigris River bridge. In this report and others that followed, two major issues of concern were discussed. One, the firebombs were said to be similar to 'the controversial napalm used in the Vietnam War'. Indeed the Marine officers described the devices as 'napalm' and the Marines' spokesman Col. Michael Daily was quoted as suggesting the firebombs' effects were 'remarkably similar' to napalm.

Second, this story had followed denials by the Pentagon made during the war that napalm bombs had been used. In March 2003 both *CNN*[2] and the *Australian Sydney Morning Herald*[3] reported that Marines had claimed napalm had been dropped. At the time a Pentagon spokesperson called these two reports 'patently false' as the US had removed napalm from service in the 1970s and destroyed its last stockpiles in 2001.[4] The *San Diego Union-Tribune* report explained the disjuncture between the denials of the Pentagon in March and the admissions in August in stating:

> Apparently the spokesmen were drawing a distinction between the terms 'firebomb' and 'napalm'. If reporters had asked about firebombs, officials said yesterday they would have confirmed their use. What the Marines dropped, the spokesmen said yesterday, were 'Mark 77 firebombs'.[5]

For officials at the Pentagon, while firebombs were indeed 'remarkably similar' to napalm bombs, they were also substantially distinct from them in terms of their chemical make-up and effects. Firebombs employ a kerosene-based fuel with some benzene instead of a mixture of gasoline and benzene in 1970s US versions of napalm bombs. The latest mixture was said to make the most recent versions of the Mark 77s less harmful to the environment.

While the Department of Defense's distinction between firebombs and napalm was supposed to insulate the US armed forces from criticism, its significance was lost on many commentators. The similarities between the two instead meant the bombs in question were indeed napalm. John Pike of GlobalSecurity.org was quoted as stating 'You can call it something other than napalm, but it's napalm'. Spokespersons for the Physicians for Social Responsibility considered the distinction 'pretty outrageous'[6] and added 'There is absolutely no difference in the impact and use of MK 77 and napalm. They're both made for the same purpose . . . Both are designed to kill as many humans as possible, attack bunkers and spread fire.'[7] On the basis of the partial resemblance noted by the Pentagon, the German television programme *Monitor* concluded 'Therefore it is a fact: The US used in the Iraq-War the same weapons as they did in Vietnam: napalm-bombs, one of the most horrible war-weapons of all times, with real heavy damages done especially to all surviving victims.'[8]

Here then was a dispute about classification: how associations should have been made between terms and objects. Were the incendiary bombs used by US forces in Iraq best understood as 'napalm' or 'firebombs'? The debate centred on a questioning of the similarities and differences between the latest Mark 77 bombs (mod 5 version) and previously deployed ones routinely designated as napalm (e.g. M-74). While admitting in some respects that the Mark 77 bombs in question were similar to napalm, Pentagon spokespersons maintained that in vital respects they were also different. Others disagreed, arguing that for all practical purposes the bombs were the same and so the same term should apply.

The dispute was not merely one about classification nomenclature that could be resolved through a technical evaluation or chemical formula definitions. Instead, all at once, the status attributed to the bombs depended on and justified assessments of the motives for their use, what counted as the germane history for understanding their deployment and what other considerations were relevant. Herein the particulars of the accounts given were highly performative in constituting an understanding of what had gone on. Consider the excerpts of reports from several media sources given in Box 5.1 that followed from the original *San Diego Union-Tribune* article. In these, various rhetorical strategies were employed to make sense of what the use of weapons identified and decried as *napalm bombs* was about. In 'US Admits It Used Napalm in Iraq', the specific phrasing of the admission by the Pentagon implied a decision was taken by it to hide these (what must be dubious) weapons (why else would they have denied them?). To state napalm is 'controversial' was to imply both that this status existed as something out there that was not the whimsical product of individual newspaper reports[9] and that the Pentagon must have made a deliberate calculation in deploying the bombs. That they were an 'upgraded version' that 'obliterated' positions implied they might be even worse by some metric than older versions of napalm. Mentioning their psychological impact highlighted a range of issues beyond the Pentagon's concerns.

In 'US Used Napalm in Iraq' the characterization of the dropping of the bombs as (yet another) instance of a return to (what are likely to be regarded by many as) the undesirable days of Vietnam suggested what evaluation should have been

Box 5.1 Napalm in Iraq

'US admits it used napalm in Iraq'

Arab News[a] *and* The Independent *(UK)*[b]

American pilots dropped the controversial incendiary agent napalm on Iraqi troops during the advance on Baghdad. The attacks caused massive fireballs that obliterated several Iraqi positions. The Pentagon denied using napalm at the time, but Marine pilots and their commanders have confirmed that they used an upgraded version of the weapon against dug-in positions. They said napalm, which has a distinctive smell, was used because of its psychological effect on an enemy...

'US used napalm in Iraq'

Alternet[c]

Here's yet another Vietnam-era flashback: Marine fighter pilots and commanders newly returned from Iraq have confirmed dropping dozens of napalm-type bombs to clear the path to Baghdad during the war. Col. Randolph Alles who commanded Marine Air Group 11 *told* the San Diego Union – Tribune, 'We napalmed both those (bridge) approaches. Unfortunately, there were people there because you could see them in the (cockpit) video.' He added, 'The generals love napalm. It has a big psychological effect...'

'Why we aren't winning the peace in Iraq'

The San Diego Union-Tribune[d]

...War should be fought only by professional armies, but scorched earth tactics are common to every war. We learned recently from the Union-Tribune's James Crawley that the U.S. military used chemical weapons (napalm-type) against Iraq in a war fought putatively to deprive Iraq of chemical weapons that may not exist. Who is the terrorist?...

a Andrew Buncombe. 2003. 'US admits it used napalm bombs in Iraq' *The Independent* 10 August.
b Andrew Buncombe. 2003. 'US admits it used napalm bombs in Iraq' *Arab News* 10 August.
c Lakshmi. 2003. 'U.S. used napalm in Iraq' *Alternet* 6 August. http://www.alternet.org/waroniraq/2003/08/001179.html
d James O. Goldsborough. 2003. *The San Diego Union-Tribune*. 21 August, p. B.9.7.

made. That people were on the bridge and pilots dropped bombs reminded the reader that this was not a story about abstractions or vaguely identified 'troops', but about particular individuals, some of who acted and others that suffered as a result. The attribution of 'love' as the generals' motivation for using these bombs proposed a rather perverse enthusiasm in the context of war. Rather than reminding us of the past, 'Why we aren't winning the peace in Iraq' asked the reader to think about the future and how the said questionable standards of the US in using bombs now labelled as 'chemical weapons' in the search for other chemical weapons will decrease the prospects of rebuilding Iraq. In suggesting chemical weapons were the reason why the war was fought at all, the report implicitly condemns the action since much discussion had been taking place at the time regarding the lack of such weapons in Iraq.

In these reports, the contention that the weapons should be understood as 'napalm (-type) bombs' both derived from and justified the critical tone taken. The problematic initial denial by the Pentagon supported the claim that controversial napalm bombs had been employed. That napalm (a term with 'push button' moral connotations for many[10]) had been dropped questioned the actions of military officials and justified linking this weapon to the category of chemical weapons.

Debates about names are not simply matters of nomenclature because they also are bound up with the distribution of social authority. In these disputes, the question was raised of who should be able to define what the bombs really were: their military users, defence commentators, NGO medical professions or senior military spokespersons. As contrasting claims were being made and all parties were proposing that in the final analysis only one term should really apply, just who had authority was of some importance. Choices about who was expert were bound up with what aspects were taken as the proper basis for establishing resemblances between the Mark 77 bombs in question and previous agreed napalm ones.

In the examples given, references to Vietnam and the label of 'chemical weapon' were part of suggesting what evaluation should be made. And yet, while evoking the history of Vietnam may conjure up for many disturbing images and the designation of napalm as a 'chemical weapon' might suggest it should have been regarded as immediately suspect, these identifications do not specify why 'napalm bombs' should be regarded as worthy of special condemnation. Regarding weapons called napalm as *per se* particularly reprehensible implies a distinction between them and other types of weapons such as conventional high explosives which kill in atrocious ways but do not receive the same attention. The contention that 'napalm' should merit immediate negative moral connotations was questioned as part of this debate. The retired Marine Lt. Gen. Bernard was reported as saying 'I used it routinely in Vietnam...I have no moral compunction against using it. It's just another weapon.'[11] Echoing the 'tool' themes of Chapter 4, herein the evaluation given to napalm should not depend on their deployment *per se*. Indeed, while incendiary devices were often associated with indiscriminate injury to civilians and infrastructure in Vietnam, napalm (along with cluster bombs, another type of weapon that often receives special attention) was justified as a weapon for minimizing secondary damage in certain situations (e.g. such as in strikes against anti-aircraft sites placed near dikes).[12]

As indicated earlier though, citing their chemical make-up, Pentagon officials maintained that the incendiary bombs used in Iraq were not the same as napalm bombs, whatever NGOs or even certain serving Marines might think. Another set of reasons that were cited for why the moral stigma of Vietnam should not be attached to these 'new firebombs' was that they had been used in much different ways and with alternative effects. In Iraq, a reported 30 firebomb canisters were released in combat situations as opposed to the widespread and extensive use of hundreds of thousands of tons of assorted types of napalm bombs in Vietnam. Various operational contingencies such as the weather, the combustibility of the materials targeted and the precision of targeting could have been cited as additional reasons for why it was highly misleading to equate the effects of selective incendiary bombs strike in Iraq with napalm in Vietnam.

That the US officially has questioned wide ranging characterizations of incendiary devices elsewhere that underlie unconditional condemnations in favour of a more consequentialist, case-by-case approach could be cited as supporting the categorization of firebombs. For instance, as noted in many media reports of the Iraq incendiary bomb dispute, the US is not a party to Protocol III of the UN Convention on Certain Conventional Weapons (CCW – colloquially known as the 'Inhumane Weapons Convention'). This Protocol does not call for a ban on incendiary devices *per se* – not every weapon that functions by burning humans is deemed as reprehensible. The Protocol does, however, prohibit air-delivered incendiary weapons in all circumstances against 'any military objective located within a concentration of civilians', limits the scope for incendiary weapons attacks on such an objective through means other than air-delivery to those instances where the 'military objective is clearly separated from the concentration of civilians and all feasible precautions are taken' to prevent harm to civilians and prohibits making plant cover on object attack 'except when such natural elements are used to cover, conceal or camouflage combatants or other military objectives, or are themselves military objectives' (see Box 5.2).

In assessing Protocol III of the CCW, the US Department of Defense Office of Arms Control Implementation and Compliance has recommended it be signed only if the US can 'reserve the right to use incendiary weapons against military targets located in concentration of civilians where it is judged that such use would cause fewer casualties and less collateral damage than alternative weapons'.[13] To cite one case mentioned by the Office, in comparison to high explosives, the heat of incendiary devices might reduce the threat of the dispersion of toxins from attacks on biological weapons (BWs) facilities. Without such an option the surrounding civilian population would be put at greater risk. As with the anti-aircraft sites near dikes in Vietnam, for the Office of Arms Control Implementation and Compliance, adhering to the principle of proportionality requires retaining the ability to use incendiary devices in certain scenarios.

Article 1

Definitions

For the purpose of this Protocol:

1 'Incendiary weapon' means any weapon or munition which is primarily designed to set fire to objects or to cause burn injury to persons through the action of flame, heat, or a combination thereof, produced by a chemical reaction of a substance delivered on the target.

   (a) Incendiary weapons can take the form of, for example, flame throwers, fougasses, shells, rockets, grenades, mines, bombs and other containers of incendiary substances.
   (b) Incendiary weapons do not include:
      (i) Munitions which may have incidental incendiary effects, such as illuminants, tracers, smoke or signalling systems;
      (ii) Munitions designed to combine penetration, blast or fragmentation effects with an additional incendiary effect, such as armour-piercing projectiles, fragmentation shells, explosive bombs and similar combined-effects munitions in which the incendiary effect is not specifically designed to cause burn injury to persons, but to be used against military objectives, such as armoured vehicles, aircraft and installations or facilities.

2 'Concentration of civilians' means any concentration of civilians, be it permanent or temporary, such as in inhabited parts of cities, or inhabited towns or villages, or as in camps or columns of refugees or evacuees, or groups of nomads.
3 'Military objective' means, so far as objects are concerned, any object which by its nature, location, purpose or use makes an effective contribution to military action and whose total or partial destruction capture or neutralization, in the circumstances ruling at the time, offers a definite military advantage.
4 'Civilian objects' are all objects which are not military objectives as defined in paragraph 3.
5 'Feasible precautions' are those precautions which are practicable or practically possible taking into account all circumstances ruling at the time, including humanitarian and military considerations.

Article 2

Protection of civilians and civilian objects

1   It is prohibited in all circumstances to make the civilian population as such, individual civilians or civilian objects the object of attack by incendiary weapons.

2   It is prohibited in all circumstances to make any military objective located within a concentration of civilians the object of attack by air-delivered incendiary weapons.

3   It is further prohibited to make any military objective located within a concentration of civilians the object of attack by means of incendiary weapons other than air-delivered incendiary weapons, except when such military objective is clearly separated from the concentration of civilians and all feasible precautions are taken with a view to limiting the incendiary effects to the military objective and to avoiding, and in any event to minimizing, incidental loss of civilian life, injury to civilians and damage to civilian objects.

4   It is prohibited to make forests or other kinds of plant cover the object of attack by incendiary weapons except when such natural elements are used to cover, conceal or camouflage combatants or other military objectives, or are themselves military objectives.

Some problems of establishing resemblance

As suggested earlier, attempts to label weaponry were crucial in justifying appraisals of the use of force. Contrasting conceptions of the main functions and effects of incendiary devices have been offered to support different designations. If the world is not to be understood as a chaotic assortment of unique objects, then they must be clustered together through terms like 'firebombs', 'incendiary devices' or 'napalm bombs' and generalizations must connect various instances of force to justify statements such as 'napalm has the effects x because of y'. And yet, just whether these terms and propositions are valid is disputable. In the debate stated, much effort was expended in advancing a definitive classification of the incendiary weapons. As argued, that has been a matter of specifying the resemblance of weapons to each other so as to determine if the term napalm should apply. Were the Mark 77 bombs in question so similar to other weapons usually designated as 'napalm' that they should be categorized as 'napalm weapons' and thus be condemned or were the Mark 77s distinct in ways that mean that referring to them as such was not so valid as the stigma associated with napalm need not follow? As argued, the exact descriptions given of objects and events in particular situations were highly suggestive of what evaluation should be made.

The significance and pervasiveness of attributions of similarity and difference in making arguments can be underscored by noting that my analysis of the napalm debate has itself relied on mobilizing notions of similarity and difference in an attempt to offer a sense of meaning. For instance, to say the US Department of Defense has approached deliberations about the acceptability of incendiary devices overall in 'the same' consequentialist, case-by-case manner it has approached deliberations about the acceptability of firebombs is to ascribe a relation of similarity. That this relation was presented in the way it was suggested that the US Department of Defense adopts a consistent basis for assessing the appropriateness of incendiary weaponry; this in contrast to more critical claims of an opportunistic logic by examining the 'firebombs' debate alone. But questions can be asked of just what cases ought to serve as the basis for deriving claims about coherence or opportunism. Likewise, the contention that quotes from individuals display the same features as brought up in earlier chapters rests on notions of similarity.[14]

While commentators to the debate have offered appraisals of why the term napalm or firebomb ought to be applied, the suggestion that the identification of similarities or differences in properties in itself would settle disputes was and is problematic. Establishing agreement through such a comparative process requires identifying what the important properties are and how these properties should be weighed against each other. However, these were the very matters under question in debates; for instance, many of those critical of the US armed forces stressed how 'firebombs' and 'napalm' operated in the same manner – by burning human beings. In contrast, the Pentagon's contented that napalm and firebombs have different environmental consequences and that the usage of firebombs in the Iraq war was simply not comparable with previous usages of napalm. Answers to the questions of what is important and how are better thought of constituting similarity rather than stemming from some understanding of it.[15]

This condition poses major problems for those that wish a definitive resolution to questions about what particular technologies really are. In a wide ranging analysis of the application of concepts and terms, Barnes contends

> there is no metric for resemblance: where an entity is discernibly the same as another or others, but at the same time discernibly different from it or them, there is no absolute scale for measuring sameness or difference and producing a magnitude of resemblance.[16]

This is not to say that every case for resemblances between objects that are said to have something is common is equally plausible. But the degree of resemblance and what this implies for the naming of objects and events are practical judgments that must be argued for, rather than being issues simply resolved once similarities (or differences) are identified. In other words, the proper usage of a concept

> is developed step by step, in process involving successions of on-the-spot judgements. Every instance of use, or of proper use, of a concept must in the last analyses be accounted for separately, by reference to specific, local contingent determinations.[17]

Following Barnes' argument, the future application of terms (such as 'napalm bombs') to objects cannot be set out once and for all. Debate is always possible about whether a bomb that shares some properties with the (itself heterogeneous) group of objects already identified as instances of 'napalm' is best understood as belonging to this group or some other. Much will depend on what are deemed the key properties for determining resemblances.[18] Assessments of the relevance of certain properties can, in turn, depend on determinations of why they are offered. For some commentators, the Pentagon's distinction between napalm and firebombs was taken as an Orwellian public relations word game motivated by the wish to hide uncomfortable facts. As such it hardly desired serious consideration.

The suggestion made in the preceding few paragraphs is that the application of terms or concepts is problematic and the potential for forwarding them as the means for resolving disputes about force is limited. Much of the focus so far has been on moving from cases where a term is generally agreed as appropriate to ask whether another object fits under the same title. Against this approach it might be argued that what is needed instead is an authoritative definition that establishes the meaning of a term so that its appropriateness for any object can be definitively determined. The prospects of such a strategy, Barnes suggests, are quite limited, 'It will not do, for example, to impose verbal definitions upon our concepts and require that future usage proceeds in strict conformity with the definitions.' Herein the 'question then arises of the proper use of the terms within the definition itself'.[19] To seek to define the terms within definitions could lead to questions about the definition of terms in definitions, and their definitions and so on. To seek to give those terms substance by applying them to objects on the basis of whether the objects in question are like others where the term applies brings one back to the original problem of how resemblances are justified.

For instance, while Article 1 of the Protocol III of the CCW establishes definitions for some of the terms of the prohibitions given in Article 2, what would count as a weapon '*primarily* designed to set fire to objects or to cause burn injury to persons' or an object that makes an '*effective* contribution to military action' are themselves matters open for debate. While the meaning of such clarifying definitions might not be disputed at a given time, where controversy takes place, then the clarifying terms will themselves require elaboration. To propose that the determinations of whether an object makes an 'effective contribution to military action' can be done by comparing it to past objects widely considered effective contributors reintroduces the problem of what basis should be employed for making determinations of similarity. Again, for practical purposes, determinations of such matters might not prove insurmountable, but such a situation is a contingent agreement rather than a condition arising from the essence of the terms. In discussions about weapon prohibitions, agreement is often far off.

The legal scholar HLA Hart spoke to the import of the problems of naming for judging standards of action (such as by setting out rules in weapon conventions) in arguing:

> Particular fact situations do not await us already marked off from each other, and labelled as instances of the general rule, the application of which is in question; nor can the rule itself step forward to claim its own instances. In all fields of experience, not only that of rules, there is a limit inherent in the nature of language, to the guidance which general language can provide... Canons of 'interpretation' cannot eliminate, though they can diminish these uncertainties; for these canons are themselves general rules for the use of language, and make use of general terms which themselves requires interpretation. They cannot, any more than other rules, provide for their own interpretation. The plain case, where the general terms seem to need no interpretation and where the recognition of instances seems unproblematic or 'automatic' are only the familiar ones, constantly recurring in similar contexts, where there is general agreement in judgments as to the applicability of the classifying terms.[20]

To say that further definitions or rules are limited in this fashion does not mean that they are thereby irrelevant, for the manner in which they are specified and enacted can act to structure disputes. How far canons of interpretation can diminish uncertainties is a matter of scholarly debate.[21] Whatever the subtleties of this discussion, in relation to prohibitions the extent of contention about the basic terms and issues at stake mean that uncertainties abound. Numerous examples in later chapters will suggest a lasting 'plain case' in the area of weapon prohibitions is hard to come by as contexts and standards of generality are called into question. All of these will justify the importance of a sceptical orientation to the potential for rules to determine proper conduct.

Part(ial) obligations

So far this chapter has focused on what is at stake in the naming of weaponry. As argued, while the names given to weapons are of some importance in constituting what they are, they rest on rather precarious footing. Although just not any term will do, in cases where competing claims of resemblances are plausible, the proper terminology is open to challenge. Contrasting appraisals stem from alternative determinations of what considerations are relevant. As such, an appeal to the similarity or dissimilarity of some object to others placed under a given category (e.g. napalm bombs) is a strategy limited in its ability to convert nonbelievers. In the given case, for instance, the doubts voiced about particular determinations of the status of the Mark 77 bombs did not compel any re-naming; indeed it would be highly notable and extraordinary if they did.

The difficultly of specifying once and for all what counts as the range of important considerations though should not just be taken as a problematic condition that stands in wait to hopelessly undermine any determinations of how weapons ought to be understood and classified. Instead, the difficultly of specifying relevance and resemblances can *facilitate* some in implementing prohibitions. This section considers one such case and in doing so further elaborates what is at stake in attempts to name and categorize technologies.

Despite the complications suggested in making evaluations of resemblances, the case of the incendiary bombs in Iraq entailed a fairly simple type of comparison: one type of bomb was being compared to others in debates about what term should apply. As indicated in Chapter 1 for leg cuffs and their components though, just what constitutes a given object can itself be a matter of much dispute. Separate components have been shipped out of the UK and later reassembled so as to evade prohibitions on the export of 'leg cuffs'. As opposed to leg restraints, modern sophisticated weaponry, such as tanks, aircraft and naval vessels, consists of numerous component parts assembled in complex systems. This section considers how place and purpose is given to 'component parts' *vis-à-vis* prohibitions regimes: how they are defined, how determinations are made of the permissibility of their export under national and international export control restrictions, and what is at stake in debates about these matters.

In order to prevent arms transfers to countries under embargo or otherwise judged as undesirable destinations, states across the world have enacted export control systems that include provisions requiring private companies to obtain licences for the shipment of military and security technology.[22] The content and terms of these controls, however, vary from country to country in ways which are highly consequential. In 2001, for instance, Amnesty International (AI) reported that while Italian 'military' small arms exports required a government licence, 'civil' arms such as handguns, sub-machine, spare parts and ammunition ostensibly used for sporting, self-defence or police purposes did not. This situation enabled a fairly open trade in such weapons. For example, the establishment of a UN embargo on arms transfer to the former Yugoslavia did not prevent the sale of small arms related weaponry from Italy. Italian companies also supplied some $1.6 million of 'civilian arms' to Sierra Leone between 1993 and 1997, approximately $6 million to Algeria and $7 million to the Republic of Congo between 1993 and 1996. In each country, numerous deaths and extensive human rights abuses were committed in armed conflict with small arms. The Italian government cited 'commercial confidentiality' as a reason for not supplying public information on the extent of such 'civil' transfers. The shipments only become public knowledge through an analysis of general foreign trade data complied by the Italian Institute of Statistics.[23]

Head-up display units

This section examines negotiations about the meaning of categories and terms in export controls in relation to one case of a component part: the export of F-16 fighter Head-Up Display (HUD) Units from the UK to the US for eventual export to Israel. The case points to the importance of considering how categories form and how they function as part of rules setting out appropriate action. In contrast to the vast majority of export decisions, the extent of public and parliamentary scrutiny given to this one makes it possible to develop at least a rudimentary sense of how export rule interpretations are justified and the practical problems of defining weapons.

Of all British arms exports, transfers to Israel for use in the Occupied Territories have proved some of the most controversial. For instance, during the autumn of 2000, as conflict heightened between Israelis and Palestinians, the Israeli Air Force used helicopter gun ships for attacks in the West Bank and Gaza Strip. Such technology was said to allow the pin-point targeting of key strategic facilities that minimized potential casualties, particularly as warnings were given in at least some situations. Human rights groups refuted each of these claims.[24] British companies supplied parts to many of the helicopter gun ships, tanks and armoured personal carriers used by the Israeli Defense Force (IDF) in the Occupied Territories. Much of the public and parliamentary questioning of these exports centred on a promise given by the Labour government in 1997 to reform export controls as part of what was dubbed in the media as Britain's 'ethical foreign policy'. Among other provisions, it was announced licences would be denied for 'Equipment where there is clear evidence of the recent use of similar equipment for internal repression by the proposed end-use . . .'[25]

With the overall heightening of violence in late 2000, France and Germany initiated undeclared embargoes on defence equipment to Israel.[26] The UK did not completely halt transfers but received an agreement from the Israeli government that 'no UK-originated equipment . . . are used as part of the defense force's activities in the territories'.[27] When attack helicopters, tanks and fighter planes of the kinds for which the UK supplied parts were employed in assaults on the Gaza Strip and the West Bank during 2002, further queries were made about which exports should be granted.[28]

Questions about transfers to Israel came to a head in 2003 when an export licence was requested for F-16 aircraft HUD units to the US for eventual delivery to Israel. HUDs present visual navigational, attack and other information to aircraft pilots. The Foreign Secretary Jack Straw justified the approval of the displays in a written statement to Parliament (see Box 5.3). The statement set out to elaborate a 'special' approach to export policy for the particular category of 'incorporation parts': these being technologies exported to one country to be incorporated into equipment there for ultimate onward export to a third country. As stated, the factors (a)–(e) are meant to elaborate the previously existing Consolidated EU and National Arms Export Licensing Criteria. These consist of eight criteria and other factors that specify the range of considerations for making

Box 5.3 8 July 2002 Statement by UK Foreign Minster Jack Straw[e]

In recent years there have been far reaching changes in the defence industry in the UK, the rest of Europe and the United States. Against the background of the end of the Cold War and the resulting reduction in defence budgets world wide, the defence industry has been subject to massive rationalization. One consequence of this change is that increasingly defence goods are manufactured from components sourced in several different countries.

This restructuring of the defence industry presents new challenges for the government's approach to export licensing. Many export licence applications are for goods which are to be incorporated in defence equipment in a second country, which thereafter may be exported to a third country.

The Consolidated EU and National Arms Export Licensing Criteria...make clear that they 'will not be applied mechanistically' to decisions on export licence applications, but rather 'on a case-by-case basis, using judgment and common sense'. The criteria do not provide specific guidance on what approach should be adopted in these 'incorporation' cases.

Other EU and NATO member states face the same rapidly changing environment for their defence industries as the UK. Enquiries by Her Majesty's Government suggest, however, that while as yet there is no common policy in such cases, many of our European partners recognize the need to adopt a special approach towards cases involving incorporation for onward export.

After very careful consideration, Her Majesty's Government has, therefore, decided that it is necessary to set out how it will in future approach licence applications for goods where it is understood that the goods are to be incorporated into products for onward export. The government will continue to assess such applications on a case by case basis against the Consolidated Criteria, while at the same time having regard to, *inter alia*, the following factors:

(a) the export control policies and effectiveness of the export control system of the incorporating country;
(b) the importance of the UK's defence and security relationship with the incorporating country;
(c) the materiality and significance of the UK-origin goods in relation to the goods into which they are to be incorporated, and in relation to any end-use of the finished products which might give rise to concern;
(d) the ease with which the UK-origin goods, or significant parts of them, could be removed from the goods into which they are to be incorporated and
(e) the standing of the entity to which the goods are to be exported.

Against this background the government has considered its response to a number of applications for the export of parts, subsystems and components to the USA for incorporation into equipment eventually destined for other countries. These include Head Up Display units (HUDs) for incorporation in F-16 aircraft scheduled for delivery to Israel in 2003. The UK content in F-16s is less than 1 per cent in value, but the supply of HUDs is part of a long-standing collaboration in this US programme. Any interruption to the supply of these components would have serious implications for the UK's defence relations with the United State...

The government continues to be seriously concerned about the situation in Israel and the Occupied Territories. There has to be a break to the cycle of violence, which has brought so much misery to both peoples, and a resumption of the peace process. We are working closely with partners including the US to reduce the level of tension and to bring about a sustainable and peaceful settlement through negotiation.

The US government maintains a strong and effective export licensing system. The Quadripartite Committee has noted that the United States' conventional arms transfer policy

'does not appear to differ in any important way from the EU Code or the UK national criteria. In some respects...it is an improvement' (HC 467 xxix 73 (25 July 2000)). Appropriate use of arms exported to Israel by the US is the subject of regular dialogue between the two countries, and when the US have concerns they make these known to the Israelis (as required by Congressional legislation). The State Department has been monitoring Israeli actions carefully and will continue to do so.

At the same time the government carefully takes into account the importance of maintaining a strong and dynamic defence relationship with the US. This relationship is fundamental to the UK's national security as well as to our ability to play a strong and effective role in the world. The importance of this role has been demonstrated repeatedly in recent months. There are also wider benefits to the UK's national security of maintaining a strong indigenous defence industrial capability.

Taking account of all these considerations, the government considered that the applications should be approved, and my right hon. Friend the Secretary of State for Trade and Industry has today granted licences for the export of the HUDs, and other equipment to the USA. The government will apply similar considerations to similar applications in future.

e Jack Straw. 'Export Controls' *House of Commons Hansard*, 8 July 2002, Columns 651–2.

export licensing decisions. The criteria are meant to be implemented in such a way that an export will not be issued when 'the arguments for doing so are outweighed by the need to comply with the UK's international obligations and commitments, by concern that the goods might be used for internal repression or international aggression, by the risks to regional stability or by other considerations as described in these criteria.'[29] The headings of the consolidated criteria are provided in Box 5.4.

Box 5.4 The Consolidated EU and National Arms Export Licensing Criteria[f]

Criterion one

Respect for the UK's international commitments, in particular sanctions decreed by the UN Security Council and those decreed by the European Community, agreements on non-proliferation and other subjects, as well as other international obligations...

Criterion two

The respect of human rights and fundamental freedoms in the country of final destination...

Criterion three

The internal situation in the country of final destination, as a function of the existence of tensions or armed conflicts...

Criterion four

Preservation of regional peace, security and stability...

Criterion five

The national security of the UK, of territories whose external relations are the UK's responsibility, and of allies, EU Member States and other friendly countries...

Criterion six

The behaviour of the buyer country with regard to the international community, as regards in particular to its attitude to terrorism, the nature of its alliances and respect for international law...

Criterion seven

The existence of a risk that the equipment will be diverted within the buyer country or re-exported under undesirable conditions...

Criterion eight

The compatibility of the arms exports with the technical and economic capacity of the recipient country, taking into account the desirability that states should achieve their legitimate needs of security and defence with the least diversion for armaments of human and economic resources...

Other factors

Operative Provision 10 of the EU Code of Conduct specifies that Member States may where appropriate also take into account the effect of proposed exports on their economic, social, commercial and industrial interests, but that these factors will not affect the application of the criteria in the Code.

The government will thus continue when considering export licence applications to give full weight to the UK's national interest, including:

(a) the potential effect on the UK's economic, financial and commercial interests, including our long-term interests in having stable, democratic trading partners;
(b) the potential effect on the UK's relations with the recipient country;
(c) the potential effect on any collaborative defence production or procurement project with allies or EU partners;
(d) the protection of the UK's essential strategic industrial base...

f HMSO. 2000. *House of Commons Hansard*, 26 October, Columns 199–203W.

The statement and linked approval of the HUDs generated immediate condemnation,[30] by some accounts even within the government cabinet.[31] The Liberal Democrat defence spokesman called the statement a 'clearly rushed and reactive change of policy [to] provide maximum flexibility and minimum accountability', one that would institutionalize a degree of discretion that would 'open the door to any arms exports of any kind'.[32] While accepting the need to revise policy in light of changing conditions, a 2003 report by the Parliamentary Committees on Strategic Export Controls criticized the policy position in stating: 'There is little doubt about the general intent of the guidelines: the Government will approve some licences for the export of military goods for end-use in particular destinations (such as Israel) if they are to be incorporated in a second country, which it would not approve if they were for export direct to those destination...'[33]

For those critical of the HUDs licence approval, the decision represented a significant breach of the Labour government's pledge not to approve licences for exports to destinations 'where there is clear evidence of the recent use of similar equipment for internal repression'. For government officials, as articulated in Parliamentary question and answer sessions, press briefings and testimonies before the Committees on Strategic Export Controls, the decision represented nothing of the sort. In these debates, alternative appraisals of similarity and difference provided the basic building blocks for justifying contrasting assessments. These appraisals of similarity and difference warranted how the boundaries of categories were to be drawn, how particular objects and decisions were identified as instances of a defined category and how the significance of technology was established.

To start with, in the written statement here, Secretary Straw attributed the impetus of the incorporation policy to the new context of the internationalized production of defence equipment. Rather than the policy deriving from the active need to justify the particular and recognized controversial approval of the HUDs, the restructured manufacturing base required the government to set out its policy – the HUDs case being just one instance of the emerging category of 'incorporation exports'. As Straw contended during Parliamentary questioning in 2003, what ministers needed 'to do was to sit down and say, "We are likely to face a number of these applications, what are we going to do about it?" then having decided what we are going to do about it, be completely open about it.'[34] He responded to voiced criticisms that the globalized production was hardly new to July 2002 (and thus the need for a specific incorporation parts policy hardly urgent[35]) by prefacing the previous comments with the justification that

> It had always been to a degree an international supply chain and an international assembly line, but this has become more formalised and much, much more extensive and it is very rare to find, as far as the UK defence suppliers are concerned, any single item of finished equipment that has not got items of import inside it and also a large proportion of the work of the defence industry is parts which are then assembled elsewhere.[36]

Indeed the policy statement in Box 5.3 makes a case for the pervasiveness of the problem in stating 'many of our European partners recognise the need to adopt a special approach towards cases involving incorporation for onward export'. In short, ministers were responding to a new environment because they were forced to respond, this rather than proactively seeking to justify a conscious choice.

While the environment was new and demanding a policy response, the policy itself was not a departure from that enshrined in the Consolidated EU and National Arms Export Licensing Criteria. If it were a break, there would be some justification for the critical assessment by the NGO Saferworld that the policy announcement set a precedent signifying that henceforth the 'Secretary of State can issue new guidance which changes licence decision-making as and when s/he sees fit. There is no compulsion for the Secretary of State to consult with Parliament on this significant change in policy.'[37] For officials, instead of representing a departure from past practices, the statement in Box 5.3 was said to provide Parliament with 'some gloss on the [consolidated] criteria'.[38] As Straw went on to say: 'I thought it better to be explicit about the principles involved because that seemed to me to be a new circumstance because of the changing nature of the defence industry, and therefore required a new statement.'[39]

As argued by government officials, the stated incorporation parts policy and linked HUDs approval amounted to an elaboration of existing policy for one particular area of export control hitherto not given proper attention; one ministers were forced to confront given the new defence manufacturing context. By articulating the said reasoning at work in making decisions about licences for incorporation parts, the government was acting in a manner accountable to Parliament and the country. Given this formulation, as suggested above, those wishing to contest the merits of the policy statement readily did so, among other ways, by arguing that the policy statement did, in fact, represent a change in export policy and/or that far from some radical change in the environment of defence production requiring a government response, the policy decision was a proactive attempt to re-draw (read: expand) the boundaries of what counted as an acceptable export so as to justify the HUDs approval.[40]

The previous section of this chapter suggested the imposition of meanings on rules and terms through marshalling notions about similarity and difference should be regarded as contingent achievements subject to re-appraisal. In principle it is always possible to suggest an alternative, and generally not completely implausible, range of similarities and differences for making sense of what is going on. Analysis alone cannot authoritatively determine once-and-for-all what characteristics of an object, action or policy should serve as the basis for making comparisons. The remainder of this section extends these initial points by considering their relevance for some of the key areas of debate about the category of incorporation parts.

Are the criteria being followed?

The question of whether the HUDs licence approval went against the Consolidated Criteria has been a predominant topic of concern. To pose such a question assumes the export policy as enshrined in the consolidated criteria and other international agreements has some definitive meaning that was or was not being adhered to. Yet, for a number of reasons, such a presumption is of doubtful merit.

One, from the start, just what the criteria ought to mean has been conceived of as a matter requiring interpretation. In the UK, prior to the Labour government coming to power in 1997, the standard practice for evaluating applications for licences – outside of those few countries under official embargos – was to examine them on a 'case-by-case' basis. Rather than deriving a formal list of acceptable weapons for approved countries or even specifying criteria for making decisions, successive British governments said they treated each application on its individual merits. Over the course of time – perhaps due to changing security assessments, recipient country policy or other factors – the acceptability of a transfer might alter. In the past just how decisions were taken by officials, and in relation to which concerns, were not clear outside of the corridors of Whitehall. At least for some, the inadequacy of this state of affairs was underscored by a series of scandals in the early 1990s regarding the destinations of British arms and their reported role in acts of torture, civil repression and military aggression.[41] The introduction of the consolidated criteria was meant to make the export control regime systematic and operate according to publicly known principles.

Yet despite the explicit introduction of principles for decision-making, as indicated in the written statement in Box 5.3, the consolidated criteria set out as part of the Labour government's reformed export control systems are not being seen as 'hewn in tablets of stone'[42] and simply applied in a mechanical way. Rather the desire to retain flexibility in interpreting the criteria was recognized during their introduction. While the criteria set out general considerations, each application must be examined on its individual merits; that is on a 'case-by-case' basis. In other words, as conceived, in making decision about exports licences 'What you have to do is weigh up all the criteria against the application and make the best judgment that you can.'[43] In this way it cannot be specified in advance what the stipulations of the criteria mean because how they are interpreted depends on contingent determinations of what is deemed relevant for particular cases.

As a second reason why the export policy should not be understood as possessing some definite meaning is that the individual criteria can be played off each other in ways which alternatively offer support or opposition for individual applications. In the case of the HUDs transfers, for instance, criterion 2 related to human rights and criterion 7 related to end-use were placed in opposition. On 22 July 2002, two weeks after the incorporation part policy announcement, an American supplied F-16 jet dropped a one-ton guided bomb on an apartment complex in Gaza City where the Hamas leader Sheikh Salah Shahada was hiding, thereby killing 15 civilians. Even after this widely condemned attack, when Jack Straw was asked in a Parliamentary question and answer session by Richard Burden MP, 'When a 150 sq. m, two-storey apartment block is hit by a missile from an F-16 killing 15 people and nine children, how is it acceptable that British equipment could be supplied for that through a third party, whereas it would not be acceptable if we did it directly?', the Foreign Secretary defended the decision by stating:

> The issue is more complicated than that. The equipment appears to have been misused in this case, but if my honourable Friend looks carefully at the criteria, he will find, first, that we have applied the criteria and, secondly, that the criteria seek to take account, under criterion 7, of 'the capability of the recipient country to exert effective export controls'.

It so happens that the Quadripartite Committee [the Committees on Strategic Export Controls] itself said that the United States' conventional arms transfer policy 'does not appear to differ in any important way from the EU Code or the UK national criteria. In some respects...it is an improvement'.

Although in a particular instance the United States may come to a slightly different decision from us or the EU, the fact is that its arms control policy and the exercise of it are, on any basis, at least as transparent and as effective as the United Kingdom's, and certainly more transparent than that of almost all of our European Union partners.[44]

The UK has thus deferred decisions about the legitimacy of the shipment of completed F-16s by locating decision making with the US and it did so through citing the criteria. By referring to the general provisions of the US export control system rather than its track record with regard to Israel, the British Foreign Secretary was able to argue the issues at stake were 'more complicated' than they might at first appear, so much so that the transfer should have gone ahead.

Of course, it would have been possible to rank each of the consolidated criteria so that when two are seen in conflict it would be clear which should prevail. However, to do so would have meant forgoing the desired flexibility in assessing what factors are relevant and how they should be weighed. In the case of the HUDs that might have meant ignoring the long-term relationship of the manufacturer of the HUDs (British Aerospace (BAe) Systems) with contractors in the US; and as argued 'no sensible government can ignore the implications for that relationship of decisions on one individual application. That does not mean that you automatically go along with the application, but it does mean you need to take account of it'.[45]

A third reason for doubting the existence of some definite meaning to export policy is that irrespective of the stated desire for flexibility, just what their 'application' might mean is something that must be worked out. Even if the human rights criterion had been deemed the most significant, just how it should be applied is another matter. As suggested in the previous section, in thinking about the application of rules:

> Every particular case differs from every other and can never be conclusively pronounced identical to any other, or identical in any attribute to any other. Hence, nothing can be unproblematically deduced from a rule or law, concerning any particular case, because there is always the undetermined matter of whether the case falls under the rule or the law – that is, whether it is *the same as* or *different to* those instances which have already been labeled as falling under the rule or law. Formally this matter of similarity or difference arises at every point of use of a concept, and has to be settled at every point by the using community.[46]

For instance, while criterion 2 of the consolidation criteria rules out the (direct) export of equipment to countries 'where there is clear evidence of the recent use of similar equipment for internal repression by the proposed end-user', just what counts as 'clear evidence', 'recent', 'similar equipment', 'internal repression' and 'the proposed end-user' are not at all clear. The meaning and specific relevance of these terms must be worked out in practice, in this case by government officials and civil servants. Outside of certain regrettable incidents, the Israeli government has insisted on the need to attack the Occupied Territories, labelling such actions as necessary self-defence measures in waging war against terror. This assessment stands in sharp contrast to descriptions of the actions as 'internal repression' or 'external aggression'.[47] Any determinations of exports would have to assess which designation was appropriate. Temporal terms such as 'recent' also provide ample scope for wider ranging interpretations. So when questioned whether the HUDs transfer indicated the Israelis' promise in 2000 not to use British equipment in the Palestinian Territory had been 'torn-up', the Prime Minister's Official Spokesman answered 'no', because that agreement 'related to a specific situation and had been written to address concerns at that particular time'.[48] As such, even if one does not take the case-by-case approach for assessing what transfers are acceptable (as embodied in the Israeli–British agreement), it is necessary to assess for each case whether the rules are still relevant.

Were the HUDs 'significant'?

The tensions associated with striving for a policy that at once seeks to maintain flexibility while laying out principles for decisions can be illustrated in relation to the (a)–(e) incorporation part factors identified by Foreign Secretary Straw in Box 5.3. The factors listed are meant to be taken into account in future export decisions and include matters such as the export control policy of the incorporating country, the importance of UK's relations with the country and the significance of the UK-origin parts in the final product (such as the 1 per cent value of the HUDs identified).

While the factors are suppose to provide further guidance and make policy decisions more transparent, they are not determinate in meaning. For example, instead of specifying what the 'materiality and significance' of an export meant, this was left open to ensure flexibility. So, when asked what counted as a 'significant' component part – whether, for instance, a component that made up 10 per cent of the total value of the F-16s would have been deemed more significant and thus unacceptable – the Prime Minister's Official Spokesman responded that such judgements would be taken on a 'case-by-case' basis.[49] The 1 per cent figure for the F-16 HUDs was only illustrative of the insignificance of the component in this particular instance. In future this might not be relevant.

The indeterminacy associated with particular factors such as material significance was compounded because, as indicated in the policy announcement, any individual factor had to be assessed in relation to the other ones listed. The Committees on Strategic Export Controls argued that this could justify conflicting conclusions. Including both the material significance and the UK's relation with the incorporating country as factors in the open-ended way done meant:

> An insignificant component, a motor part, for example, might well be considered of little relation to any end-use of concern, and therefore more likely to be licensed. A component might also be more likely to be permitted for export if it is more significant, because, for example, of the impact that refusing the licence might have on the defence relationship between the United Kingdom and the incorporating country.[50]

In response the government reiterated the Prime Minister's Official Spokesman earlier contention in stating there is 'no direct correlation between the materiality and significance of the UK-origin good in relation to the goods into which they are to be incorporated and the likelihood of their being licensed for export...'.[51] The relevance associated with this criterion is a matter that must be determined for each case.

With these competing criteria, technology simultaneously can be conceived of in competing ways. On the one hand, the HUDs are an insignificant percentage of the overall value of the F-16s and thus do not significantly enable possible abuses with the fighters. On the other hand, the displays are vital because they are not easily withdrawn. The status of the HUDs as both insignificant and vital is maintained by considering them in relation to different systems: the physical assemblage of the aircraft or the customer-contractor relations of production agreements.

Whatever ethical and economic evaluation is made of the HUDs approval and the incorporation parts policy, given the qualifications stated and the range of possible concerns that might be brought to bear in decisions, the government's contention in Box 5.3 that in the future 'similar' decision-making processes will take place for 'similar' applications does not resolve or necessarily even clarify how any individual incorporation part factor (or any individual criterion of the consolidated criteria for that matter) will be handled for the purposes of export decisions.[52]

Moreover, returning to the themes of Chapter 4 regarding the dilemmas associated with evaluating technology, highly diverging assessments can be made of what the factors set out should mean for determinations of appropriateness. Rather than pointing to the material insignificance of exports as a reason for reducing unease, critics can make a diametrically opposed interpretation: that being it reflected how easily (read: cheaply) the government was willing to go back on its stated principles. In other words, the material insignificance of the HUDs component was not a reason for diminishing concerns but signified the gravity of the approval. This example resonates with another case involving Israel. When four Israeli soldiers living in West Bank settlements were arrested for supplying ammunition to Palestinian militants, a Jewish settler injured in an attack by them commented 'To think – there were the terrorists in front of me, firing away... and one of our own might have supplied them with the bullets... [The Israeli men] sold us for half a shekel [about 10 cents], the price of one bullet that ruined my life'.[53] In this case, the insignificant value of the 'component' in question provides no defence against condemnation. At stake in these interpretations is how one gives meaning and place to 'components' of technical systems.

Did the government go back on its commitments?

The debate about incorporation part transfers can be characterized as one that involved a series of categorizations and particularizations. Government officials contended that the specific category of incorporation parts required a special approach, which in the end amounted to a mere elaboration of existing policy. As argued, for the purposes of making decisions on exports, transfer licences such as the one for the HUDs should be treated as instances of the category of 'incorporation parts' rather than being 'component parts' or general 'arms' exports. If the HUDs application had been placed under the latter two categories, it may well not have been approved or at least required a different justification. In response to efforts to demarcate the boundaries of incorporation parts, questions have been raised about whether the similarities and differences of these parts with other exports makes this distinction necessary or justifiable.

Following Billig's analysis of the dynamics of categorizations and particularizations, this case can be treated as not just about the meaning of categories or particulars, but as involving arguments about arguments about categories and particulars.[54] So, much of the political commentary that followed the policy announcement centred on whether this decision represented a mere re-drafting of rules for exports in light of specific concerns over the growing importance of incorporation parts (that this, whether it represented an attempt to particularize) or whether it signalled that the government had forgone its principles regarding exports (that is whether it represented a shift to different sort of policy). In other words, debate about the approval of the HUDs and the export policy centred on whether they represented a mere redrawing of the existing policy or a fundamental change in the essence of decision making.

Government officials argued that incorporation policy represented a mere re-drafting because the considerations employed in assessing exports had not changed. Critics suggested otherwise, in part by noting that human rights violations in the Occupied Territories meant it was highly doubtful that the direct export of the HUDs to Israel would have been permitted. Yet, for members of the government, even if this were the case, it did not imply a change in the essence of policy. So when asked whether the approval of the HUDs signalled a retreat from its ethical foreign policy, the Prime Minster's Official spokesperson pointed out there had never been an 'ethical foreign policy'; rather the government phrase was an 'ethical dimension' to foreign policy. Herein human rights related criteria were one, but just one, type of criteria. In the case of incorporation parts, the human right considerations had to be assessed against matters such as the export controls in incorporating countries and their relation with the UK. In the context of the far-reaching changes in the defence industry and the increasing out sourcing of production facilitates, the British government had to adopt a special approach to cases involving incorporation for onward export. The government's principles had not altered; what had changed was the recognition of the new 'modern reality which we are confronting'.[55]

For critics of the HUD export, the approval represented a break with the past or business as usual, depending on the scruples attributed to previous practices of the Labour government.[56] The Liberal Democrat Foreign and Defence spokesman Menzies Campbell regretted the decision, in part, because the Labour government had 'a list of achievements' in controlling British arms exports, and 'that is why it is so dispiriting that an announcement of this kind appears to being made really in a way which one can only describe as being rushed and reactive'.[57]

In a more critical assessment, defence analysts Dunne and Freeman situated the HUDs approval as just one in a long list of questionable exports of subsystem 'parts' in cases where the export of 'whole' systems would be rejected.[58] For instance, though as part of a limited embargo on China the UK prohibits the export of 'lethal weapons' (e.g. bombs and guns and missiles), their component parts and 'weapon platforms' (e.g. whole aircraft and helicopters) this embargo does not extend to the components of weapon platforms. This has allowed companies to gain licence approval for a 'considerable number of categories of equipment that would clearly be for use in or with a weapons platform which would itself be subject to embargo'.[59] So in 2001, exports in relation to aircraft licences to China were granted for:

> Aircraft military communications equipment, components for airborne radar, components for aircraft military communications equipment, components for aircraft radar, components for combat aircraft simulators, components for military aero-engines, components for military infrared/thermal imaging equipment, military aero-engines, software for the use of military aircraft navigation equipment, technology for the use of combat aircraft simulators, technology for the use of military aero-engines (temporary), test equipment for military aircraft navigation equipment.

As such, the approval of the incorporation component HUDs was not so much a break with past commendable initiatives, but a continuation of the dubious practice in relation to the category of export component parts.

A more thorough critique of the HUDs decision could be offered by situating it within a broader history of questionable export practices of the Labour government not restricted to the category of components. As part of this a variety of decisions might be cited, such as:

> * The failure of the government after in coming to power in 1997 to revoke licenses granted under the previous one for over one hundred licenses for arms and equipment to Indonesian; this despite the human rights conducted

by Indonesian military and police forces, particularly in relation their then occupation of East Timor.[60]

* In February 2000, Prime Minister Tony Blair reportedly personally helped push through seven license applications by BAe Systems for Hawk spare parts to the Zimbabwe despite the latter's partaking in an illegal war in the Democratic Republic of Congo with Hawk jets.[61] While government cited the need to comply with commercial obligations at the time, later that year after internal strife in Zimbabwe centred on the distribution of land between white and black citizens, the commercial obligations cited were over-ruled by the British government and no further licences were granted. The Committees on Strategic Export Controls concluded the recent spare parts supply involved a 'serious error of judgement' and that the government response to questions proved 'factually inaccurate'.[62]

* In July 1999, the UK granted a license to Morocco for products under a number of military categories covering the refurbishment of 30 105 mm artillery guns and the transfer of six further guns. The weapons in questions were deployed along the border between Western Sahara and the Saharawi refugee camps in Algeria.[63] The transfers went ahead with government assertions that it received assurances about the suitability of the transfers from the UN, a claim denied by the latter.[64]

Many other such questionable instances could be cited.[65] Here the HUDs decision can be taken not as a break with past good practice or a continuation of problematic practice for the limited category of component parts, but instead as an expression of the dubious essence of past policy. As in other debates about weaponry, what evaluation is made depends on what is taken to be the relevant history for assessment. Views about whether the HUDs approval represents a change in the essence of policy or a mere redrafting of previous policy are highly significant in making assessments.

What is like what?

This chapter has examined the dynamics of attempts to identify what objects and events are and how they should be named. While in much of daily life the meaning of words is a matter of shared understanding, the same cannot be said of attempts to impose terms and categories for the purpose of evaluating weaponry. Contention can take place regarding whether particular weapons should be understood as following under some categories (e.g. is this a napalm bomb?) and the nature of those categories (e.g. what is a 'significant incorporation part'?). In many ways, determinations of these matters depend on mobilizing a sense of the similarity or difference of objects and instances from other objects and instances. Attributions of similarity and difference pervade attempts to give meaning to objects and actions as well as ascribe condemnation or praise, as indeed they have been central to my analysis. For instance, in arguing that (in many respects) the

British Labour government has continued the long-time practice of previous Conservative governments in seeking case-by-case flexibility in export decisions or in suggesting this chapter has extended themes of earlier chapters, my argument has relied on notions of similarity and difference.

While only two cases were given detailed attention in this chapter, it has been intended that the analysis presented has a more general relevance. The terms and categories given to things are not ordained somehow by the things themselves but are matters of social negotiation. As a result, just how technologies and acts of force are defined and categorized are topics of potential dispute where considerable latitude exists for making alternative determinations. Just what is like what – what is sufficiently similar to something else to be considered the same for the practical purposes sought – is a relationship that must be secured. Any agreement achieved at one time is open to later reassessment as the proposed meaning of terms and the range of factors deemed relevant are unpacked.

These considerations have significant implications for the status of the stipulations of prohibitions. The terms and categorizations given in prohibitions such as export control are supposed to fix a sense of what is important. Yet, final agreement about what prohibitions mean and whether they are even relevant is hard to pin down. This is not to say that rules or criteria are simply inconsequential, but the analysis here would suggest they are better thought of as providing resources for argumentation about what should or should not be done rather than simply specifying what constitutes appropriate conduct. Even if it is agreed that rules should be followed in some particular case, the analysis here contended just what following rules means can be a topic of varied argumentation. Criteria conflict, their import for particular cases must be established, and the meaning of terms can be matter of much disagreement. As suggested in the case of the HUDs, such conditions need not be an impediment to making practical determinations about what action should be taken; indeed open-ended rules combined with established procedures for decision making can provide conditions quite convenient for some. Later chapters will reiterate similar overall themes (or so I wish to contend) by examining similar disputes about what counts as a nuclear weapon, a landmine and an offensive biological weapons programme.

In making these arguments I am not advocating treating all claims about what technologies are and how prohibitions ought to be interpreted as equally valid, but the categories and terms used to make sense of the world and to lock down meaning are limited in their ability to do so. While we seek to grasp the world by naming it, such naming fails to provide a lasting way of understanding. Categorizations made are supposed to locate 'the heart of the issue'.[66] Yet, any characterizations are necessarily fallible, approximate and provisional. In the case of weaponry, expecting the meaning of terms and categories to be a matter of unanimity over time is unrealistic. With every attempt to define and classify, more questions can be asked about the basis of the definitions and classifications made. Determinations of the similarity between objects and events should be approached as 'relative and variable, as undependable as indispensable'.[67]

As suggested in this chapter, by offering a sense of the proper 'context' for consideration (e.g. the previous use of napalm in Vietnam, the absence of chemical weapons in Iraq, the Labour government's track record in defence exports, etc.), individuals attempt to pre-empt or resolve disputes about the meaning of controversial events and objects. Determinations of similarity or difference are always made in relation to some sense of the context in question. Context is also central in constituting a sense of individuals' ability to act. As Foreign Secretary Straw argued 'against the background of the end of the Cold War and the resulting reduction in defence budgets world wide' the defence industry was going through a time of major upheaval that demanded governmental acknowledgement. The export policy for incorporation parts then was not a deliberation re-interpretation of words by those assuming a Humpty Dumpty position of 'master'; rather the policy was a response by those with little choice to do otherwise. The next chapter considers the importance of 'context' in more detail by examining debates about the purpose of weaponry.

Chapter 6

Weapons

What are they for?

'A bomb is a bomb is a bomb'.
(Unnamed US State Department official (2001)[1])

On 4 September 2001 the *New York Times* reported that 'Over the past several years, the United States has embarked on a program of secret research on biological weapons that, some officials say, tests the limits of the global treaty banning such weapons.'[2] As noted in Chapter 4, while the Biological and Toxin Weapons Convention (BTWC) allows states to undertake defensive activities to counter possible attacks, just what, if anything, distinguishes the knowledge, equipment and techniques necessary for such protective steps and that required for the production of biological weapons is much disputed. The *New York Times* article questioned the legitimacy of three activities: (1) plans by the Defense Intelligence Agency (DIA) to genetically enhance the potency of the bacterium that causes anthrax, purportedly to test existing vaccines against a variant identified by Russian scientists,[3] (2) the Central Intelligence Agency's assembling and testing of an old Soviet cluster germ bomb and (3) a project by the Pentagon to determine if a bioweapon plant could be fashioned from commercially available materials. The latter two completed projects made use of stimultants.

In this article and the subsequent debate that followed, the question was posed of whether these activities were permissible under the terms of the BTWC; that is, whether they should be classified as activities that serve defensive or offensive purposes. As with the cases considered in Chapter 5, various analysts offered competing appraisals of the proper classification and desirability of the projects and plans. For instance, with the BTWC forbidding the production of 'weapons, equipment or means of delivery designed to use such agents or toxins for hostile purposes or in armed conflict', the quote at the start of this chapter was offered to suggest how the production of cluster germ bomb should be evaluated. That the US government had not listed these 'biodefence' activities as part of the BTWC annual declarations was cited as a ground for suspicion that the projects might be a sign of something more ominous.[4] In light of such considerations and the US' rejection of verification mechanisms for the BTWC in 2001, Wheelis and

Dando contended:

> It seems the US government has concluded that the global proliferation of bioweapons is inevitable. Having made this decision, the United States may have concluded that an offensive biological research program was necessary to evaluate the threat, devise countermeasures, and possibly even to eventually develop sophisticated bioweapons.[5]

Pentagon officials and others rejected any insinuation that the activities were proscribed or that their undertaking signalled some essential departure from its past commitments to honouring its international obligations. Rather, the three disputed cases went through stringent legal approval procedures ensuring they adhered to the terms of the BTWC. When asked by a reporter 'What's the rationale for having kept this work a secret up to now?' spokesperson Victoria Clarke from the Department of Defense responded that:

> Well, the DIA, for instance, doing this work, is trying to protect us and protect the men and women in uniform against threats of chemical and biological warfare. There are certain countries that we know are trying to do very bad things out there. The less information we give them about it, the better. Intelligence activities tend to remain secret.[6]

The overriding concern for national security thus required the US to make certain, relatively minor omissions from annual declaration requirements designed to promote international confidence.

In debates about the appropriateness of the US plans and projects, reference was made to alternative considerations for making sense of what had taken place including: the stated intention of officials, the quantity of agents and equipment produced, the wider background of biological weapon treaty negotiations, the history of US practices, the robustness of its legal approval procedures, the extent of public transparency, and the potential of the initiatives to facilitate offensive ends. As well, Barbara H. Rosenberg and Milton Leitenberg argued, attention should have been given to the implication of any designation of the US activities for the evaluation of other countries' 'biodefence' programmes. Was not it true that 'Similar activities in other countries have led the United States to label them biological weapon proliferators. Yet no doubt those countries would ascribe their activities to benign "threat assessment" necessary to develop appropriate military defenses and medical treatments, just as the U.S. is now describing its activities.'[7]

The dispute about the status of the projects reported in the *New York Times* was not the only case at the start of the twenty-first century where the legitimacy of biological weapons 'programme-related activities' were called in question. Neither was it unique as a case where the purpose of objects and acts was multiply conceived *vis-à-vis* weapon prohibition regimes. What looks like a strictly defensive and necessary action from one perspective can seem rather different from another. Following from some of the preliminary points raised in Chapter 7, this one examines the complicated business of figuring out what something is for; that is, how purpose is attributed to actions and objects. As already argued in Chapter 4, purpose is a rather slippery notion. Determinations of it are dependent on often complicated and disputable assessments of the foreseeable outcomes of action, which themselves are contingent on how actions and events are characterized.

Substantively, this chapter focuses on the prohibition of chemical and biological weapons. The 1972 BTWC and 1993 Chemical Weapons Convention (CWC) are major facets of the existing system of international arms controls. Unlike the export regimes examined in Chapter 5 that set restrictions mainly on the basis of whose hands should get a hold of what sort of weaponry, the BTWC and CWC primarily limit activities on the basis of their purpose.

Conceptually, this chapter extends previous points made by examining the importance of 'context' as an interpretative resource for attributing purpose. If Chapter 5 was concerned with how relations of similarity and difference are forwarded so as to box the world into categories, this one addresses the wider landscape against which those boxes are situated. As Chapter 5 argued the notion of resemblance is as indispensable as it is problematic in resolving disputes, so this one primarily considers the ever present and ever elusive attempts to marshal a sense of 'the context' to determine the intention behind acts and objects.

The purpose in prohibitions

From at least the start of the twentieth century, arguments have been made about the categorical unacceptability of chemical and biological weapons as means of warfare. Those seeking to justify why these weapons should be deemed more morally repugnant than 'conventional' weapons that kill, maim and cripple have done so by arguing their effects are particularly severe, their development perverts the goals of medicine, they are likely to be devastating to civilian populations and that 'the public' has a deep psychological aversion to them.[8] The Preamble to the BTWC, for instance, states that the weaponization of biological agents would be 'repugnant to the conscience of mankind and that no effort should be spared' to minimize the possibility of this taking place.

How such overall appraisals ought to translate into workable restrictions though has required careful judgement. Simply deriving a list of prohibited and permissible materials and activities has been deemed unworkable. In time, with constant developments in science and engineering, the comprehensiveness of any list of prohibited chemical and biological weapons would be in doubt. Perhaps more problematic though is the matter of 'dual use'. The chemicals, chemical precursors, biological agents, techniques, processes and equipment necessary for devising chemical and biological weaponry can be employed in industry, agriculture and health care for peaceful purposes. Thus imposing bans on any of these through deriving a list of prohibited chemicals and agents would hinder many civilian sectors of society. A further complication in relation to dual use is that the scientific and technical developments that inform the production of chemical and biological weapons can also be used to set up countermeasures against them.

Partially in order to maintain flexibility and respond to the dual-use problem, both the BTWC and the CWC employ the so-called General Purpose Criterion. Article I of the BTWC states:

> Each State Party to this Convention undertakes never in any circumstances to develop, produce or stockpile or otherwise acquire or retain:
>
> 1 Microbial or other biological agents, or toxins whatever their origin or method of production, of types and in quantities that have no justification for prophylactic, protective or other peaceful purposes.

In other words, the prohibition embodied in the BTWC is not against biological weapons *per se*. Instead, it is a general restriction of certain purposes served by science and technology.

In terms of policing adherence to the BTWC, the open-ended nature of this prohibition is at once both its strength and its weakness. The General Purpose Criterion has the strength of being flexible enough to accommodate new technologies and it also does not seek to limit the use of biological agents for benign purposes. However, it also has the major weakness of failing to elaborate just what is and is not permissible.[9] The BTWC draws on a number of terms such as 'development', 'acquire', 'prophylactic' and 'protective'. The meaning of these as they relate to determinations of the permissibility of particular activities has been a matter of considerable contention since the inception of the Convention.

Following on from the cases reported in the *New York Times*, in this section I only want to consider one aspect of contention as it relates to the question of what technology is for: what activities under the heading of 'biodefence' are permissible for 'prophylactic and protective purposes' as part of the BTWC.

The BTWC allows states to undertake measures intended to prevent and counter a bioattack, such as the production of vaccines and treatments. Traditionally though 'biodefence' has occupied a shadowy space where competing assessments have been given about what should rightly fall under its scope. Few have advocated a halt to all such programmes, let alone civilian studies of naturally occurring infectious diseases that might aid in understanding virulence. Yet, citing the potential for defensive activities to further offensive capabilities or for the former to serve as cover for the latter, many have expressed unease about the wisdom of partaking in biodefence work. As has been maintained:

> With modern technology, much that can be carried out in the name of biological threat assessment is indistinguishable from preparations for the offensive use of biological weapons, activities such as creating new, genetically engineered pathogens and testing how well they work as aerosols delivered under simulated battlefield conditions. Stockpiles of bacteria, viruses or toxins no longer are necessary; they can be produced rapidly on demand.[10]

Whatever the intent, activities undertaken in one locale might facilitate the prohibited production of bioweapons elsewhere.

For these reasons and others, the purposes served by ostensibly labelled 'biodefence' programmes have been a topic of significant controversy. Since the establishment of the BTWC, pressing questions have been posed of whether and how legitimate and illegitimate activities can be differentiated. In relation to the Convention's terms, that has meant finding ways of determining the intent behind and purposes served by biodefence programmes. An additional complication is that while the BTWC limits the 'development' of biological weapons, it does not place any limits on 'research' itself. Thus, any appraisal of the rights and wrongs of a biodefence programme must not only find a way of specifying the real intent of activities that could serve multiple ends but also distinguish mere research from actual development.

David Huxsoll, former director of the US Army Medical Research Institute of Infectious Diseases (the base for much of the past US medical biodefence work). suggested that while some similarities exist between developing preventive countermeasures and weapons, there were also differences that enabled individual projects (such as those carried out by the US Army) to be evaluated.[11] Both vaccine and weapon development isolate viruses, determine their biochemical properties and culture them. Subsequently, however, the required activities begin to diverge, particularly in relation to the quantities used. Offensive programmes include the mass production and storage of micro-organisms along with attempts to enhance the virulence of agents and finding ways of disseminating them. In effect then, Huxsoll argued intent could be surmised from the characteristics of the activities undertaken. Despite the stated desire in the US for clear lines in relation to its assessing its own programme, arguably a much different approach has been taken in relation to other countries' biodefence programmes. For the latter some have argued that appraisals have been made on a highly contextualized all-things-considered basis.[12]

Others have cast considerable derision on any assessment procedure that attempts to set apart defensive measures. Novick and Schulman argued that attempts by military establishments to find vaccines are generally of questionable value, because there is little prospect they will work effectively when a determined attack takes place.[13] Here military vaccine research serves more or less as a 'cover' for activities that can easily be turned to purposes other than those permitted under the BTWC. Others concur with this assessment, further suggesting that attempts to identify prohibited bioweapons development on the basis of considerations about the quantity of materials stored is unrealistic because of the potential speed of reproducing organisms.[14]

Attempts to offer sweeping approvals (e.g. Huxsoll) or dismissals (e.g. Novick and Schulman) of whole areas of biodefence on the basis of the characteristics of the activities undertaken have had limited appeal. Rather, for many commentators, there has been an uneasy recognition of both the promise and problems associated with biodefence. This has led to rather ambivalent and qualified assessments of what ought to be done. After decades of dispute within the American Society for Microbiologists about the wisdom of partaking in biodefence initiatives, in 1985 it adopted a code of ethics (later reaffirmed in 2001) that discouraged 'any use of microbiology contrary to the welfare of humankind'.[15] This abstract call though rather left unanswered the question of exactly what activities should and should not be done. Determinations of whether certain activities were ruled would depend on potentially contestable assessments regarding the ability to separate defensive and offensive implications and the ultimate purposes of activities. As a further complication, post 9–11 many argue that the fundamental (as opposed to applied) knowledge gained about biological processes may enable states, terrorists or even sociopaths to produce bioweapons.[16] As such, attempts to elucidate basic life mechanisms might end up directly furthering offensive possibilities. If accurate, a wide range of activities across many countries may merit concern.

Despite the said difficulty of making appraisals though, some means for categorization and assessment has been sought. Leitenberg argues that the allowance of 'prophylactic, protective or other peaceful purposes' in the BTWC opens up a category just too abstract to function as a basis for differentiating specific projects on the basis of whether they are 'offensive' or 'defensive'.[17] Similar techniques and know-how have underpinned past prohibited offensive biological programmes, Western biodefence programmes and benign medical research. Almost any activity can be justified as contributing to defensive 'threat assessment' at some level; so, for instance, the cases discussed at the start of this chapter which entailed engaging in (limited) 'offensive' developments.[18] While ascribing purpose to activities in cases involving extensive and known offensive biological weapon programmes (such in the past programme by the former Soviet Union terminated in the early 1990s) might be non-controversial, elsewhere this is not the case. As a result, he argues nothing like consistent criteria are employed internationally to make determinations of the real purpose of activities. Following from these points Leitenberg concludes that it is impossible to say whether individual activities in isolation are intended to serve biological warfare. Instead, the wider 'context' in which individual R&D activities take place must be considered, this in order to give them meaning and purpose. As part of this analysis, Leitenberg cites examples of numerous aspects of the US biodefence programme of the 1980s and 1990s deemed questionable – such as efforts to reveal the mechanism of agent pathogenicity, to produce powdered anthrax and to build aerosol test facilities – to raise doubts about the ultimate appropriateness of the programme overall.

Adopting a somewhat comparable line of analysis, Piller and Yamamoto conducted a review of unclassified information on the US biological defence research programme in the 1980s.[19] In doing so, they acknowledged activities could be interpreted in multiple ways. So, while projects taken individually might not indicate inappropriate offensive ends – for example, a project to make E. coli attack human cells – when taken together with other projects – say, an effort to modify their bacterial pathology – a much different picture emerged. Since full-funding figures were not available to Piller and Yamamoto, they concluded it was not possible to know the scale of potentially offensive activities and thus whether only limited measures necessary to test defences were conducted. That only 9 out of 329 projects studied related to the stated priority in biodefence (i.e. devising generic vaccines) was taken to indicate that the actual agenda being pursued was different from the one publicly portrayed. Piller and Yamamoto stressed this indeterminacy, as well as concerns about funding patterns and transparency measures, in concluding that the US biodefence programme was ambiguous at best, and strongly suggestive of inappropriate offensive goals. That US administrations in the 1980s took a confrontational stance in international affairs made the biodefence work provocative as well.

Wright and Ketcham likewise treated the problem of interpreting biodefence as one of contextualization.[20] Although recognizing any interpretations about the 'ultimate' goals of biodefence are highly charged politically and legally, these authors wished to avoid 'an indefinite suspension of judgment on the significance of ambiguous research.' Wright and Ketcham stressed the need to examine 'the pattern of support for the program as a whole and to ask to what extent this pattern indicates interest in either defensive or offensive goals'. However, they then went on to assess the merits of particular types of activities. For example, efforts to develop vaccines and even diagnostics were treated as inherently more offensive than defensive, because of the limited effectiveness of such measures. Detection and decontamination activities were more easily classed as defensive, but such activities constituted only a limited part of the US effort. In the end they concluded that the US programme

> has rapidly expanded since 1980, particularly in the use of new biotechnology; it remains partially secret, classifying policy documents and research results; and it indicates repeated military interest in exploring dimensions of biotechnology that an outside observer could reasonably construe as having potential for offensive application.[21]

In different ways and with different focuses, the commentators in the last few paragraphs contend that rather than examining the characteristics of particular activities in isolation, a sense of purpose can be gained from examining programmes 'in context'. The importance of a sense of context to guide determinations can be further underscored by considering how, when under scrutiny, attempts to appraise activities in a decontextualized manner often resort to marshalling a notion of context. For instance, should the criteria Huxsoll set out be followed irrespective of wider contextual factors, the plans and projects to genetically enhance the potency of a bacterium that causes anthrax, assemble a cluster germ bomb and set up a bioweapon plant would seemingly justify labelling the US biodefence programme as partially 'offensive'.[22] Huxsoll though is not completely opposed to drawing on contextual factors in the attempt to resolve controversy about the acceptability of some actions. In relation to what he regards as mistaken concerns about the potential offensive ends suggested by the US biodefence programme he argues:

> Critics of the US Biological Defense Research Programme have suggested that the programme could easily and quickly be turned into offensive efforts. To accomplish this, however, we would have to assume that all the military personnel, including the civilians employed by the Department of the Army, are unethical and willing to break the law and run the risk of placing the US in a noncompliance status.[23]

While the suggestion that a critic would have to 'assume that all the military personnel . . . are unethical and willing to break the law' might be somewhat overstated, the thrust of his argument is that whatever the worry about the potential for defensive activities to raise offensive possibilities, in the context of the US programme, such concern is not justified. If the 'same' activities are conducted elsewhere, a different evaluation might be merited. Here benign national and organizational motives attributed to the US buttress considerations of the character of the activities, a suggestion not likely to be accepted by everyone.

Context, context, context

So far this chapter could be said to examine many of the same themes in Chapter 5: debates about acceptability of biodefence activities entail competing appraisals of the similarity or difference between acts and objects in order to justify classifications as 'offensive' or 'defensive'. As suggested in both chapters, a sense of the proper 'context' in question is often marshalled in attempts to resolve classification and categorization disagreements. Few would suggest that determinations of purpose can be made by examining individual phenomenon in isolation. Yet, however widespread the turn to context, I want to suggest it is a fickle aid in resolving disputes about meaning and purpose. Consider some initial difficulties.

The proper context: disputed and disputable

In different ways Wright and Ketcham, Piller and Yamamoto, and Leitenberg all suggest drawing on a sense of the wider context to understand US biodefence activities. Yet, just what counts as the relevant background, pattern or context is multiply conceived. For Wright and Ketcham the range of programme activities undertaken by the US provides the context for making appraisals of ambiguous biodefence projects. While Piller and Yamamoto are also concerned with this, they attribute greater importance to a broad range of considerations such as funding patterns and transparency measures. Leitenberg compares US assessment practices for biodefence programmes in other countries with the standards by which it evaluates itself. Such alternative formulations of context are highly consequential in suggesting what information is needed, what needs to be done and who is best placed to decide. Wright and Ketcham's focus on the importance of abandoning certain areas of funding, Piller and Yamamoto stress the significance of further transparency and Leitenberg mainly stresses the need for international standards tied to verification procedures under the BTWC. As argued earlier, many US officials would dispute the necessity of such recommendations.

Alternative assessments of the proper context can fundamentally alter the sense given to activities. Whatever the ambivalence accorded to past biodefence activities by those in the US, post 9–11 one dominant policy answer has been given in government and biomedical circles regarding what biodefence work should be done: that being *more*.[24] In many respects, the limits placed on biodefence in the past have been set aside because of the spectre of bioterrorism. Although there are voices highly critical of the 'war footing' posture resulting from the recent substantial increase in biodefence activities[25] and of their limitations in protecting the population against biological attack,[26] these are being drowned out amid the clatter of the construction of new biodefence labs.

Take another example. Chapter 5 argued, starkly contrasting determinations of what the Head-up displays (HUDs) export decision represented have been justified by referring to alternative contexts for consideration. Similarly, contrasting assessments have been made of the outright significance of the decision through appealing to alternative senses of context. Consider the following comments made by the secretary of the House of Commons All Party Palestinian Group, Brian Iddon MP. Despite criticizing the transfer, he argued that in light of concerns about contractual obligations and the likelihood that someone else would supply the HUDs if a British company did not,

> this whole fuss is probably a red herring in the middle of a huge debate about peace in the Middle East and that is the ultimate thing we ought to be discussing, how peace in the Middle East can be achieved and I think the Americans have to put huge pressure on the Israelis to get back around the table.[27]

Thus, in the context of attempts at the time to get back to the road to peace, the HUDs controversy took attention away from the really vital issue: the said lack of US pressure on Israel. Whether or not in these instances 9–11 or Middle East peace talks are seen as credible and overriding contexts, the more general point is that any particular appraisal made of the appropriateness of acts and objects can be fundamentally questioned by situating them within some 'bigger picture'. Each of the bigger pictures offered might be regarded as legitimate in some respects, just as contrasting descriptions of acts of force might be regarded as applicable. Thus, as contended in relation to descriptions in Chapter 3, in this situation analytical attention should be dedicated to how the relevancy of contexts are secured and what citing specific notions of contexts accomplish in particular situations.

Contextualization is always partial

Attempts to consider the 'wider context' or the 'bigger picture' though should not be understood as only involving contextualization. In necessarily only treating certain topics in light of a wider context, the contextualization of some issues is simultaneously reliant on treating others in a decontextualization fashion. For instance, even while acknowledging the importance of context in their efforts to give meaning to the US biodefence programme, many of the commentators in the previous section maintained certain activities were of dubious standing outright (e.g. the establishment of sophisticated aerosol testing facilities) for which no justifications or excuses could be proposed. Taking the merits of certain activities as given was key in then substantiating the sceptical appraisal made of the US biodefence programme overall. Yet, rather than taking activities that might at first glance appear suspect as questionable, such as the establishment of aerosol facilities, others have defended these actions by situating them within an alternative wider context.[28]

The complete contextualization of any topic is unattainable because any contextual factors identified to suggest how individual objects or acts should be understood could themselves be contextualized. For instance, any of the claims made in support of how the establishment of aerosol facilities should be contextualized could themselves be contextualized, etc. In theory if not in practice there is no final ending of efforts to see things in context.[29]

Just how disputes about categorizations should be resolved can depend on how one orientates to dilemmas. Against criticisms of its failure to declare certain biodefence activities as part of the BTWC annual declarations, for instance, US officials could point out the context of the long standing limited nature of declarations made by other countries under the BTWC; countries that likewise cite concerns about disclosing security information to would-be aggressors. Against such a contention it might be countered that as the only remaining superpower in the world, the US should adopt stringent standards that serve as a model to others. A possible counter counter-argument could be that as the sole remaining superpower the US faces security threats that other countries do not and therefore it must take exceptional measures to protect itself.

Contextualizing contextualizations

As suggested so far in this section, the contention that 'the context' can resolve questions about the meaning and appropriateness of certain activities is problematic. Not only are contexts multiply conceived, once the effort to 'contextualize' begins, specifying where it should end is difficult. With the complete descriptions of the world well beyond our practical reach, the call to situate some activities necessarily faces practical limits that mean other activities are not subject to the same treatment. So, in the case of debates about the legitimacy of the US biodefence programme, both critics and defenders engage in persuasive strategies that have an uneasy simultaneous reliance on both contextualization and decontextualization. While agreement can be reached regarding what for-all-practical-purposes should serve as the context for consideration, unanimity is a contingent product of social agreement rather than resulting from some logical necessity.

The problems faced with contextualization are more deep-seated than overtly mentioned so far because they apply to the analysis given earlier. As the Chapter 5 examined how characterizations of similarity and difference are mobilized to justify categorizations through itself employing characterizations of similarity and difference, so too in this chapter I have examined how notions of context are mobilized through forwarding a sense of the context in question of various topics.[30] In focusing on some issues more than others, in extracting statements by individuals out of a given situated dialogue and inserting them within a wider argument, and in noting some issues but ignoring others, analysts are continuously putting the topics of their study into 'context'. In this way, it can be said analysis:

> involves delinking or disarticulating connections in order to link or rearticulate others [and] is a continuous struggle to reposition practices within a shifting field of forces, to redefine the possibilities of life by defining the field of relations – the context – within which practice is located.[31]

As such, any choice taken about what to study and how inevitably involves particular forms of contextualization at the exclusion of others. Indeed, the very call to consider context is a claim which itself could be contextualized.

Two programmes and numerous contexts equal many programmes

The previous section argued context is at once vital in appraising purpose but contestable as well. That context is simultaneously so pervasive and deficient should serve as reason for caution and reflection. We can further develop an appreciation for the dynamics and dilemmas of contextualization by undertaking an intellectual exercise.[32] Consider Table 6.1. This lists a variety of extracted claims about biological and chemical weapons-related activities that purportedly have been conducted by countries 'A' and 'B' at the start of the twenty-first century. The allegations were made by two organizations that set out to investigate such matters. Although for neither organization making the accusations were the said activities taken as iron-clad proof that the country was actively engaging in the extensive stockpiling of chemical and biological weapons for offensive use, in both the appropriateness of the activities were called into significant doubt. At best it was claimed there was a clear indication of the scant regard of each country for its international obligations. The reader is asked to appraise the activities listed.

Although many of the activities associated with chemical and biological defence are generally regarded as ambiguous, without any reference to just who is making what claims against who and in what sort of situation, it is especially

Table 6.1 What does it all indicate?

Programme A	Programme B
• Involvement of intelligence service in 'a secret programme of biodefence research that, in the opinion of many experts, violates' a major international agreement	• 'The involvement of the [intelligence service] in possible BW activities, and deliberate concealment activities'… including 'a clandestine network of laboratories and facilities within the security service apparatus'
• The undeclared genetic modification of weapon bacterium	• Failure to declare reference strains to the appropriate international body
• Advanced mortar munitions development which may involve 'testing of mind-altering, sleep-inducing or cramp-causing chemicals on human volunteers'	• 'Human testing activities using chemical and biological substances'
• National defence laboratories and military Special Forces plans to harness 'natural environmental microorganisms' and develop 'non-pathogenic genetically modified' strains to degrade 'highway and runway surfaces, metal parts and coatings of weapons, support equipment and vehicles' along with 'vaccination' strategies for friendly forces[33]	• Possession of mobile research trailers, of which 'nothing we have discovered rules out their potential use in BW production'
• This nation 'unilaterally blocked the creation of a multilateral inspection system for [biodefence] laboratories'	• Said interest by government officials in reconstituting a chemical weapons programme
• Research sponsored by defensive department into the development of psychopharmacological drugs (e.g. Valium) as weapons	• 'May have engaged in proscribed or undeclared activity since 1991, including research on a possible VX stabilizer, research and development for CW-capable munitions, and procurement/ concealment of dual-use materials and equipment'
• Massively expanded and highly secretive 'biodefense' programme that may trigger a bioweapons research race	• 'Clandestine capability was suitable for preserving BW expertise, BW capable facilities and continuing R&D
• R&D work in testing mock biological bombs and construction of a bioweapons production facility with non-pathogenic organisms serving as surrogates	• 'R&D work that paired overt work with non-pathogenic organisms serving as surrogates for prohibited investigation with pathogenic agents'
• Interest in developing new dissemination techniques for chemical and biological agents including unmanned aerial vehicles, biological submunition prototypes, and a rifle-launched projector (the latter for which a patent was sought)	• 'Dramatic' breach of international obligations regarding the development of ballistic missiles, cruise missiles, cruise missiles and unmanned aerial vehicles. Past interest in such devices to dispense chemical and biological agents and 'open question' of whether recent interest in delivery system intended for such agents

difficult to evaluate the claims specified in Table 6.1. By way of furthering an appreciation of context, in this section I want to reflect on how determinations of it can suggest a way of making sense of the equivocal activities listed. In the text that follows the reader is asked to attend to how the contextual factors discussed later help you make sense of the similar points in the table.

Programme A

Programme A refers to activities said to be undertaken by various US government agencies under the banner of biodefence and also as part of its 'non-lethal' weapons programme. As mentioned in earlier chapters, although chemical and biological weapons are often categorically condemned in public discussions, within military establishments some question the appropriateness of such designations. Herein biological and chemical weapons with selective or short-term minor effects might offer highly valuable force options. There is at least some scope for such weapons within the CWC which makes allowances for developing chemicals in the types and quantities that would be used for 'law enforcement including domestic riot control situations'. This provision has enabled the continuing use of 'tear gas' and other such options by police forces around the world. In addition, since the inception of the CWC the US has insisted on its right to use riot control agents in certain 'military operations other than war', such as peacekeeping missions.[34] Many of the military weapon projects in the past and today have been justified by the US under such exceptions, and as part of this what should count as 'law enforcement', a 'riot control agent' and a 'peacekeeping mission' have been topics of some dispute.[35]

The particular allegations in Table 6.1 were made by an NGO called the Sunshine Project in a series of reports and press releases.[36] By making use of the US freedom of information law, over a number of years the organization has criticized many of the biological and chemical weapons-related activities in the US, some of which it maintains 'violate international agreements on chemical and biological warfare as well as human rights'. Against claims about the humanitarian advantages of so-called 'non-lethal' weapons, for instance, it has argued their less than non-lethal effects (including how they might multiply the destructiveness of conventional weapons), their potential use for use in civilian repression and the possibility of their deployment to foster retaliatory weapon development cycles mean '[t]hese weapons must be rejected for what they are: chemical and biological weapons – not as deadly as a vial of anthrax or bottle of nerve gas; but enormously provocative and pertaining to same class of arms'.[37]

To substantiate the critical appraisal made of US chemical and biological weapons-related programmes that others might be deemed equivocal and ambiguous, the Sunshine Project has drawn attention to a variety of additional contextualizing claims. First, the activities listed have been shrouded in secrecy and vital documents have been deliberately suppressed from the public, including the official government legal interpretations of the CWC *vis-à-vis* 'non-lethal' chemical weapons. Much of the non-lethal chemical weapons programme represents a revival of the DoD Advanced Riot Control Agent Device programme which was terminated because of the negotiation of the CWC.[38] The Sunshine Project also cited Congressional testimony by Secretary of Defense Donald Rumsfeld of his 'regret' prior to the 2003 Iraq war of the restrictions placed on incapacitating weapons as evidence that legal obligations might well have been forgone by the US had the war taken a different course.[39] In light of such considerations and the extent of questionable activities documented, the Sunshine Project has called for a UN weapons inspection team to be sent to the US to investigate its chemical and biological programmes.

Programme B

The activities under 'Programme B' in Table 6.1 were included in an Interim Report of the Iraqi Survey Group (ISG) and refer to efforts said to be undertaken by the Iraqi government under the leadership of Saddam Hussein. The report was presented to the US Congressional House Permanent Select Committee on Intelligence, the House Committee on Appropriations, Subcommittee on Defense and the Senate Select Committee on Intelligence by Iraqi special advisor David Kay on 2 October 2003. The 1400-member ISG was sent into Iraq after the end of the war in 2003 to search for WMD. While not having found any stockpiles of weapons, Kay stated 'we are not yet at the point where we can say definitively either that such weapon stocks do not exist or that they existed before the war'. Numerous security and physical considerations were pointed out that hampered documenting the extent of Iraqi's activities. Yet from what was found as listed in the Table 6.1, 'it is already apparent that these undeclared activities would have at a minimum facilitated chemical and biological weapons activities and provided a technically trained cadre'. Kay concluded, Iraq had 'dozens of WMD-related program activities'.[40]

Unlike many of the highly technical disputes surrounding weapons verification in the past, the claims of the ISG have been subject to widespread public discussion. Were the said indications of WMD-related programme activities significant enough to prove Iraq was partaking in illegal and illegitimate activities? Were these activities sufficient justification for war? The Interim report, however provisional and qualified, was taken as indicating something for many. For the British Secretary of State, the report showed the military intervention into Iraq was 'justified and essential'.[41] Here as elsewhere though, the true meaning of the activities could not be fathomed by simply taking them on their own. Consider the following exchange between Secretary of State Jack Straw and presenter John Humphrys on 3 October 2003 on the BBC *Today* Programme. Prior to the start of the war the British government claimed Iraq's WMD capability posed a 'clear and present danger' to the UK. The question being considered was whether or not this was justified:

JACK STRAW: ... because if I read this report, and it is only an Interim report, what do I see? I see a regime incontrovertibly establishing a clandestine network of laboratories ...

JOHN HUMPHRYS: Yes, sorry can I stop you just for a second? I want you to make those points, of course, and you will make those points I am sure, but let us just deal first with the clear and present danger.

STRAW: I am just dealing with that . . .

HUMPHRYS: Except that is not in the report, they found no weapons, so therefore there was not a clear and present danger.

STRAW: John, John the fact that they have not found weapons as Kay said obviously does not mean that the weapons were not there. What we know for certain . . .

HUMPHRYS: Well where were they then?

STRAW: Well. Look, what we know for certain is that the Saddam regime had had substantial chemical, biological and nuclear weapons.

HUMPHRYS: Had had, nobody disputes that . . .

STRAW: Well, some people do.

HUMPHRYS: Well not if you go back far enough, because he used them, so we know he had them at some stage.

STRAW: Allow me to continue. Had had substantial chemical, biological and nuclear programs and had used the chemical and biological programs, and we know too that there was a record of concealment and deception by that regime in the clearest possible breach of United Nation's sanctions. We also know that the environment that the inspectors, the previous inspectors, were able to operate was made so difficult that the inspectors had to leave in December 1998 and that notwithstanding a further United Nation's Security Council resolution, Saddam Hussein refused to allow the new inspectors back for four years, until there was a threat of force. Now, you take that behavior, put it with what is already in this Interim Kay report – which is a network of clandestine laboratories and safe houses within the Iraqi intelligence service, for example, a prison laboratory complex possibly used in testing of biological weapons . . .

HUMPHRYS: Possibly, yes.

STRAW: . . . Ahh, that Iraqi officials preparing for UN inspections were explicitly ordered not to declare to the United Nations reference strains of biological organisms concealed in a scientist's home and a far . . .

HUMPHRYS: Hang on, we found one vial. One vial of botulinum! Was that threatening to us as a nation, one vial of botulinum?

And so the interview continued, with the participants oscillating back and forth between arguments about individual activities cited and the wider context in which they should be understood. As expressed by Straw, when one listed and added up all of the various facts about Iraq under Saddam Hussein, then the only conclusion that could be reached was that the regime was 'dangerous [and] carrying out illegal activities in complete defiance of United Nation's resolutions'; that is, it presented a 'clear and present danger'.[42] Herein one vial of botulinum certainly was threatening because it did not exist in isolation. In this antagonistic exchange, Humphrys questions the importance of the individual bits of evidence suggested by Straw, the inferences he makes, and just what might serve as the proper context for making determinations.

The Straw–Humphrys interview, like so many regarding the ISG report, was characterized by dispute regarding just what the report said[43] and what it should be taken to mean. Such disagreements were evident in other statements about WMD in Iraq. In January 2004 David Kay testified before a US Senate committee that in relation to claims prior to the war that Iraq possessed stockpiles of chemical and biological weapons 'It turns out we were all wrong, probably, in my judgment, and that is most disturbing'. While this statement was widely reported in the world media, it was not taken as a significant admission of failure by the British Prime Minister Tony Blair who argued 'All I ask, again as I said earlier, is that people do not clip one part of what he is saying and not take the rest of what he is saying because the rest of what he is saying is ample justification for the decision to go to war'[44] (readers are asked to consider whether this extract clip of Blair is adequate or what would count as the relevant context for his statement). Yet, here as elsewhere just what should be inferred from claims made depended on various considerations and judgements about the necessary justification for military intervention.[45]

Consider another bit of commentary, coming to a rather different appraisal of the situation at hand. A few days after the release of the ISG Interim report the former UN Iraq weapons inspector Scott Ritter was interviewed as part of the BBC programme *Hardtalk*.[46] Ritter's direct experience in Iraq and Republican Party political background gave him a credible basis for voicing dissent about WMD in Iraq in many media circles. Instead of drawing on past practices by 'Saddam's regime' as Jack Straw did, he directly questioned the motivations behind 'Kay's report' and whether it should even be taken seriously:

DAVID JESSEL: Let us go back to what the ISG actually said it found. It said it found significant amounts of equipment and weapons-related activities all of which had been successfully concealed from the UN. Is that a lie or is that what they found?

RITTER: Again it is political spin.

JESSEL: Well now, sorry is it true? Did they find weapons-related activities and significant amounts of equipment related to that which had been hidden from the UN? That might be spin, but it is either true of untrue?

RITTER: Then what is it? I cannot tell you if it is a lie until David Kay y'know articulates exactly what he found. What equipment did he find? Did he find a lathe that was purpose built to produce nuclear weapons related material or did he find a lathe that was being used in legitimate civil purposes that was brought in in violation of economic sanctions and he is speculating that it could have used in a future date in a program as of yet unidentified? I don't know what David Kay reported, I do know.

JESSEL: Let's say one thing that he found, he found a network of laboratories suitable for chemical and biological weapons research.

RITTER: What does that mean a network of laboratories? You know I could I could go to London right now and go into every hospital...

JESSEL: It was not there for research on the human genome, I don't think.

RITTER: No, I think it was there for research on how to protect the Iraqi people from diseases. Let us remember that Iraq is a modern nation state of 25 million people who have every right to access to the kind of research and development that other states have, so let us not assume that everything the Iraqis do is nefarious and evil. There are plenty of work, there is a lot of work to been done in a biological laboratory that is legitimate. And David Kay has gone in and basically said, in my opinion, that if the Iraqis had a university research project, my gosh, that had to be used for nefarious activity.

Following from this, against claims made by President Bush and Prime Minster Blair that the report vindicated the war, Ritter responded that these are 'politicians who misled their respective constituencies, lied about the threat posed by Iraq, and right now are desperate to spin any data which they can get their hands on in a way that is advantageous to them'.

As illustrated in these contrasting responses to the ISG report, 'facts' do not speak for themselves. The process of speaking for them is not one of the mere representation of given knowns, instead the specific descriptions given constitute an understanding of the facts under discussion. In relation to the ISG report, just what had been found by way of evidence of illegitimate chemical and biological weapons in Iraq and what it meant had to be made sense of. Bound up in the strategies for doing so were concerns about where the burden of proof should rest and who should be attributed responsibility. While Ritter reserved scope for the Iraqis to undertake activities that might be regarded as ambiguous and located responsibility with finding and publicly documenting factual evidence of WMD programmes or weapons with the ISG; for Straw, Blair, Bush and others the history of Saddam and the range of activities found meant the mays and mights expressed in the ISG report were not sources of unease. While Ritter treated the ISG findings as primarily reflecting the political bias of Kay and lumps him together with Bush, Blair, Straw and others who are seeking to hide the truth; for these government representatives the Interim report was treated as 'something-out-there' that had been produced by distinct others and so the validity of the conclusions were not open to fundamental doubt.

In relation to the biological and chemical weapons mentioned, dispute took place regarding the range of relevant factors for judging just what inferences should be drawn from evidence.[47] For instance, in debates about the ISG interim report, as with the final ISG report, that included matters such as the past defiance by of Iraq of UN resolution, the past defiance by others countries (e.g. Israel) of UN resolutions, the 'serious consequences' specified in UN resolution 1441, the claims that France's proposed veto of another UN resolution in 2003 would have been an 'unreasonable veto', the opportunity for Saddam to comply with UN demands, the further options short of war, the possibility of later gaining international support for war if the United Nations Monitoring, Verification and Inspection Commission inspectors had been given more time, 9–11, and varied other issues. Attempts to discussion one topic – whether the ISG report indicated Iraq had posed a 'clear and present danger' – quickly became implicated in a range of considerations which some may regard as tangential and others as core.

Elaborating contexts

Considered on their own, it is problematic to state the nature of the activities listed under Programme A and Programme B in Table 6.1. The listing itself is not, however, completely devoid of a sense of context. Citing the activities together in the manner done does suggests a pattern of practice which indicates some cause for concern. Yet, just what the pattern illustrates is disputable. The sort of contextual matters cited in the discussion given are central in rendering activities intelligible.

As hinted earlier though, attributions of context should not be approached in an acontextualized manner; that is to say notions of context are not inert backdrops that are simply drawn upon to support appraisals of particular ambiguous activities. To treat context in this way provides a rather limited understanding of what is taking place in making sense of accounts. Rather in disputes about what ought to serve as the context, the appropriateness of its definition must be justified, and often this is done through reference to the very equivocal and ambiguous activities cited.

Consider again my listing of the extracted activities in Table 6.1. Adding various elaborating details as done previously enables you as the reader to reflect on the process whereby individual activities are made sense of. As part of this, questions can be considered about when and how you felt assured regarding what the activities were really about and whether that changed as more details were provided. For instance, for some an evaluation of the activities might have been warranted after reading of the list irregardless of who said exactly what referring to whom. For others, a definitive evaluation might have been justified after reading who sponsored the programmes or discovering who was making the allegations.

In much of the public debate about these programmes however, neither of these approaches has dominated. While a sense of contextual factors might give place and purpose to objects and acts, those objects and acts are also significant in making sense of what should be taken as 'the context'.[48] Following the work of the sociologist Mannheim, Garfinkel labelled the mutual constitution between contexts and individual instances in accounts of the world as 'the documentary method of interpretation'. Herein:

> The method consists of treating an actual appearance as 'the document of'. as 'pointing to', as 'standing on behalf of' a presupposed underlying pattern. Not only is the underlying pattern derived from its individual documentary evidences, but the individual documentary evidences, in their turn, are interpreted on the basis of 'what is known' about the underlying pattern. Each is used to elaborate each other.[49]

In other words, a sense of context is both constituted by and constituting of the individual activities listed in Table 6.1. It is 'this process of contextualization in which descriptor and context mutually elaborate one another contributes immense refinement and definition to an apparent crude and undifferentiated descriptive system'.[50]

Consider this sort of interpretative process might have been working in the accounts cited previously. So for Straw and others, the ambivalent activities identified in the ISG report obtained their meaning from the context of practices under Saddam Hussein and those activities gave credence to claims about the depravity of that regime. In a similar fashion, for many analysts in the previous section, the extent of disputed activities undertaken as part of the US biodefence programme has served to raise questions about the goals of US administrations and doubts about those goals further reinforced a sceptical appraisal of the purely 'defensive' orientation of the activities under question. Without an understanding of 'the context' the meaning of individual activities are often difficult to assess, but without an understanding of the events in question it is difficult to justify what understanding of 'the context' should apply. With regard to the latter, for instance, unless Straw and others are able to persuasively point out a wide range of dubious 'WMD program-related activities' undertaken by the Saddam regime, individuals such as Ritter can easily argue the said questionable activities are nothing of the sort by seeking to alternatively categorize them as acceptable examples of biomedicine done for the benefit of the Iraqi people or by labelling them as marginal activities that did not pose a significant security threat.

When contexts and instances are treated as mutually defined, then determinations of purpose of acts and objects can be characterized as forming through a succession of piecemeal and iterative judgements. The process is also somewhat circular and self-elaborating in nature – new evidence gets added to the existing understanding held. Certainly in public statements made about the disputed chemical and biological weapons activities considered in this chapter, the understanding given to the situation at one time has lead groups such as the Sunshine Project and the US and UK governments to seek out further activities that might be questionable and, once found, these activities have been taken as reaffirmation of their previous programme appraisal. In this way, the manner in which specific determinations are made by individuals can be treated as an ongoing process that is constantly being modified but one generally resistant to rapid revision because new pieces of evidence are interpreted in relation to previous notions of the overall context in question and an understanding of the context is justified from the evidence accumulated to date. Both shift together.

In recognizing how contexts and activities are mutually defined, it is possible to gain a greater appreciation of the grounds for and intractability of disagreements about the purpose served by acts and objects. As suggested in the analysis of biodefence activities and the ISG report, any determination can be questioned by alternatively framing many contextual and activity-specific issues at hand. Contrasts in the contextual features identified lead to alternative sets of relevant activities and then debates about the relevancy and import of these activities could lead to considering still further contrasting contextual features, and so on. In this way arguments can facture as particular senses of the range of relevant issues at stake proceed along different paths. Herein little hope exists that divergent ways of making sense of context and instances can be reconciled by simply marshalling some new decisive fact. Divergent assessments held by commentators of whether, in fact, the non-lethal weapons programme of the US is a prudent one designed to save lives or a reckless breach of international obligations are not likely to be resolved by the next piece of evidence.

The issues that might be deemed relevant to making determinations of purposes need not be limited to the issues noted earlier about Programmes A and B. By recounting other controversial weapon activities, previous chapters of the book have suggested a range of issues that might be deemed relevant for appraising what these programmes are an underlying pattern of. As the reader, you may well have not simply reflected on the issues noted here, but brought to bear an alternative sense of the range of relevant contexts and activities for making determinations of the purpose and appropriateness of the programmes. Other documents and arguments could have been marshalled to suggest alternative assessments. That may have resulted in questioning the adequacy or motivations of what evidence was presented in this analysis. Inevitability discussions about the complex matters considered here have relied on generalizations and simplifications of the issues at stake. As there is not one absolute context, in marshalling quotes and citations, my account – just as those given by Kay and biodefence commentators – can be challenged for inappropriately dis-embedding and re-locating interview clips, news reports and publications out of their 'proper context'. For those convinced of the justifications for the US' chemical and biological activities, that its programme should be compared to the previous one in Iraq at all would be quite unfitting.

As has been suggested here, such possible points of criticisms should not be understood as mere failings of particular analyses.[51] Rather, any attempt to describe the relevant context can be contested through the marshalling of an alternative account that seeks to contextualize in an alternative fashion. Just what ought to count as the proper context is a topic of potentially endless dispute. Reports such as those by the ISG and the analyses of US biodefence commentators necessarily entail attempts to extract and abstract particular and partial accounts of the world in order to bring them together to suggest what is really going on.

Concluding remarks

Chapter 4 suggested that specifying the purpose of weaponry is exercise full of difficulties. Just whether weapons should be understood as fulfilling their aims or what the intent is behind particular instances of force depends on disputable determinations regarding the extent to which individuals and organizations foresee and are responsible for the outcomes of their actions. This chapter has extended that analysis by considering in some detail how determinations of purpose are made *vis-à-vis* weapons prohibition conventions; particularly regarding how the purpose of objects and acts are evaluated in relation to 'their context'. It has focused on one distinction: how ambiguous biological and chemical weapons-related activities are deemed offensive or defensive in nature.

As argued, context is a problematic aid at making appraisals. Accounts of the world at once involve attempts to contextualize, decontextualize and recontextaulize that can be unpicked and alternatively contextualized themselves in varying ways. Moreover, while acts and objects are given meaning in some context, it is also important to attend to how they give meaning to that context. A sense of context both constitutes and is constituted by a sense of the instances under question. Agreement might be reached about what acts and objects are for, but such a state of affairs is a contingent social achievement secured in relation to particular set of concerns, rather than one necessarily resolved once 'the context' is identified. The question of 'what is the proper context?' has no simple solution. Part III builds on the analysis presented in this chapter to shift the focus of analysis. Before this, Chapter 7 moves on to the final aspect of characterizing weaponry: how determinations are made of what weapons do. Here too, context establishes and evokes a contested ground for making sense of the world.

Weapons
What do they do?

Richard Ottaway MP: The Prime Minister says that all the intelligence about the 45 minutes [in the September 2002 British dossier] was made available. As he will be well aware, it has subsequently emerged that this related to [Iraqi] battlefield weapons or small-calibre weaponry. In the eyes of many, if that information had been available, those weapons might not have been described as weapons of mass destruction threatening the region and the stability of the world. When did the Prime Minister know that information? In particular, did he know it when the House divided on 18 March?

Prime Minister Tony Blair: No. I have already indicated exactly when this came to my attention. It was not before the debate on 18 March last year. The honourable Gentleman says that a battlefield weapon would not be a weapon of mass destruction, but if there were chemical, biological or nuclear battlefield weapons, they most certainly would be weapons of mass destruction. The idea that their use would not threaten the region's stability I find somewhat eccentric.

(UK House of Commons 4 February 2004[1])

In this exchange during Prime Minister's questions, Ottaway MP queried claims made by Tony Blair and other government ministers about Iraqi's weapons of mass destruction (WMD) capabilities in the run up the 2003 war. With no stockpiles of chemical, biological or nuclear weapons discovered after the war, questions were subsequently asked not just about the import of what was found by way of WMD programmes-related activities (as examined in the previous chapter) but what government officials thought might be found prior to the start of the conflict. When it became public knowledge after the war that the British government warnings that Iraq possessed a chemical and biological WMD capability that could be activated with 45 minutes of an order to do so referred to 'battlefield weapons' such as mortars and shells, many questioned the prominence given to the claims in the build up to war. Irrespective of why stockpiles of these munitions were not found, the question was asked of whether what was expected to be found should have been characterized as 'weapons of mass destruction'. Such questions were not asked out of mere curiosity, rather the distinction between battlefield and other types of chemical and biological weapons was said to cast doubt on the claims made about the security threat posed by Iraq, the extent to which its government had violated restrictions placed upon it, and thus the necessity and timing of military intervention. The UK was not alone in making claims about the severity of the threat faced. Statements made by US officials, such as Secretary of State Colin Powell's address to the United Nations in February 2003, arguably left little doubt about the severity of the threat faced.[2]

This chapter examines disputes about what weapons do; specifically how claims made about the effects of weapons are forwarded *vis-à-vis* weapon prohibitions. While determining the capabilities of weapons might be thought a fairly undisputable technical undertaking, this is a rather limited way of conceiving of the issues at stake. When it comes to establishing prohibitions, agreement about seemingly 'self-evident' facts often evaporates. Establishing controls on the basis of effects means cutting through complex, uncertain or confusing situations (perhaps involving multiple technologies and individuals) to specify just what is the main cause for certain effects: whether that be the intent of users, the situations of use or the inherent characteristics of the weapons. Assessments made of the primary source of concern affect determinations of what, if any, controls should be enforced. Attempts to deem some weapons as 'indiscriminate' or 'disproportionate' can be and often are questioned as scrutiny turns to the unstated assumptions, categorizations and qualifications informing appraisals.

Substantively, these issues are addressed with particular focus on how determinations are made about the effects of what are commonly referred to as 'weapons of mass destruction', especially nuclear weapons. Such weapons are frequently said to have 'indiscriminate' or 'disproportionate' effects and thereby their use or even possession is often condemned. While it might be assumed that there is widespread agreement about the effects of such weapons, in many debates about prohibitions this is not the case. The first half of this chapter considers several general points and dilemmas associated with specifying the effects of weapons and the second then focuses on the case of nuclear weapons.

Establishing prohibitions and limiting certain acts or objects inevitably requires relying on and forwarding generalizations. To have more than a one-off or *ad hoc* relevance, prohibitions must establish rules that are applicable over time and across situations. Yet any such generalizations can be unpacked and questioned by pointing to specific instances where the characterizations and rules set out are of doubtful merit. As with many of the other topics considered in this book so far, a key consideration in this chapter is how efforts to justify determinations of the acceptability of the use of force attempt to cut through the world to characterize what is really going on despite the disputability of any such characterization.

The general and the specific

Calculating the effects of weapons has long been a preoccupation of weapon designers and others. Deriving probability figures about how many deaths and how much damage might be expected from particular uses of force has been central to the development of new weaponry and the formulation of military strategy. Attempts to establish such measures rely on the identification and specification of the range of issues that might be pertinent to making estimations.

Of central importance to characterizing the effects of weapons is how contextual considerations regarding the situations of use are factored into or stripped out of assessments. At one extreme the military historian Colonel Trevor Dupuy has sought to understand changing tactics and injury in war in relation to the lethality of weapons.[3] On the basis of measures such as the rate of fire, accuracy, reliability, range and radius of damage he calculated a theoretical lethality index for weapons. In this index, for instance, the sword gets a rating of 23, a First World War machine gun 3,463, a Second World War fighter-bomber 6,926 and a one-megaton nuclear bomb 695,385,000.

Such abstract figures are open to numerous lines of questioning, however reasonable in spirit. A great deal of judgement is required in determining how factors such as reliability and radius of damage should be measured and weighed against each other for the purposes of deriving a single number. Perhaps more fundamentally, such figures give little indication of diverse factors that might factor into the lethality of weapons in any specific instance. Figures for death and injury in recent major wars compiled by the International Committee of the Red Cross (ICRC) indicate a complex set of situational factors contribute to casualty rates from conventional weapons.[4] The terrain of conflict, the distance at which force is used, the ability of people to defend themselves and a host of other issues all significantly influence the statistical rate of injury and death probable from a given weapon. Elsewhere I have suggested that tallying overall lethality figures for weapons, as done by Dupuy and others, can lead to counter-intuitive findings.[5] Field experience with rifles in conflict over the course of the twentieth century, for instance, indicates that hundreds of thousands of bullets are fired for each death in warfare. Yet, few would feel comfortable concluding rifles are therefore of low lethality.

While many might readily concur that effects depend on situational and user considerations, just how and to what degree is not often so readily agreed. Rather than just proposing single abstract lethality figures, attempts have been made to determine effects for particular situations. The former US Office of Technology Assessment compared the potential for various weapons to cause mass casualties in urban areas.[6] Assuming a 1,000 kg Scud missile warhead is effectively employed with substances of particular densities, the results are given in Table 7.1. After 11 September 2001 and the anthrax attacks that followed, assessing the threat posed by such weapons (particularly bioweapons) has become a high priority. The figures given in the table have informed analyses of US homeland defence.[7]

While this sort of assessment gives greater specificity and qualification to effects than abstract lethality figures, it still entails a fair degree of generalization. The basis of these figures can be unpacked. So, it could be pointed out that the danger of biological weapons are highly dependent on environmental conditions in a way nuclear and even some chemical ones are not. Many security analysts

Table 7.1 Comparative effects of biological, chemical and nuclear weapons

Type	Weapon description	Area covered (km²)	Fatalities (assuming 3,000–10,000 people per km²)
Biological	30 kg of anthrax spores	10	30,000–100,000
Chemical	300 kg of sarin nerve gas	0.22	60–200
Nuclear	1 megaton hydrogen bomb	190	570,000–1,900,000

have taken the limited employment of biological weapons around the world despite the historical interest in such capacities as indication of the difficulty of effectively employing these devices.[8]

A basic issue in the cases given here is that making determinations of the probable effects of weapons requires generalizing about the likely outcomes of actions across a range of circumstances. Any figure is inevitably open to challenge regarding the appropriateness of the simplifications it entails. Specific cases can be pointed out where generalizations made are not prudent. This might be done in relation to particular employments or cumulative effects. For instance, with regard to the latter, much is made of the ability of precision guided bombs to pin point accurate targeting and thereby minimize harmful effects. However, claims that their use will minimize damage may well be misplaced in some bombing situations as:

> ... one must take issue with the assertion that the systematic destruction of the civil infrastructure through the use of precision weapons actually reduces the harmful effects of war. Ironically, the very capability of precision potentially augurs greater collateral casualties, not less ... [precision guided munitions are] clearly an efficient and effective application of force.... Unfortunately, such a methodology not only impedes the enemy in some respects, but it also eliminates civilian life-support systems.[9]

Following such arguments, the extensive use of precision guided bombs in a conflict on its own could hardly be reason in and of itself for optimism regarding the extent of civilian suffering.

A further sense of the pervasiveness of questions that might be asked of generalizations can be developed by attending to the conventions of language. As contended in Chapter 3, generalizations are commonplace in accounts of the world. Language serves to typify through employing approximate terms for objects and actions that by some metric might otherwise be regarded as unique or distinctive.[10] To discuss the effects of 'leg-irons' or 'incendiary devices' implies there are definite sets of things with defined characteristics that can be understood by these labels. As indicated in previous chapters though, when scrutiny is brought to bear, just what counts as a leg-iron or incendiary device is readily disputed. While in many aspects of everyday life the generalizing conventions of language might not be a topic of heated dispute, when it comes to debating the rights and wrongs of weaponry accord is often far from secure. Consider a vivid example of this in the exchange given between BBC *Today* Programme interviewer John Humphrys and UK Minster of Defence Geoff Hoon on 5 February 2004. This exchange followed on from the statement given at the start of this chapter from the British Prime Minster regarding whether 'battlefield' chemical and biological weapons should have been labelled as 'weapons of mass destruction' prior to the start of the 2003 Iraq War:

JOHN HUMPHRYS: You are telling us that you knew they were battlefield weapons, that Robin Cook knew they were battlefield weapons but the Prime Minister did not know they were battlefield weapons. He seemed to think they were pretty much bigger than that.

GEOFF HOON: I made clear when I was asked this question yesterday in the House of Commons that following the publication of the dossier in that time-frame, and forgive me I can't precisely remember when this conversation took place, I asked a question in the Ministry of Defence as to what kind of weapons we were talking about.

HUMPHRYS: So let me be clear, even you didn't know, when that dossier was published, the dossier carried forward by Mr Blair with this information in it, even you didn't know what it was all about. Is that what you are saying?

HOON: I am not saying I didn't know what it was all about, I am saying, and the intelligence as we've made clear in our evidence very recently to the House of Commons, we did not refer specifically to any kind of delivery system. What we're talking about here is something fundamentally important, we are talking about weapons of mass destruction that we feared were in the hands of Saddam Hussein and he was capable of using them within 45 minutes.

HUMPHRYS: Is a mortar shell a weapon of mass destruction?

HOON: Of course it is.

HUMPHRYS: Is it really? Because that is not what the military says, they say in no way can a mortar shell be described as a weapon of mass destruction. Air Marshall Sir John Walker, who was on this programme just a few days ago, said in no way possible can a mortar shell be described as a weapon of mass destruction. He's a military man, I'm not.

HOON: I didn't actually hear that interview.

HUMPHRYS: Well, I can quote you from it.

HOON: It's what the mortar shell contains. The kind of shells used in Halabja, for example, were battlefield weapons munitions, if you like, but they were causing devastating death and destruction across a huge area because they contained a chemical agent. Now that is a weapon of mass destruction.

HUMPHRYS: You believe that when that dossier told us about weapons of mass destruction that threatened us, threatened this nation, people had in mind battlefield munitions; artillery shells, mortar shells, that sort of thing. You believe that is the message you were delivering, do you?

HOON: The dossier, as I said earlier, did not set out the nature of the delivery system.

HUMPHRYS: That's not what I am asking.

HOON: I know it's not what you're asking me. That is what we published to the British public at the time. This was not a great issue of public concern at the time. This was not a great debate, it became a debate only after the *Today* Programme and Andrew Gilligan made it an issue in May the following year. Many months later it became a matter of public controversy.

A great deal of semantic foot work takes place in this exchange regarding the meaning of 'weapons of mass destruction' and 'battlefield munitions'. Central to the discussion is what basis weapons should be labelled as WMD. As argued by Hoon in this interview and Tony Blair and members of the British Intelligence Service elsewhere,[11] that the weapons referred to in the 45 minutes claim related to 'battlefield munitions' was not important. That Iraq was thought to possess *any* chemical and biological weapons was enough to justify their categorization as 'weapons of mass destruction' to both the public and the Prime Minister. Humphrys challenges this general categorization by drawing attention to the specific type of weapon delivery systems under question. So 'the military' (in this abstract formulation a highly credible source) says mortar shells cannot be characterized as 'WMD'. When Hoon contends that weapons of a kind similar to mortars had been used to devastating effect in Halabja, Humphrys shifts attention to the specific claims made in the dossier regarding the ability of weapons to threaten 'this nation'. In this exchange the rights and wrongs of labels are not just abstract matters, but rather their suitability for some practical purpose and in relation to some set of concerns is debated. Alternative notions of just what was said in, implied by or later inferred from official statements and what functions those proclamations were supposed to serve (e.g. 'when that dossier told us about weapons of mass destruction that threatened us') are also at work in appraisals of the appropriateness of the label 'weapons of mass destruction'.

Whatever government ministers might have assumed was acceptable in the build up to the war, since then the definition of the phrase 'weapon of mass destruction' has been a topic of considerable controversy. That chemical or biological weapons should be placed under this category has been questioned elsewhere by senior officials. Testifying before the inquiry into the death of Dr David Kelly, for instance, the former branch head of the UK Defence Intelligence Analysis Staff Brian Jones said:

My personal opinion is that almost all – almost all – nuclear weapons truly fit this concept of being a weapon of mass destruction, that some biological weapons are perhaps reasonably described in that way because they could be used to produce very large numbers of casualties on the same sort of scale perhaps even as nuclear weapons, but there are many biological weapons that struggle to fit into that. Some are incapacitants, for example, rather than lethal ... I think chemical weapons almost struggle to fit into that category. There are certain agents and certain scenarios where I would think that chemical weapons truly are describable as weapons of mass destruction.

Rather than a distinction between battlefield and strategic being the main determiner of what counts as a WMD, for Jones (in this statement given for a particular inquiry) even at the level of the general categories of biological and chemical weapons, it is not clear they should be treated as falling under the category of WMD. As with many other general pronouncements though, the limitations of this one are also readily acknowledged. The statement is itself qualified first by Jones as a personal account and second as one where exceptions to the general assessments proposed can be made. Given the argument in Chapter 5 about the contestability of categorizations and the often commented fuzziness of the term 'weapons of mass destruction', disagreement about what it entails is not unexpected. Yet in general, any attempt to offer a characterization of what weapons do will involve a constant tension between the generality and specificity of the claims made.

Effects and prohibitions

In response to what has been said so far about the disputability of generalizations about effects, it might be countered that probability figures or estimations of injuries are merely that – qualified statements that provide a rough guide to likely effects but do not and could not be said to specify effects once and for all for any circumstance. When it comes to assessing the effects of weaponry, in the end what matters is a combination who uses what weapon, how and in which situation. Yet, prohibiting certain weapons on the basis of their *effects* relies on mobilizing persuasive generalizations about what weapons do and why. The prospect of establishing prohibitions that are at once of general relevance and yet responsive to specific instances is daunting.

For instance, international humanitarian law provides the basis for banning weapons that are deemed cruel (i.e. that cause 'unnecessary suffering' or 'superfluous injury') or indiscriminate through the UN Certain Conventional Weapons Convention (CCW).[12] Past attempts to negotiate bans on CCWs such as cluster munitions, flechettes, incendiary devices and others because of their cruelty or indiscriminate qualities have floundered as government officials have sought to point out the numerous ifs and buts hidden within general characterizations of effects. Various precautions might enable relatively acceptable use of what would otherwise be condemned as 'inhumane weapons': the precision of targeting mechanisms, the specific characteristics of the weaponry (e.g. not all incendiary devices are the same, see Chapter 5), the aftercare provisions made available to those wounded, the amount of intelligence gathered about the location of enemy targets, etc. What counts as a workable, good enough generalization has been a matter of ongoing dispute.

Rather than evaluating individual weapons on a case-by-case basis to determine if they should be characterized as inhumane, in 1997 the ICRC proposed general criteria for determining what counted as unnecessary suffering and superfluous injury. As suggested here, determinations of what kind of controls should be established depend on determinations made about where the cause of effects is principally located – whether that be in the weapons themselves, the way in which they are used or the circumstances of their use. While, as noted earlier, members of the ICRC have recognized a role for contextual factors in determining the lethality of weapons, these criteria attempted to specify the design inherent effects of weapons; that is a base rump of non-contingent materialism which would be founded on 'clear and objective' medical effect-based standards. Weapons that cause superfluous injury and unnecessary suffering were defined as those that inflict:

- specific disease, specific abnormal physiological state, specific abnormal psychological state, specific and permanent disability or disfigurement;
- field mortality of more than 25% or a hospital mortality of more than 5%;
- grade 3 wounds as measured by the Red Cross classification (skin wounds of 10 cm or more with a cavity);
- effects for which there is no well-recognized and proven treatment.[13]

In drawing up these standards, the ICRC did not just rely on predictions of effects from testing laboratories but years of battlefield hospital experience that served to establish an empirical baseline for assessing weapons.

As discussed elsewhere,[14] enthusiasm for the criteria has not been universally shared. In the abstract it might readily be acknowledged as mere common sense that some weapons cause greater injury than others, but trying to define such matters for the purpose of establishing controls leads to any number of objections. Representatives from the US and elsewhere have made various criticisms of the ICRC criteria.[15] Following similar lines of argument to those mentioned here, numerous 'contextual' considerations have been said to invalidate the general standards. Criterion two and three, for instance, were derived from ICRC hospital casualty data for injuries sustained in conflicts over the past 50 years, but generally between warring factions in the South. As such the data has been said to be unrepresentative of the effects of modern, technologically sophisticated forces; so modern forces should not be bound by injury data derived from elsewhere. Officials from the US have further argued that the criteria did not take into account how the quality of available medical assistance affects recovery rates. Critics also pointed out that highly discriminate force employments, such as sniper fire, would be deemed unacceptable due to their high mortality rates. Following these criteria then might lead to more (not less) death and injury as other options will be resorted to in lieu of those banned.

In such criticisms, not only were questions posed about the appropriateness of generalizing about what weapons do, the degree of generalization in the criteria themselves was a source of concern. Responding to the criticisms made while seeking to maintain the generalizability of any standards would be problematic. Making allowances for particular weapons in particular contexts, or modifying the criteria by differentiating them in relation to certain factors (such as the nature of accessible medical facilities), would undermine the possibility that the criteria would serve as reasonably straightforward, practical guides. Making specific exceptions would be unlikely to establish agreement, but to provide the seeds for further cycles of generalization and particularization.[16] When allowances are made for certain circumstances, such as lowering or raising hospital mortality rates because of the quality of medical care, then new general standards will be established for a more circumscribed range of situations. These in turn may draw objections that highlight other circumstantial factors (say, the physical terrain) which undermine the generalizability of the already more restricted criteria. As new or modified technologies are used in varied circumstances, questions can be asked constantly about the applicability of standards. In principle there is no end to the number of factors that can be brought to bear in determining why particular injuries and deaths take place, and thus no end to possible exceptions for forming limited general standards that are supposed to govern conduct in particular situations.

It was partially the prospect of a similar dynamic regarding the acceptability of anti-personnel landmines that reportedly led many NGOs to campaign for a total ban on such technologies.[17] For quite some time as part of the CCW, member states debated whether restrictions should be placed on anti-personnel landmines because of their alleged indiscriminate effects. In 1983, various precautionary steps were required by member states to protect civilians against mines and booby-traps. In 1996, amid growing public concern about the destruction wrought by 'mines', further requirements were put in place stipulating standards for their detectability and longevity. Because these additional amendments to the Convention defined anti-personnel landmines as being 'primarily' designed to injure or kill, they did not prohibit mines that had not primarily been designed to inflict casualties (e.g. mines that 'primarily' marked out an area in order to restrict military movements). Moreover the unlimited deployment of so-called 'smart' deactivating mines was permissible. With such provisions, groups seeking to limit the placement of landmines would have to establish persuasive claims about their real purpose or their probable self-destruction rate (itself regarded as dependent on environmental conditions and placement practices).

The (slight) prospect of policing such restrictions led concerned NGOs and governments to go outside of the CCW. In 1997, the Anti-Personnel Mines (APM) Convention was agreed upon by 97 governments. It prohibits the use, development, production, acquisition, stockpiling, retention and transfer of all such mines. Its passage has not resolved debate about what is acceptable. What distinguishes

APMs and anti-tank mines remains contentious.[18] Moreover, countries such as China, Russia and the US have not signed the APM Convention. Instead these governments argue that mines remain highly effective and discriminate in their effects *if* the right precautions regarding their placement and deactivation are taken. To say that landmines *per se* kill and maim thousands of people per year then is to misinterpret the source of the problem. Injuries to civilians are contingent on who uses which devices and how. Banning mines will not end conflict, but require that hostilities be resolved by perhaps more indiscriminate means than (properly placed) APMs. Successive US administrations have pointed to areas such as the boundary between North and South Korea where anti-personnel landmines (complementing anti-tank ones) are said to offer clear benefits in relation to other options. The US has also sought to develop technical solutions to the problems of landmines by actively promoting new 'smart' self-destructing and non-lethal mines,[19] a policy most recently reaffirmed in February 2004 by the Bush Administration. The APM Convention makes no allowances for potential 'humane' or appropriate uses of anti-personnel landmines in particular situations: it simply deems these weapons illegitimate.

Such debates are fuelled by alternative assessments about what ought to be done by way of responsive actions. In the example of APMs, organizations have taken different positions regarding how to respond to the current level of technical know-how. The US is allocating more than a billion dollars into finding ways of making safer mines. The attempt is being made to differentiate the general category of 'landmines' into sub-categories such as 'smart' versus 'long-lived' mines. Many human rights NGOs have argued such attempts will fail to make affected communities feel safer, hamper demining efforts and undermine the total ban on landmines.[20] A question being posed in such debates is whether time and energy should be dedicated to trying to improve and disaggregate a category of weapons or whether the limits of technical modifications and other considerations mean that for all practical purposes such alterations are ill advised.

Consider another example. As mentioned earlier, since efforts have been made to ban 'chemical weapons', some have argued that certain incapacitating agents may provide relatively humanitarian force options. As such they should be exempted from any bans. Against such a contention, Klotz, Furmanski and Wheelis argued that 'genuinely non-lethal chemical weapons are beyond the reach of current science'.[21] Even making quite optimistic assumptions these authors argued that incapacitating chemical weapons (as opposed to chemical sensory irritants) will cause fatalities for 10 per cent of those exposed to them, a figure comparable if not higher to the field rates of fatalities experienced in the First World War from 'lethal' chemical weapons such as mustard gas.[22] Rather than relying on current states of knowledge, those supporting research into the use of incapacitating agents have argued that resources should be spent to overcome existing technical limitations. Such arguments are hardly unprecedented. For instance, in the 1960s a US Army Brigadier General advocated continuing work into the incapacitating chemical agents despite the difficulties of achieving the desired results by arguing:

> Some military leaders feel that we should not consider using these materials because we do not yet know exactly what will happen and no clear-cut results can be predicted. But imagine where science would be today of the reaction to trying anything new had been 'Let's not try it until we know what the results will be'.[23]

In diverse ways, in all the debates considered in this sub-section, questions have and are being asked about the appropriateness of generalizations and what they mean for the permissibility of weapons.

Some general tensions

So far this chapter has considered the validity of general statements regarding what weapons do. Often determinations about the merits of controls turn on where the principal cause of the effects is located – whether that be in the design of the weapons themselves, the way in which they are used or the circumstances of their use. Appraisals of this are bound up with determinations of the relevant issues for consideration and who or what is responsible for any unacceptable consequences. While broad and loose characteristics of the effects of certain weapons (e.g. X is a WMD, Y is abhorrent) are not queried all the time, when attention turns to deriving statements so as to ground formal prohibitions, intense scrutiny often follows. Attempts to survey across diverse instances of the use of forces to establish controls require setting aside or freezing constant some elements in order to highlight others. Proposals for controls can be undermined by questioning the appropriateness of disentangling individual elements of varied complex human and technical systems.

In addition though, not only must prohibitions rely on generalizations about the effects of weapons, agreements consist of generalizations about what needs doing.[24] In debates about the merits of weapon controls, questions about the appropriateness of generalizations of the effects of weapons dovetail with questions about the degree of generalizations of the prohibitions set out. While wide-ranging prohibitions might establish agreed standards of conduct, their responsiveness can be questioned. As suggested, any attempts to establish general proscriptions on actions or weapons are open to counter by pointing out the diversity of things under discussion. Certain prohibitions (e.g. all anti-personal landmines should be banned) can be countered through pointing to specific incidents of the use of technology where deleterious outcomes do not result (e.g. 'smart' 'non-lethal' or self-deactivating APMs used as tactical protection aids). Moreover though, where only a very narrowly defined set of specific contexts or technologies are within the remit of proposed prohibitions, it can be said that nothing much of general applicability is being offered. Prohibitions restricted to highly limited types of employments of weaponry are often deemed ineffective, irrelevant or unworkable and therefore given low priority in international negotiations.

The need to forward claims of general relevance and the problems of doing so are pervasive in analyses that purport to provide authoritative accounts of the world. As this chapter has sought to provide convincing general commentary about the nature of debates about weapon controls that is responsive to particular cases, it has been steeped in various tensions associated with managing the general and the particular.

This state of affairs is made even more complicated because what is taken as general or specific cannot be set out once and for all but is a relative characterization that depends on a sense of the situation in question. While landmines might be a specific category of all weapons, in relation to past efforts to establish an international ban, it is a rather general category which itself has been disaggregated into categories such as 'anti-vehicle' and 'anti-personnel' mines. Arguably the boundary between these two is less than clear-cut. In the field, an anti-vehicle mine might be triggered by a person if it is improperly placed, intentionally misplaced, designed poorly or because of environmental conditions. Efforts to establish a ban on 'APMs' have in turn brought criticism that this specific category is itself too general and a distinction must be made between persistent and self-destructing landmines. Self-destructing landmines can themselves be broken down between those that fully self-destruct and those that merely deactivate. At any stage in the process of trying to establish a workable prohibition on some types of mine, queries can be made whether the terms set out are too general or specific by referring to some consideration relevant to another level of analysis. The remainder of this chapter further illustrates the difficulties, dilemmas and disputes about the effects of weapons by examining the specific (and general) case of nuclear weapons.

Nuclear weapons: distinct, conditional, indiscriminate, abhorrent and invaluable

Perhaps unlike any other category of armaments, nuclear weapons have been the subject of extensive global discussion. The devastation caused by the bombings of Hiroshima and Nagasaki and the ever pending peril of their use in the Cold War generated wide ranging commentary about their place and purpose in international security. While dispute has taken place about just how long term and catastrophic a large scale nuclear war between the major powers would be (e.g. the possibility of a nuclear winter), the prospect of hundreds of millions or even billions of deaths was and is surely possible from such a conflict. Whatever the disagreements about the wisdom of labelling chemical or biological weapons as 'WMD', this category would seem almost designed for describing nuclear weapons.

In relation to the negotiation of prohibitions, it might therefore be assumed that these weapons would have a given and agreed status that could provide a solid basis for making judgements about what should be done. So along these lines, today nuclear weaponry is generally regarded as a special class whose abhorrence is not merely a function of the destructiveness of such weapons. They are not just 'big bombs' in certain states' arsenal suitable when major firepower is required, rather they are deemed distinctive and the epitome of unconventional weapons.

Whatever the present general revulsion accorded to the use of nuclear weapons, Tannenwald[25] suggests their present status has developed over time in a gradual fashion. During the Second World War for instance, with the ravages of the Allied fire-bombing of cities in Japan and Germany, the use of atomic bombs was not said to be a discontinuity with past practices of top US officials (at least on some occasions). For US Secretary of War Henry Stimson atomic bombs were 'as legitimate as any other of the deadly explosive weapons'.[26] With the Korean War and the development of thermonuclear bombs, however, this assessment came under widespread doubt in government circles and public discussions. Despite his initial decision to bomb Hiroshima and Nagasaki, President Truman later argued to his senior policy makers that:

> You've got to understand that this isn't a military weapon... It is used to wipe out women and children and unarmed people, and not for military uses. So we have got to treat it differently from rifles and cannon and ordinary things like that.[27]

As Farrell and Lambert suggest, the need for a distinction between weapon types was not confined to political or public circles. One could find traces of it in military forces at the time, though the standing accorded to nuclear weapons has always been inter-laced with institutional politics. So shortly after the Second World War:

> Navy leaders also opposed counter-city targeting, ostensibly on moral and strategic grounds, but really to deflect budget cuts. In the 'Revolt of the Admirals' in late 1949, senior Navy leaders publicly denounced nuclear attacks on cities as barbaric. A decade later, they strongly advocated the targeting of Soviet cities because the Navy was acquiring a highly inaccurate submarine-based nuclear weapons system that could hit little else.[28]

While President Eisenhower fought against efforts to set nuclear weapons apart from other force options, a stigma against the use of the former was building in the public conscious in the 1950s.[29] Tannenwald maintains that by the time of the Vietnam War little serious attention was given to the use of nuclear weapons by senior politicians. Although the targeting of Soviet cities remained in place and throughout the Cold War some military officials pressed for their limited use, nuclear weapons gradually became further and further designated as special or unique options[30] which could only be used as extreme retaliatory measures. Today an extensive range of treaties and agreements exist limiting the general scope for the use of nuclear weapons. Calls for a ban on these weapons are often made by members of civil society, governments and even international bodies such as the UN General Assembly.

Whatever the shared overall public and political resistance to the use of nuclear weapons, the reasons that lay behind this are arguably not shared. An important distinction can be made between absolute condemnations and contingent evaluations. In the former, nuclear weapons *per se* are deemed unacceptable whereas in the latter their acceptability is dependent on various considerations. General, wide ranging and absolute condemnations of nuclear weapons are typically justified on the basis of their said effects. In 2003, for instance, Amnesty International (AI) adopted the position that it 'opposes the use, possession, production and transfer of nuclear weapons, given their indiscriminate nature'.[31] This sweeping decision represents a significant break with AI's position regarding many conventional weapons (e.g. small arms, tanks, combat aircraft) where their appropriateness depends on the practices and precautions of users.

Nuclear states, of course, have not treated these weapons in such an absolutist manner. Instead they have maintained nuclear weapons have an important deterrent role in securing international peace and that their use by certain major powers, at least, might be legitimate. As part of justifying an (albeit) limited role for nuclear weapons in warfare, sweeping general statements about their indiscriminate effects have been challenged. As presented in Chapter 2, for instance, the British government argued that 'It is by no means the case that every use of nuclear weapons against a military objective would inevitably cause very great collateral civilian casualties'.[32] Such a conditional appraisal of the acceptability of nuclear weapons stands in sharp contrast to public condemnations often made about the outright abhorrence and devastation of biological or chemical weapons.

As part of the effort to challenge general categorizations of nuclear weapons as distinct and abhorrent, some nuclear states have sought to differentiate this category of technology. In recent years, countries such as Russia and the US have renewed long-standing interest in developing and acquiring nuclear weapons for use against underground bunkers, biochemical weapons sites and battlefield concentrations of enemy forces.[33] Proponents contend that such weapons can have limited and controlled blast and radiation effects, a suggestion readily contested by others.[34] Distinguishing 'tactical' from more common 'strategic' and 'sub-strategic capabilities is a central part of efforts to make a space for useable nuclear weapons. However, no widely held agreement exists for the criteria that ought to be used to demark the two.[35] The explosive yield, range, targets and effects of nuclear weapons labelled as 'tactical' and 'strategic' overlap in substantial ways. The lack of definition is both a product of and a further hindrance to attempts to prohibit nuclear weapons. Past treaties such as SALT I and II and START I and II have dealt with particular types of delivery systems and warheads on an *ad hoc* basis. Left largely unaddressed in such international agreements has been the effort to set out universally agreed terms and categories for types of weapons. While the *ad hoc* method served certain pragmatic purposes at the time, with the attempts today by some to set apart the category of 'tactical nukes' as legitimate options and the efforts by others to establish controls, the adequacy of the situation has come under sharp question.[36]

Alternative determinations of whether nuclear weapons are absolutely illegitimate or whether their legitimacy depends on how and what types of weapons are used has infused public and policy debates. Limited formal attempts have been made to adjudicate between these competing appraisals. In December 1994, the UN General Assembly requested that the International Court of Justice (ICJ – or 'World Court') offer an advisory opinion on the question 'Is the threat or use of nuclear weapons in any circumstance permitted under international law?'[37] The ICJ functions as the main judicial branch of the UN and as such it is one of the most authoritative courts regarding the interpretation of international law. By way of addressing the question 'what do weapons do?', it is worth considering in some detail how it went about assessing the legality of nuclear weapons.

The process of referring the legality of the threat or use of nuclear weapons to the ICJ was steeped in questions about who should be able to credibly comment on such issues, how any determinations might be made of the consequences of the resort to nuclear weapons and what future importance could be placed on the advisory decision offered. Initially, wildly divergent factors were cited as part of the debate about whether the ICJ ought to even be able to consider the matter. For instance, countries such as the US, the UK, Germany and France contended that the issues at stake were simply too complex and hypothetical to be resolved through judicial analysis. Adding to this, the UK argued the ruling might distract attention away from other more pressing issues such as the accumulation of conventional arms and the proliferation of WMD. In contrast, the Mexican representative suggested the judges consider as a relevant factor the view said to be held in many developing countries that the past agendas and actions of the ICJ have served the priorities of highly developed countries.

Despite the objections from some quarters, on 8 July 1996 the ICJ delivered its opinion on the legality of the threat or use of nuclear weapons. In the discussion that follows, I want to focus on how the ICJ judges marshalled and justified a sense of the effects of 'nuclear weapons' as part of attempting to 'apply' the principles of treaty, customary and humanitarian law.

The argument so far in this chapter would suggest that the ICJ faced (at least) two major difficulties in judging the legality of the threat or use of nuclear weapons. To the extent the judges generalized about the effects of 'nuclear weapons', their judgements could be challenged. In addition, if the opinion was to provide workable guides for future action it had to offer a general opinion about what should be done, one whose applicability over time and across varied situations therefore could be challenged.

The ICJ decision can be interpreted as exhibiting the tensions associated with offering definitive determinations while acknowledging the importance of contingent considerations and specific circumstances. The judges agreed that the existing rules of international law neither universally prohibited nor authorized the threat or use of nuclear weapons. As with other weapons, it was further agreed that the use of nuclear weapons had to comply with the tenants of international law. To the central issue of permissibility though, by a vote of seven to seven decided through the second vote of the President of the Court, the judges ruled that:

> the threat or use of nuclear weapons would generally be contrary to the rules of international law applicable in armed conflict, and in particular the principles and rules of humanitarian law;
>
>   However, in view of the current state of international law, and of the elements of fact at its disposal, the Court cannot conclude definitively whether the threat or use of nuclear weapons would be lawful or unlawful in an extreme circumstance of self-defence, in which the very survival of a State would be at stake.

So while the threat or use of nuclear weapons was *generally* held to be against international law, the judges could not determine that it *always* would be. Just what would constitute 'the very survival of a State' was not defined in the ICJ opinion. In many respects, the decision could be characterized as a decision not to decide, at least not to determine once-and-for-all the matter of legality.

As no explicit legal prohibition existed on nuclear weapons *per se*, in coming to their decision the judges set about to determine whether the envisioned threats or uses of these weapons would necessarily violate the principles and rules of international humanitarian law; particularly the need to discriminate between combatants and non-combatants and to avoid causing unnecessary suffering to combatants. Central to determining this was the categorization of nuclear weapons; that is, whether they should be regarded as similar to other weapons or in some sense special. In reaching the judgement that nuclear weapons were generally but could not always be said to be contrary to international law, the ICJ judges treated them in a rather ambiguous fashion. They both had 'unique characteristics' in relation to their 'destructive capacity, their capacity to cause untold human suffering, and their ability to cause damage to generations to come'[38] but also they had to be subjected to similar contingent and contextual restrictions that applied to other weapons.[39] Responding to the claims forwarded by the UK and others regarding the potential relative acceptability of nuclear weapons in a limited range of situations and of low yield varieties, the judges ruled that while the use of nuclear weapons seemed 'scarcely reconcilable' with respect for international law they could not 'conclude with certainty that the use of nuclear weapons would necessarily be at variance with the principles and rules of law applicable in armed conflict in any circumstance'.[40]

This overall conditional and contextual approach to assessing effects was not shared by all the judges, three of who argued a sweeping prohibition could be supported. In a lengthy dissenting opinion, for instance, Judge Abdul Koroma argued 'In my considered opinion, the unlawfulness of the use of nuclear weapons is not predicated on the circumstances in which the use takes place, but rather on the unique and established characteristics of those weapons which under any circumstance would violate international law by their use.'[41] Whereas in the ICJ opinion nuclear weapons were categorized in a tension-ridden manner of being simultaneously unique and not unique, in this dissenting opinion there was no disputing they were 'not just another kind of weapon, they are considered the absolute weapon and are far more pervasive in terms of their destructive effects than any conventional weapon'. As he argued, the qualifications made in the ICJ opinion meant decisions about the legality of nuclear weapons were ultimately left to individual states, a situation that was both practically dangerous and 'legally reprehensible'.

Just as physical contextual circumstances were alternatively taken into account in justifying deceptions of the effects of nuclear weapons, so too were alternative renderings made of the legal context for consideration. In justifying his dissenting opinion, Judge Koroma suggested the other judges might have concurred if they had considered the context of 'the whole spectrum of the law, including international conventions, rules of customary international law, general principles of international law, judicial decisions, as well as resolutions of international organizations'. While the ICJ opinion acknowledged that the decision should rest on 'international law viewed as a whole' it gave a rather different rendering of that whole. Instead of determining that the accumulation of varied aspects of the law meant the threat or use of nuclear weapons was illegal, the advisory opinion pointed to the need to regard particular legal grounds 'in the light of the others'. Specifically, this meant weighing those aspects of international law that prohibit indiscriminate or cruel weapons against the right of states to their survival (and thus the right to defend themselves) as enshrined in Article 51 of the UN Charter. In other words, humanitarian concerns had to be weighed against military defence. As the effects of nuclear weapons were not deemed unconditionally unacceptable, there might be situations (however limited) in which they are proportional. In response to similar contentions made in some states' court submissions, others argued that even the limited use of nuclear weapons might well escalate into a much wider nuclear exchange. Consistent with its highly conditional and somewhat ambiguous appraisal of what nuclear weapons do, the ICJ suggested 'the very nature of all nuclear weapons and the profound risks associated therewith are further considerations to be borne in mind by States believing they can exercise a nuclear response in self-defiance in accordance with the requirements of proportionality'.[42] At issue in such disputes about the proper context for consideration were questions of what principles ought to guide the interpretation of principles and who should determine this.

Despite the conditional and context dependent character of the ICJ advisory opinion, it is not neutral on the long term desirability of the existence of nuclear weapons. Rather by considering the question of the permissibility of the threat or use of nuclear weapons 'in a broader context', the judges offered certain suggestions for the way forward. As argued in earlier chapters, just what constitutes the relevant context is a contingent but highly significant matter. In this case, the broader context was defined through citing the obligations on states specified in Article VI of the Treaty on the Non-proliferation of Nuclear Weapons (NPT) to pursue good faith negotiations to devise a 'complete disarmament under strict and effective international control'. Further to this, the ICJ expressed concerns about the decidedly limited efforts by major nuclear powers to achieve this goal.

Following from this definition of the relevant context, the ICJ concluded unanimously that 'There exists an obligation to pursue in good faith and bring to a conclusion negotiations leading to nuclear disarmament in all its aspects under strict and effective international control.' What is not highlighted – but well could have been as part of the ever present potential for debate about what constitutes the proper context for consideration – is that Article X of the NPT enables states to withdraw from the treaty should they decide that extraordinary events 'have jeopardized the supreme interests of its country'. Just what such events might be and what they might justify by the way of a withdrawal are matters for future argument and persuasion. No doubt, conditions where the 'very survival of a State would be at stake' would be a prime candidate for a supreme interest.

What do weapons do?

This chapter has examined something of how this question has been asked and handled as part of attempts to appraise actions and devise arms prohibitions. As with user- and purpose-based prohibitions reviewed in previous chapters, establishing limits on the basis of weapons' effects is fraught with complications and contestation. The suggestion that weapons simply 'have' certain capabilities that must be acknowledged in deciding about prohibitions provides a quite shallow understanding. The difficultly of specifying effects has been conceived of as a problem of generalization: that is, a problem of how to abstract from various specific instances involving weapons in order to offer a general characterization of what they do.

The topic of generality has been explored here in relation to how determinations are made about the effects of weapons and how workable prohibitions are established. With regard to the first, in attempts to justify restrictions on weapons, the exact source of effects is a matter of considerable importance. General claims about 'what weapons do' (e.g. this is a WMD, this one causes a given profile of injuries, etc.) set out to identify probable effects notwithstanding certain contextual and use-related contingences. For the purpose of justifying standards of permissible conduct, however, for many such contingent factors are not notwithstanding. How likely or inevitable a certain effect is, depends whether it is attributed as resulting from the inherent features of a weapon itself, the circumstances in which it is used or the choices made by users. Alternative determinations of the primary source of concern lead to alternative determinations of what, if any, controls are prudent. As the adequacy of descriptions comes under scrutiny in debates about the merits of prohibitions, hard and fast characterizations often give way to various 'ifs' and 'buts'.

The tensions associated with generalization are not only prevalent in effects-based controls. Prohibitions intended to be applicable across contexts and over time must themselves offer standards with a general relevance can be responsive to specific objects and acts. Just how the general and the specific are brought together is central to the legitimacy and practicality of prohibitions.

Part III

Prohibiting weapons

Chapter 8

Predicaments with prohibitions

Predicament: A situation, especially an unpleasant, troublesome, or trying one, from which extrication is difficult.[1]

The disputability of just what ought to be done by way of humanitarian inspired prohibitions has been a central theme of this book. The reasons for this contestation are many. Disagreements in the necessity and appropriateness of the use of force are pervasive. Many competing descriptions are routinely made of particular acts so as to support alternative evaluations. The role of technology in acts of force is likewise multiply conceived. Parts I and II sought to develop a greater appreciation of the intellectual and ethical difficulties associated with establishing bounds for the acceptability of weaponry and force. While there are no doubt acts and deaths to decry, formally specifying just what counts as 'appropriate' versus 'inappropriate' force is problematic. As argued, attempts to authoritatively name 'the trouble' with weaponry are as vital as they are vexed.

While there might be widely recognized and perennial problems with attributing some definite character to objects, attempts to devise prohibitions invariably entail delineating certain actions or artefacts as inappropriate, unacceptable, etc. In doing so, efforts to establish workable and legitimate standards must find ways to address a range of persistent problems in specifying the relation between humans and technology, the categorization of related but also dissimilar phenomena and the ethics of developing and modifying technologies used for killing.

The initial sections of this chapter summarize and extend many of the points raised in Parts I and II. The aim is to evoke a sense of the tensions and dilemmas associated with determining the acceptability of weaponry through addressing the questions 'What and where is the problem?', 'What is like what?' and 'So what?'. Building on this, following sections establish the analytical agenda for the remainder of this book: attending to what is accomplished in and through the management and distribution of binds, tensions and dilemmas. Chapter 9 complements the general analysis given in this chapter by considering in some detail the case of cluster munitions. On the basis of these chapters, the question is posed on how individuals go on despite the problems of doing so. Chapter 10 examines some of the practical strategies for negotiating the difficulties associated with specifying the appropriateness of weaponry.

Classifications and contention

In this book I have approached the difficulties associated with determining the acceptability of force first and foremost as problems of classification. Accounts of the world attempt to lock down the meaning of events and objects. The basic problem in doing so is that our intellectual constructs never provide lasting or completely adequate ways of understanding. While we may seek to classify phenomenon into definite categories so as to suggest what needs doing, the quest for some final sense of order is ever elusive.[2] In our messy and mutable world, classifications are not revelations of some pre-existing order, but active attempts at ordering. Chapter 1 discussed the case of leg-irons to suggest that for even the simplest of objects, classification schemes routinely fail to provide a durable basis for prohibitions; not least because some actively seek to pry apart classes and categories.

As contended, the problems of classification can be seen as rooted in basic questions about the satisfactoriness of accounts of the world. The concepts used for defining the appropriateness of force – notions such as escalation, power, primary, intent, proportionality, suffering, necessity and purpose – are brittle and crack without too much strain. The ability of language to provide an adequate representation of actions and objects is constantly in doubt because the meanings of terms are approximate. And yet, nonetheless, it is through specific and contingent descriptions we seek to characterize what is taking place to justify a course of action.

The overall limitations of language have been taken here as cue to examine how individuals offer particular descriptions that attempt to secure working agreement about 'what is going on'. Through examining various public speeches, press conferences and interviews, it was argued that just how a 'weapon of mass destruction', a 'chemical weapon' or an 'incendiary device' are defined in particular settings is of considerable importance in how prohibitions are interpreted. In this sense accounts should be understood as forms of actions.

The chapters in Part II took off from these basic points about language-as-action to consider some of the issues associated with assessing the place of technology in the use of force; specifically addressing the questions of what weapons are, what they are for and what they do. By going through a diverse range of cases, attention was given to various problems with establishing workable and legitimate standards for the acceptability of weaponry. In sites of contestation, discussions often oscillate between categorizations and particularizations, contextualized and acontextualized accounts, as well as general and specific claims. In this, the dynamics with controlling force through formal rules do not have some invariant standing and import; rather these are constituted in relation to specific situations.

Having said this, in order to bring order to the study of prohibitions, the remainder of this section offers an understanding of some of the recurring problems in establishing standards. The range of possible issues that might be included in such an analysis is substantial. Yet, through the previous argument, three inter-related and dilemmatic questions could be identified as central to discussions of the acceptability of weapons:

1 What is like what?
2 What and where is the problem?
3 So what?

The manner in which these questions are handled is bound up with how distinctions are made between what is apparent versus hidden, what counts as adherence or deviation from a rule and what is social or technical in nature. In suggesting what needs to be done and why, diplomats, political commentators, corporate spokespersons, NGOs and others explicitly or implicitly address these questions in order to offer credible accounts. Following previous comments given in earlier chapters,[3] to say that the questions are dilemmatic is not just to assert that disagreement exists, but rather that any particular answers contains the basis for counter arguments. Let us briefly consider each of the questions in turn.

What is like what?

A recurring theme throughout this book has been how credible characterizations can be made of acts and technologies. Determining whether something or some group of things is unlawful, unadvisable, prohibited or reprehensible entails distinguishing it or them from what is legal, advisable, allowed or above suspicion. In marking off certain acts or objects, boundaries must be drawn and relations of resemblance and difference established. In general, the possibility of conducting analysis at all depends on the ability both to group things together as well as to separate them apart. Each must have its limits if the world is not to be treated as an undifferentiated goo or a chaotic assemblage of unique things.

In previous chapters, the question of 'what is like what?' has been most evident in the debates about the categorization of weapons. Problems arise both in terms of what ought to be put under the 'same' category and how such categories should be treated for the purposes of evaluating what is taking place. So, are leg cuffs and leg-irons really the same type of technology deserving the same appraisal? Are the Mark 77 incendiary bombs sufficiently similar to napalm bombs to be properly classified as instances of them? Are the controversial activities undertaken by 'biodefence' establishments essentially defensive or offensive in nature? Should incapacitating so-called non-lethal weapons 'be rejected for what they are: chemical and biological weapons' or embraced as valuable options?[4] Do the differences between components for onward incorporation and other parts really merit establishing a new category of weapon for the purpose of export controls? Has the incorporation parts policy brought a minor refinement to British export policy or a significant shift in its very essence? In answering such questions, situations and devices are grouped together or separated apart for the purpose of offering general appraisals of what is going on.

Particular controversies about what is like what are not inevitable. It was only after the lack of evidence of major stockpiles of chemical and biological weapons in Iraq at the beginning of 2004 that critical attention in the UK focused on what members of the government expected to find in the run up to war. When it was acknowledged that intelligence claims that Iraq possessed biological and chemical weapons capable of being activated with 45 minutes of an order to do so referred to 'battlefield munitions', only then did many question the appropriateness of referring to biological and chemical weapons as 'WMD'. Likewise, what should count as a leg-iron only became an issue of significant debate once evidence had indicated a seeming breach of export controls.

While categorizations of specificity or attributions of similarity or difference in general might not always be contested, when they are, prolonged debate can ensue with little prospect for resolution. What should be compared to what and on what basis those things are deemed 'similar enough' are not narrow perfunctory matters that can be answered once and for all. As suggested previously, determinations of the similarity between objects and events should be approached as 'relative and variable, as undependable as indispensable'.[5] Real world contentions about whether a particular prohibition on X category of weapons applies to the specific device #1 inescapably involve assessing things that are neither completely dissimilar nor exactly alike. For that reason there is ample room for a range of plausible classifications. Debates about the appropriateness of categories can turn on a wide range of issues, such as the assumed motives of commentators, competing senses of what counts as a germane history and alternative assessments of what would constitute a 'practical' generalization. Relations of likeness are always relations in a particular context, where what counts as the pertinent context can itself be questioned. Moreover, what is deemed a categorization from one perspective (e.g. the grouping of 'dumb' and self-deactivating landmines together as anti-personnel landmines) can be a particularization from another (e.g. anti-personnel landmines are just one form of mine). With this interrelationship, it is always possible to challenge some determination of what is like what by framing the issues at stake in an alternative fashion.

Whatever the extent of debate about the appropriateness of designations of similarity or difference, making such attributions is pervasive. The arguments of this book, just like that of this sentence, have necessarily employed notions of what is similar to what. How this is done is highly performative and often consequential. In Chapter 5, for instance, it was noted that how relating a discussion of the US government's case-by-case approach to appraising Mark 77 firebombs to its case-by-case approach for appraising incendiary devices was itself highly suggestive of the existence of pattern of behaviour. Comparing the Mark 77s to a different class of technology where the case-by-case was not employed might render a fair less favourable conclusion about the appropriateness of how the Mark 77s were handled. In Chapter 6 allegations about Iraqi's former chemical and biological programmes and that of the US were juxtaposed to suggest (though never explicitly state) that they shared a certain 'likeness'. Much of political debate entails an active contest over what can be realistically compared to what. Various critical questions can and indeed are routinely asked of assertions about what is or is not like something else: What basis exists for making this claim? What is the significance of bases offered? Why are certain comparisons being made and not others?

What and where is the problem?

Another central concern in the previous chapters has been with how proposals for prohibitions attempt to cut through complex issues so as to offer a characterization of just what is taking place and why. By setting a certain basis for restrictions, controls identify some particular aspect associated with the use or the development of weaponry as the principal source of the problem. As we have seen, that might be the intrinsic effects of weapons, the purposes they serve, the situations in which they are used, the intentions of their users or who they are used against. Alternative bases for prohibitions suggest alternative answers to the questions of 'what and where is the problem' and therefore what, if anything, needs doing.

In the preceding argument, the contingencies associated with delineating 'the problem' were most evident in how objects and acts were understood in relation to 'their context'. The extent to which contextual factors were said to play a part in determining the acceptability of weaponry varied considerably. In the case of the category of nuclear weapons, for some their acceptability depended almost entirely on the physical terrain in which they were used, while for others such factors were irrelevant. Likewise, when death or injury results from the use of force, questions are often asked about just why this was the case; whether the individuals involved were really responsible or whether situational features had the most explanatory relevance. Analyses have tried both to recognize the importance of physical context in determining the effects of weapons, while isolating a sense of those effects necessarily 'built-into' the weapons themselves.

The importance of the relation between weaponry and its context in identifying 'what and where the problem is' extends far beyond concerns about the physical terrain of combat. Different notions of context can suggest radically alternative casual backdrops against which to understand events. In past disputes about the real purpose of ambiguous 'biodefence' activities, commentators have identified a wide range of contextual factors including the attributed motives of individuals as part of the relevant historical background. More recently, the US increase in biodefence funding after 9–11 might be represented as a massive destabilizing expenditure of funds or insignificant against the global backdrop of current pharmaceutical and medical R&D.

The marshalling of a sense of context is widespread in attempts to provide a sense of meaning. And yet, following from points mentioned earlier, just how this is done is contestable. The suggestion that the elaboration of 'the context' can resolve debates about the acceptability of objects and events is problematic. What counts as the proper context in areas of controversy is often multiply conceived. Just how far one should look outside of the text of an agreement to find its true meaning is a recurring theme in the interpretation of rules. The 'spirit of a rule' can be said to derive from the text in question, the original stated intent behind the agreement, its implied purposes, the history of its interpretation, etc. Efforts to take context into account are also inevitably partial. The question 'where should the story end?' has no definite answer. Should the assessment of incapacitating agents focus on their probable health effects in particular situations or instead consider the possible detrimental effects of their development on securing agreement about ever fragile prohibitions such as the Chemical Weapons Convention (CWC) and the Biological and Toxin Weapons Convention (BTWC)? Are the possible detrimental effects on such conventions the main issue or is it the inflexibility of the conventions to make way for said beneficial technology? Yet any response to such questions could themselves be contextualized. With regard to the point about the CWC and BTWC, others might respond that if we are really interested in preserving such conventions then we should not draw attention to the ramifications of weapons deemed marginal to their real objectives.[6] In the wider context of preventing biological warfare (BW) and chemical warfare (CW), non-lethals are insignificant.[7]

Seeing things 'in context' is thoroughly tension-ridden. As Scharfstein[8] notes, on the one hand situating something in context individualizes it as the uniqueness of the specific considerations entailed are noted. On the other hand, the very noting of such points provides the basis for connections between different things. Thus the British government's decision to formulate a policy for incorporation export components in the new 'modern reality which we are confronting'[9] was presented as an attempt to draw attention to the specific implications of the restructuring of the defence industry for the said narrow category of incorporation component parts. Yet in doing so, it also begged questions about the potential corrosive effect of this restructuring for other areas of export control and the viability of adhering to the principles the British government said it was adhering to.

Not only is the attempt to see things 'in context' tension-ridden because it points in different directions, as argued in Chapter 6, in practical situations a notion of the context is itself defined in relation to the things under question. Implicitly or explicitly, many analysts of 'biodefence' projects have suggested that their status can be properly determined only by situating them within the wider programme in which they were undertaken. Depending on assessments of the wider programme's purpose, individual activities – such as the production of aerosolization testing devices – are given wholly different interpretations. The process at work is one in which presumptions about the overall intent of actions inform characterizations about specific activities. Such characterizations, in turn, are used to inform determinations of intent. Many critics of the US 'biodefence' programmes treated the secrecy surrounding it and the wider political posturing of American administrations as indicators of the dubious intent of the undertaking. Seemingly acceptable individual projects were re-considered regarding how they might inform offensive weapons development. In turn, the number and character of such ambiguous activities provided justification for concerns about the ultimate aims served by the programme as a whole. Although circular, such reasoning is central to how judgements are made about the status of programmes. Instead of treating such iterative processes as misguided, we can understand them as part and parcel of how meaning is attributed to activities and artefacts. The progressive mutually definition of contexts and activities means disagreement about the meaning of acts and objects can prove quite intractable.

For the reasons stated, attempts to identify some sense of the 'the problem' with weaponry so as to suggest what needs doing are likely to be fraught with complications. As with categorizations, the resort to context can be treated as indispensable but yet undependable. Context is as much as an explanation as the thing to be explained.[10] Any determination of the problem can be challenged through mobilizing a different sense of the thing or context in question or through alternatively relating them to one another. The reader is asked to pause to reflect on arguments given so far in this book and how they have been varyingly accepted, rejected or qualified through drawing on some sense of the 'real' context for consideration.

So what?

Another recurring issue associated with establishing workable standards, rules and principles for the acceptability of weapons centres on the scope and relevance of claims made. Prohibitions involve a degree a generality both in resting on generalizations about what a particular category of weapons is, does and why as well as in setting out rules that are meant to guide action across varied settings. One-off, throwaway claims about weapons or applications of rules are of limited utility in forming workable prohibitions. And yet, the generalization entailed must to some degree be regarded as true to the individual objects or acts under question.

Making general statements and rules that are responsive to specific objects and acts is a tension-ridden process. With generality in prohibitions comes vagueness but with specificity comes insignificance. In the previous chapters, numerous instances were considered where individuals contended that the effects or purpose of some weapon did not fit the common claims made about it; either by it being more horrific or benign. Through such arguments, questions were asked of whether the generalizations set out (e.g. leg-irons are tools for torture and other cruel treatment; nuclear weapons are indiscriminate) were appropriate. While in the abstract few would vehemently disagree that some categories of weapons cause greater harm than others, when it comes to establishing formal prohibitions the assumptions and contingencies underlying such generalizations can become a topic of much dispute. As contended in the case of the ICRC standards, some national representatives have challenged the criteria by pointing to their failure to account for just who was fighting with what technology and with what sort of medical facilities. In response exceptions could have been made where specific contingent contextual factors were determined to be relevant, but this would undermine the criteria as practical guides. The generality of a claim is central to determining whether in case of controversy, a general exemption is being offered for a rule, an exception is made for some certain case, or whether an exception is being made at all.

Whatever the problems with generalizing though, unless policies about what is and is not acceptable are simply going to be ad hoc, it has to be done. Ad hoc procedures may indeed be advocated in some situations but often their legitimacy is questioned.[11] By what measures 'tactical' and 'strategic' nuclear weapon should be distinguished or what counts a weapon that causes superfluous injury have long been defined in an ad hoc manner in international control regimes, but with the renewed attention to the desirability of tactical nuclear weapons and search for ever novel forms of weaponry, the lack of shared criteria has become a source of some disquiet.

This book has argued the pervasiveness of the tensions associated with managing the general and the specific are at work in the very language used to describe these tensions. For language to function at all depends on some common meaning to be attributed to terms and phrases. This analysis – in its discussion of leg-irons, nuclear weapons and the like – has utilized generalizations to say something about the world, generalizations that can and have been unpacked. Our language does not simply function to aggregate though; descriptions also specify, disaggregate and distinguish. What counts as a general versus a specific claim, furthermore, is not something that can be established in the abstract, this designation depends on the situation (read: context) in question. These points suggest the importance of attending to how accounts of the world seek to be sufficiently general but suitably specific at the same time.

In practice, the questions 'What is like what?', 'What and where is the problem?' and 'So what?' do not exist in isolation from one another. To employ generalizations about what weapons do relies on a sense of what those weapons are and to what extent their effects are (in)dependent of some proposed situation. Not only do the tensions associated with each question make it difficult to secure some lasting agreement about the wisdom of prohibitions, the matters involved in addressing each can be played off one another. That might mean challenging generalizations about a weapon through offering alternative categorizations of it or categorizations can be questioned by proposing alternative contextualizations, etc. So, for instance, securing adherence to a ban on all anti-personnel landmines requires being able to forward general claims about a category of technology. In the case of the APMs Convention, such mines are deemed indiscriminate irrespective of their context of use. Even if some professed agreement exists about the general abhorrence and moral stigma of landmines (or nuclear weapons, chemical weapons, etc.), whether certain technologies are regarded as instances of this category can be a topic of dispute. As suggested in the previous chapters, those engaged in debates are highly adept in adopting alternative and varied lines of argumentation that challenge attempts to provide some definitive appraisal of what is taking place and what needs to be done in response.

Attempts to survey across diverse instances of the use of force to establish controls entail an uneasy process of balancing various difficulties with how relations of similarity and difference are defined, the way categorizations and generalizations are made as well as the manner in which events and objects are contextualized. In theory, it should be possible to offer clear-cut guides for what constitutes acceptable force. Attempts to lay down definite and lasting rules specifying what is and is not acceptable though face basic questions about their meaning and flexibility. The case of the 'application' of UK consolidated criteria to the HUDs transfers (Chapter 5) perhaps most vividly illustrates the way in which the meaning of standards for acceptable action, categorizations and context for considerations are open for negotiation and re-interpretation. The attempt to pin down the meaning of any of these aspects would entail foregoing a certain degree of flexibility, something resisted by both members of Her Majesty's Government and Her Majesty's Opposition.

Building on such points, through examining the scope for negotiation about the meaning of prohibitions, it was argued the rules and criteria seeking to establish what is acceptable are not merely applied but actively interpreted. This is not to say that characteristics of weapons as silent, deadly, indiscriminate, unknown, severe, etc. are not prominent in, or even central to, arms control discussions. Just which criteria are deemed important in which situations and just what they mean in relation to specific prohibition regimes though are negotiated matters. In general discussions about the rights and wrongs of weapons, certain criteria or factors may seem of obvious importance, but when the question is asked 'what must be done in *this* case?', agreement often evaporates as definitions and assumptions are scrutinized and alternative notions of what is relevant to the discussion are forwarded. How rules about what is and is not acceptable are made relevant for specific situations should be seen as managed accomplishments.[12] The rules set out in prohibitions cannot determine proper conduct for all situations. In other words:

> The importance of rules-for-human-actions to actions themselves is not merely one of governance or of rule-following. It is something that depends on how the actors themselves, as part of their actions, as part of how they account for actions, treat rules as relevant. This might involve participants *treating* rules as constraining, or needed to be followed, or, as inapplicable, or optional, or indeed, there may be some dispute as to what the rule, or the relevant rule, actually is. In fact, the invocation of a rule is part of defining what kind of action it was to start with.[13]

'Following' the terms of some prohibition regimes then involves attempts to argue just what following means.

As argued throughout this book, determinations of what counts as an application of a rule, a 'good enough' categorizations or an appropriate level of generalization are forwarded, negotiated and accommodated in relation to what is deemed the practical purpose at hand. There is no final, absolute, unwavering, for-all-purposes answer to questions such as 'What is like what?', 'What and where is the problem?' and 'So what?'.

The points stated speak to the pervasiveness of problems of imposing meaning through offering characterizations and classifications. While there might not always be contention about such matters at a given time, the world does not stand still. The terms of prohibitions can structure and frame questions about the acceptability of force, but they cannot resolve them. Debates about limitations for weaponry are confronted and often confounded by our means of knowing.

Contrasting orientations

The previous chapters have sought to develop an initial understanding of the problems associated with establishing what counts as acceptable forms of violence and technology. In attempting to offer some sense of what (if anything) might be needed by way of prohibitions to prevent deleterious outcomes, a sense of order must be imposed on the world. The argument has proposed significant questions regarding the advisability of initiatives that are supposed to reduce the suffering caused by force: would banning certain types of weapons on ostensible humanitarian grounds actually serve to favour the agenda of particular nations or groups? To what extent are the consequences from the use of weaponry foreseeable? At a basic level is the attention to drawing lines about the acceptability of weaponry misconstruing the real problem: the existence of conflict? Does an approach of taking-all-things-into-consideration really allow for responsive policy or does it result in one without an ethical spine?

The perennial difficulties discussed previously have no, in principle, final resolution, they are the moral and intellectual problems of naming, classifying and evaluating phenomenon so as to impose a sense of order. How then we respond to this situation through further analysis is a topic of some importance. In this section I want to consider three different types of responses and in doing so establish the agenda for the final chapters of this book.

Response 1: the what – better labels for tighter prohibitions

One set of responses would be to seek ever more precise classifications and decisive facts to provide a firm grounding for prohibitions. Better labels could be sought to name phenomenon, the scope for interpretation in controls could be narrowed by removing 'if' and 'but' qualifiers, bright lines demarcating what is acceptable and unacceptable could be laid out and further data could be marshalled to offer definitive determinations of what weapons are, what they are for and what they do. Such aims are often pursued as part of convention review conferences, international legal proceedings and official analyses of policy. This book could contribute to such discussions by taking as its main preoccupation the advancement of authoritative assessments and classifications. Interpretations could be forwarded for prohibitions and arguments made for the legitimacy or illegitimacy of acts and technologies so as to persuade the reader what course of action is required. Many thoughtful analyses cited previously have offered such evaluations.

While this type of response is of obvious practical import, the previous chapters of this book have attested to the contingency, scope for disagreement and fragility of attempts to marshal facts or lock down meaning through the search for more rigorous classifications. Assertions that the latest batch of factual data will resolve debates about what needs to be done often prove doubtful. Frequently such facts are missing or not available, when available their validity and significance is doubted and the procedures employed in identifying and interpreting facts can be unpacked. So, while necessarily drawing on analyses regarding the 'facts' associated with leg-irons, nuclear warheads, cluster bombs or other weapons, this analysis has not sought to provide an authoritative resolution of debates.

Much of the resistance to pursuing this type of authoritative analysis has stemmed from the sceptical orientation adopted towards the potential for rules to function as straightforward means of governing behaviour. As argued, though agreement might exist regarding what it means to follow a prohibition, this is a contingent state. The application of rule is always a process of interpretation and so the hope to regulate actions through unambiguous (but necessarily general standards) is ever difficult. Without the ability to know the full range of future sit- uations, it is impossible to specify once and for all what any given rule should mean. Definite rules can only be set at the expense of ignoring future contingen- cies. While there are reasons for questioning what it means to follow a rule in general, with regard to weapons prohibitions ample scope exists for questioning how rules should be applied. The previous chapters have proved many examples of the scope for and the importance of citing 'relevant' contingencies in debates about what control measures should mean. The situation is in part a result of the lack of an institutionalized international legal framework in which some final arbitration can be given to the meaning of the rules set out in agreements. Disputes over jurisdiction, the non-binding status of many agreements and their overall lack of enforceable sanctions mean debates abound about what particular rules imply. Of course, many types of prohibitions are not formal agreements amenable to legal dispute at all but instead rather ill-defined arrangements. The points given are not meant to imply that how and what rules are devised are mere irrelevancies, but rather that the search for ever more specific prohibitions suffers from basic difficulties.

Perhaps more importantly though, this analysis has sought to question the priorities pursued and the issue frames embodied within current prohibition debates. In doing so it has stressed the need for caution rather than confidence in distinguishing what is and what is not an acceptable way of killing and injuring. A central goal has been to clarify what is troubling with the very pursuit to make such distinctions. As such, rather than concerning myself with offering further prohibitions, I have tried to reflect about what is going on in attempts to establish them in the first place.

Response 2: the why – offer analytical explanations to predict behaviour

Another cluster of responses to the problem of ordering would be to seek explanations for the contentions experienced and agreements reached. So rather than just noting disagreement takes place regarding the merits of weaponry, the underlying reasons for this could be sought. That could entail marshalling a sense of economic and strategic interests to account for why certain categorizations and classifications are offered by specific individuals, groups or states. As noted in previous chapters, attributions of interests are widespread in the study of debates about the appropriateness of force. For instance, just why Western governments have (recently in historical term) deemed (most) biological or chemical weapons as inherently abhorrent – this despite the potential for more indiscriminate and extensive destruction with other weapons – has been explained through suggesting it serves their geopolitical interest to do so.[14] The explanatory repertoire need not be limited to traditionally dominated notions of power and interests. In recent years in the study of world affairs, power and interests have been increasing being supplemented or supplanted by considerations about the role of culture, ideas and identity. For instance, authors such as Price and Tannenwald have drawn on notions of social taboos to account for why some weapons become regarded as abhorrent or unusable.[15] This book could attempt to settle whether certain prohibitions are motivated out of self-interests, out of pre-existing convictions of what ought to be done or because those involved became convinced of their merits through argumentation.[16]

As part of any such explanation, questions could be asked about the significance of agency versus structural constraints in producing and sustaining appraisals of what counts as acceptable force. Cases could be dissected so as to isolate independent variables that could provide a general account for why certain prohibitions are agreed. In short, a scientific explanation could be sought for who says what and why. In its more positivistic overtones, such theories might offer predictions regarding future developments.

A number of insightful analyses of national security and weapons prohibitions have been produced under this rubric.[17] However, for a variety of reasons, theorizing in this manner is not my preoccupation. Even for those undertaking such endeavours, the predictive power of explanations in disciplines such as international relations has been acknowledged as limited in potential and poor in practice.[18] Another reason is that in this book, notions of interest or norms have not simply been employed as resources to build further theoretical constructs, they are topics for analysis in themselves. As in debates about WMD in Iraq (Chapter 6) or HUD transfers (Chapter 5) determinations of the motivations for and interests behind decisions are often the very topics addressed as part of debates about what needs doing. Therefore what individuals do in accounting for interests or norms is part of what needs to be being analysed.

Another danger of theorizing about the reasons that lay behind determinations of acceptable force is that it risks building yet an additional layer of interpretation on much interpreted events; one that obscures the role of analysts in crafting explanations.[19] As contended in earlier chapters, developing a thorough sense of the ethical and intellectual problems associated with devising prohibitions means considering the way this analysis shares with those examined the tensions associated with making generalizations, offering characterizations and drawing on a sense of context. To propose a definitive meta-analysis that gets 'under the skulls' of others, this analysis would have to know answers to questions of what counts as the relevant context, the criteria for a strong relation of similarity and the proper categories under which to label objects and events.

Rather than disregarding the conditions of analysis through seeking a traditional explanation that reveals the basis of others' actions and beliefs (while passing over the role of the analyst), this book seeks to work in the problems of associated with setting standards for the humanitarian acceptability weaponry.[20] It is then not an attempt to master or escape the contradictions and difficulties of analysis, but rather a constant struggle to understand the problems faced.

Response 3: the how – asking what is accomplished in what we do

This is done by attending to what is accomplished through accounts of the appropriateness of the use and development of weaponry. Accounts of what is acceptable, what issues are at stake and what must be done entail a constant marshalling of contingent notions of similarity and difference, of partial contextualizations and of generalizations that pass over many details. The choices made or not made in the course of analysis have important consequences for suggestions about what is taking place and thereby what needs doing.

The argument given up to this chapter has not been merely aimed to convince the reader of the pervasiveness of the difficulties of establishing humanitarian prohibitions on weaponry, let only induce a state of paralysis. Rather, paraphrasing the philosopher Wittgenstein, the intent is to give a view of what is troubling in attempts to determine what needs to be done.

The remainder of this book will attend to what sorts of management strategies are employed in attempts at ordering – this despite the aforementioned scope for contestation – and what is done through them. The point is not to ignore or transcend the difficulties of approaching prohibitions, but rather to consider how individuals go on despite them. As such the truth claims sought are more modest than those that would be made in attempts to resolve debates about the merits of particular prohibitions or explain why certain agreements are reached. What is sought is an understanding of what is taking place in attempts to provide accounts of the world.[21]

A central component of this is considering how 'actors' and 'analysts' alike move between treating the world as fixed, known and structured and as fluid, unknown and unruly. As contended in previous chapters, prohibitions often attempt to identify a principal or sovereign source of concern: the users of weaponry, how, in what sort of circumstances they are employed, the overall category of equipment or particular types of it. In doing so, meaning and significance can be attributed to objects and actions and proposals forwarded. In the ways illustrated in Part II, however, such efforts are constantly open for unpacking as the presumptions and limitations underlying accounts are scrutinized. In the following chapters I want to suggest how an examination of what is accomplished through accounts of what needs doing (and as part of this the movement between treating the world as fixed and variable) can enable making constructive connections and proposing alternative considerations. The following two chapters seek to justify this contention. Chapter 9 takes forward many of the points raised in this chapter to structure a description of the case of the prohibition of cluster munitions. Chapter 10 examines the strategies whereby individuals and organizations attempt to manage the difficulties of attempting to 'resolve' questions about how to demark acceptable from unacceptable weaponry and what is done therein.

Chapter 9

Fractured worlds

The case of cluster munitions

Horrible as it may sound, the world needs better cluster bombs.
(Jaap de Hoop Scheffer.
Dutch Minister of Foreign Affairs (2003))

In recent years, renewed attention has been paid to the legitimacy of a class of weapons commonly know as 'cluster bombs' (or cluster munitions). These devices consist of a large metal casing that contains multiple (from a few to hundreds) of sub-munitions 'bomblets'. After being fired, in mid-air the bomblets are released from the casing and they disperse over a large area, in the order of several hundred to many thousand square metres. Critical assessments by NGOs, governments and others have focused on this large 'footprint' of damage combined with their use in populated areas as well as the failure of many of the sub-munitions to initially explode. Those 'duds' can be set off later by someone who disturbs them; be they a solider, a farmer or a child. Cluster munitions of some description have been used in thirty countries since the Second World War. Debate about their necessity and appropriateness has often centred on whether they are permissible under International Humanitarian Law (IHL). Recommendations for what needs to be done range from a total ban through to carrying on without change.

The quote at the start of the chapter from Jaap de Hoop Scheffer, then Dutch Minister of Foreign Affairs before being appointed NATO Secretary General in 2004, indicates one option often voiced by many Western governments possessing cluster weapons. Rather than seeking a ban or denying that any problems exist, a strong emphasis is placed on developing more accurate dispersers and more reliable sub-munitions. The quote is part of a speech which continued:

> This is on the assumption that wars will be with us for some time. We need cluster bombs whose submunitions are more reliable and therefore cause fewer exploded ordnance to lie around once the battle is over. If bombs are to be thrown, grenades to be fired, then let their effect make itself be felt on the battlefield, there and then, and not when civilians believe that it is safe enough to leave their shelters.

This speech was given at the first meeting of Cluster Munition Coalition, a group of NGOs dedicated to highlighting and reducing the humanitarian problems with such weapons; a meeting in large part funded by the Dutch government. De Hoop Scheffer's comments on cluster weapons were just one part of speech on explosive remnants of war, one that included a discussion of the problems of landmines, the Dutch government's past support for disarmament efforts and the importance of pursuing limitations to weapons under the Certain Conventional Weapons Convention (CCW). The call for better cluster bombs signalled a refusal by the Dutch government to take a leading role in international efforts to ban these weapons, accounted for that policy by framing the problem with cluster bombs in terms of technical issues about the reliability of sub-munitions, and in citing the past work of Dutch government refuted possible negative motivations that might be attributed for the refusal.

This chapter examines debates at the turn of century about what cluster weapons are, what they are for, what they do and through these issues what should be done. Previous chapters have considered numerous controversies associated with the appropriateness of weaponry and the often dynamic, fraught and situated process whereby proposals are offered for what steps should be undertaken. As argued, attempts to establish workable and legitimate standards must find ways of addressing problems associated with specifying the appropriateness of force. Commentators often move back and forth in an uneasy manner between making categorizations and particularizations, offering general and specific claims and situating technology in and specifying its relevant context. While in the main the chapters of Part 2 focused on one of these dynamics, this chapter considers the relevance of all three as well as the themes and predicaments identified in Part I. In debates regarding just what should be done about cluster bombs, wide ranging issues have been identified as pertinent and the appropriateness of basic terms have been thoroughly disputed. As such, questions have been posed about nearly every aspect of their use. In doing so, in a preliminary fashion this chapter follows through the suggestion in Chapter 8 to attend to what is accomplished through the accounts given of weapons and the use of force. Further reflection on this topic is given in Chapter 10.

Cluster bombs: a description

This chapter started with a short description of cluster bombs. The details of descriptions are often highly suggestive in defining the key issues for consideration, promoting a particular evaluation and establishing what further information might be relevant. Consider the following account of cluster bombs from a 1999 *Newsweek International* article entitled 'Seeds of carnage: after the war in Kosovo, unexploded cluster bombs continue to kill and maim dozens of victims':

> Imagine a crate full of soft-drink cans, about 200 of them. Imagine the crate is falling from the sky and spills its contents hundreds of feet in the air. The cans sprout little rubbery parachutes. Slowly, they drift toward

the ground. As they hit, they start to explode. Some blast out razor-sharp shrapnel. Others are hot enough to bore through metal before they blow up. And some- between 5 and 30 percent-don't detonate at all. They just lie there on the ground, or hang from their parachutes in tree branches, or drift in lakes and seas. Many are bright yellow-very inviting, especially for kids. Until, at some moment impossible to predict, they explode. That's a cluster bomb.[1]

The article goes on to discuss competing views about what needs to be done. As argued, cluster bombs have not received 'the same attention over the years as land mines'. As a result, major States Parties to the Ottawa Anti-Personnel Mines (APM) Convention rejected the inclusion of clusters within the terms of the convention and concerned NGOs and others were said to have compromised on this point. An analyst from the US Center for International Policy is cited as arguing that while a ban is unrealistic there may be hope in the future that American self-destruction and deactivation technology in place for landmines could be transferred to cluster bombs. The article ends by stating that 'If cluster-bomb "duds" could be made to do the same [i.e. self-destruct and deactivate], the world would be a safer place. Now that American and European troops in Kosovo are at risk...there might be a chance to do just that.'

Even this short account is quite evocative in establishing what cluster bombs are and what they do. They are highly lethal weapons, particularly problematic because of the manner in which they so often fail to explode as intended across varied terrains. They can be triggered off for a variety of reasons or no reason at all. Children, rather than adult civilians or combatants, are identified as prime victims. Clusters bombs are related to landmines and said to be (at least potentially) open to the same arms control or technical modifications. The risks being posed to Western troops in Kosovo (rather than the dangers to Kosovars) raises the prospect that Western governments will now be motivated to act against long-known dangers, most likely by employing the technical fixes already applied to landmines.

This account is but one of many given in recent years of the dangers with cluster bombs. The next few sections examine how these weapons have been characterized in the past, how commentators have forwarded alternative conceptions of the issues at stake and formulated recommendations. It does so by posing the questions identified in the previous chapter: 'What is like what?', 'What and where is the problem?' and 'So what?'. As argued, the responses given to such matters are both highly variable and highly consequential.

What is like what?

As illustrated in both the *Newsweek International* article and the speech by Jaap de Hoop Scheffer, cluster bombs are often discussed in relation to or explicitly likened with other types of weaponry, most often mines and other explosive remnants of war (ERW). The Geneva Centre for Humanitarian Demining[2] includes four groups of technology within the overall category of ERW:

- Mines and unexploded ordnance.
- Abandoned armoured fighting vehicles.
- Small arms and light weapons, and their ammunition.
- Abandoned and/or damaged stockpiles of explosives and ammunitions.

In this classification, unexploded cluster bomblets are considered unexploded ordnance (UXOs), a category defined by NATO as 'Explosive ordnance which has been primed, fused, armed, or otherwise prepared for use or used. It could have been fired, dropped, launched, projected yet remains unexploded either through malfunction or design or for any other cause.'[3] Other types of UXOs include rockets, shells and grenades.

As contended in previous chapters (see esp. Chapter 5), classifications, categorizations and relations of similarity are often central to shoring up a particular understanding of what is taking place and why. These characterizations indicate what – for some practical purpose – is important about a technology, the use of force or whatever. Yet, the basis for reaching such designations is often problematic. What makes one thing sufficiently similar to another to make them 'the same' is something that must be substantiated.

Clusters as mine-like?

Much of the attention given to cluster munitions as ERW relates to their post-conflict impacts.[4] In its 2003 study *Explosive Remnants of War*, the International Committee of the Red Cross (ICRC) examined the injuries and costs associated with ERW.[5] The ICRC contended more lives are often lost post-conflict because of UXOs than anti-personnel landmines. The effects go beyond human causalities to include the costs of coping with injury, the denial of land areas known or suspected of containing ERW and the undermining of individuals' feeling of safety. Laos, for instance, has suffered some of the most horrific effects, with some 11,000 deaths and injuries attributed to ERW since the end of fighting in 1975. Even by 2003, between 9 and 27 million unexploded sub-munitions were thought to remain in this country. The failed sub-munitions from cluster bombs are identified as a significant element of ERW in many conflicts. The ICRC cites NATO estimations that 30,000 unexploded sub-munitions (10 per cent of the total number used) remained in Kosovo from the military intervention in 1999. As stated 'While the use of sub-munitions is lawful, when they fail to explode and become unexploded ordnance they are then as indiscriminate in their timing and choice of victim as landmines.'[6]

The resemblance between landmines and unexploded cluster sub-munitions has been a long-running topic of commentary. Many of those calling for changes regarding if, how, where and what cluster munitions are used have contended they are 'in effect' the functional equivalent of mines.[7] Handicap International has argued the high failure rate of cluster munitions means they 'act essentially like antipersonnel mines, in terms of their effects and the consequences for nearby civilians'.[8] Other groups such as Pax Christi[9] and Mines Action Canada (MAC)[10] have repeatedly referred to unexploded sub-munitions as '*de facto* landmines'.[11] On some occasions, such an equivalence has been made by those promoting these weapons. The newspaper *The Guardian* reported in 2003 that an Israeli manufacturer exhibited 'cluster weapons'[12] at a London arms fair and claimed the failed bomblets from it were 'in essence mines'.

The similarity between failed cluster bomblets and mines has been proactively denied elsewhere. During a news briefing on 21 April 2003,[13] US Secretary of Defense Donald Rumsfeld and General Richard Myers of the Joint Chiefs of Staff were asked:

Q: Mr. Secretary, prior to the conflict, human rights groups complained about the use of cluster bombs by the United States. Now that the major combat phase is over, we're seeing the evidence that this, in fact, is a weapon that can continue to kill after the hostilities are over. There've been a small but significant number of people maimed or killed, including some children and some American forces as well. Would you consider limiting the use of cluster bombs in the future, or perhaps even eliminating them from the U.S. arsenal in response to this kind of – type of criticism?

MYERS: I think it gets back to – well, first of all, cluster bombs are not like mines, completely different subject. Cluster bombs are set to go off when they strike their target or whatever they do, so they're not like a mine that lies there until it's activated. I have not heard of injuries due to cluster bombs, but we'll look into it. It's possible, of course, but we'll have to look into it. And –

Q: Well, we've been seeing pictures of unexploded sub-munitions in various residential areas –

MYERS: We'll have to find out who's they are, and do all that sort of thing. I just – I have not seen those pictures, but I'll –

So against past claims that cluster bombs would continue to kill after the conflict and calls for limiting them,[14] General Myers chooses to define the issues at stake in terms of the complete dissimilarity of cluster bombs to mines due to the different designs of the technologies. Asked to account for evidence of unexploded sub-munitions in residential areas where civilians will be exposed, he declined to do so through citing a lack of specific information. This did not deny injuries might have taken place, but it did postpone having to account for whether they have to do so, and if so why, until such time that more information can be gathered.

While many have taken issue with the suggestion there have been no injuries from cluster bombs in Iraq,[15] a need for some distinction between landmines and

ERW has been made elsewhere. MAC echoed the statement by the ICRC above when it said:

> The major distinction between explosive remnants of war and landmines is their design. Whereas anti-personnel mines are intended to be victim-activated and long-lasting, most other weapons are not designed to indiscriminately harm civilians long after hostilities have ended. However weapons that fail to detonate as designed or are abandoned, pose a threat similar to landmines.[16]

So while unexploded bomblets may be characterized as *de facto* mines, a distinction is acknowledged between the design of ERW (of which failed cluster sub-munitions are one type) and landmines. The similarity between the two is in the threat posed to individuals post-conflict. MAC further argues the threat from cluster sub-munitions may even be greater given the large area the bombs disperse over and the difficulties this makes for clearing areas.[17]

Relying on a design distinction but coming to a rather different conclusion, US Air Force Major Herthel has argued that rather than being like landmines 'in reality, however, properly working cluster munitions are far more akin to traditional air-dropped munition as both are designed to explode at or near impact'.[18] Since both cluster munitions and traditional air-dropped bombs can be aimed inaccurately and result in duds, the analogy with mines does not hold.[19] Herthel quotes US Major General Ward's comments during a Department of Defense press conference that:

> Now these cluster bombs... there are some duds in there. Very few. But when they are, it's like any other unexploded ordnance. This is not a mine. There's no proximity on it where if you walk by or make the ground rumble or anything like that it's going to go off. So they're just like any other unexploded ordnance any place in the world. But they are not a mine. They have no timers on them whatsoever or anything like that. I think it's just like a 500-pound bomb, except there are several of them in a cluster. That's the way I'd characterize it.[20]

Being just another instance of unexploded ordnance, clusters are not exceptional weapons and should not be subject to extraordinary restrictions. Being like other unexploded ordnance, no special blame or responsibility follows from their use.

Others have challenged Ward's distinction between landmines and unexploded sub-munition and his evaluation of the overall problem. In a study of ERW for the ICRC, Colin King (editor of *Mines and Mine Clearance*) makes a more complicated division between the two in arguing effects and threats need to be broken down according to the reliability and design of the fusing mechanisms employed for different weapons. Where these are poor, the 'submunition can present a threat similar to that of a mine'.[21] Another factor in deciding about the validity of the comparison between mines and sub-munitions is the way in which local populations treat the weapons. King states mines are generally more feared than other UXOs, so civilians are willing to take risks by going into cluster bomblet-affected areas in a manner they would not if they were mined.

The discussion so far has mapped out some of the ways in which cluster bombs are varyingly made sense of through attributions of resemblances. While unexploded or failed sub-munitions are not in all respects exactly like mines, questions are being posed regarding just how much they are like, similar to or the functional equivalent of mines. Distinctions between types of weapons have been offered on the basis of their effects on different groups, how they can be triggered to explode, the danger they pose, why and how often they fail to explode, their design and the perceptions held about them. These distinctions identify different notions of where the problem rests. Exactly what is being compared to what varies, that includes terms such as clusters bombs, unexploded sub-munitions, explosive remnants of war, mines, landmines and APMs. The competing claims about cluster bombs surveyed in the given few paragraphs involve dispute about the relevant comparative framework for which they should be judged. In this heterogeneous mix of causes and objects, what is like what – what is sufficiently similar to something else to be considered the same – is a central matter of dispute.

Which prohibition regime?

Classifications and categorizations schemes about cluster bombs are not offered in the abstract, rather attributions of similarity and dissimilarity are part and parcel of debates about what, if any, prohibition measures such weapons should be subjected to. As stated in previous chapters, the APM Convention that came into force in 1999 places wide-ranging prohibitions on 'anti-personnel land-mines'. In relation to cluster bombs it has been argued that '[s]ince unexploded bomblets from cluster bombs or land-based systems are largely indistinguishable in their effect from APM there is a logical case for bringing them under similar sort of control'.[22] After the agreement of the APM Convention, the CCW held a series of meetings to conclude a Protocol on ERW in 2003. These two agreements contain contrasting stipulations, apply to different State Parties and include different provisions for the policing of prohibitions. The manner in which cluster bombs are defined directly bears on assessments of which prohibition agreement is deemed most pertinent.

The remainder of this sub-section considers the characterizations offered of cluster bombs for the purposes of evaluating the imposition of limitations. It asks how specific categorizations and relations of resemblance are implicated in definitions of what cluster weapons are and thereby what should be done with them. Attention is given to attempts to advance a persuasive sense of what is important about cluster bombs, mines and other weapons that could provide a basis for making conclusions about their relative similarity and dissimilarity. Following on from previous chapters, I want to illustrate the issues at stake in fixing down relations of resemblances.

Consider the managed, accomplished status of 'cluster bombs' in relation to whether they fall under the APM Convention. Box 9.1 lists the general obligations and some definitions under the treaty. As indicated, the APM Convention places wide-ranging restrictions on the use, development, production, stockpiling and transfer of APMs which it defines on the basis of their design. The APM Convention was the product of many years of negotiations and campaigning efforts by concerned governments and NGOs (many coordinated together in the International Campaign to Ban Landmines).[23]

In terms of whether or not unexploded cluster sub-munitions are restricted as APMs, some have lamented that they should have been but are not. For instance, Rae McGrath, cofounder of the Mines Advisory Group, argued that the failure of concerned NGOs and others to secure a Convention with an *effect*[24] rather than *design* based definition amounted to a betrayal of the founding principles of those that sought to ban weapons that inflicted indiscriminate injury.[25]

Other key campaigning organizations have considered the question of whether cluster bombs are the legal equivalent of APMs and reached more complicated

Box 9.1 The Convention on the prohibition of the use, stockpiling, production and transfer of APMs and their destruction

---

Article 1 general obligations

1   Each State Party undertakes never under any circumstances:

   (a) To use APMs.
   (b) To develop, produce, otherwise acquire, stockpile, retain or transfer to anyone, directly or indirectly, APMs.
   (c) To assist, encourage or induce, in any way, anyone to engage in any activity prohibited to a State Party under this Convention.

2   Each State Party undertakes to destroy or ensure the destruction of all APMs in accordance with the provisions of this Convention

Article 2 definitions

1   'Anti-personnel mine' means a mine designed to be exploded by the presence, proximity or contact of a person and that will incapacitate, injure or kill one or more persons. Mines designed to be detonated by the presence, proximity or contact of a vehicle as opposed to a person, that are equipped with anti-handling devices, are not considered APMs as a result of being so equipped.

2   'Mine' means a munition designed to be placed under, on or near the ground or other surface area and to be exploded by the presence, proximity or contact of a person or a vehicle.

assessments. In a lengthy report in 2001 entitled *The Campaign Against Cluster Bombs*,[26] MAC set out the main humanitarian issues with cluster bombs and recommended campaigning options. As an organization that has as its mandate 'a complete ban on the use, production, stockpiling, and trade of anti-personnel mines and other weapons which function like anti-personnel mines, including cluster bombs and anti-vehicle/anti-tank mines with anti-personnel effect', the exact manner clusters were like and unlike APMs was highly significant. While the report concluded 'there are strong humanitarian reasons to move forward and they are consistent with and reminiscent of the campaign to ban antipersonnel mines', the manner of this consistency and reminiscence was acknowledged as not straightforward. As noted earlier, MAC accepted a distinction between APMs and cluster bombs on the basis that mines cause indiscriminate victim-activated injuries by design, whereas cluster bombs cause such injuries when they fail to function as designed. As such it was argued in *The Campaign Against Cluster Bombs* that even in the NGO community there is fairly broad agreement that the latter are not prohibited by the APM Convention.[27] As further contended, when seen as a failure in design, both engineering and humanitarian issues became relevant to considering the appropriateness of cluster bombs.

Despite this acceptance of the distinction between APMs and failed cluster munitions on the basis of their design, the MAC report noted that others had said that the design-based definition in the APM Convention would include a wide range of technologies other than those more routinely designated APMs, including cluster bombs given their high failure rate. US military officials are quoted as stating:

> ...[A] number of groups and institutions out there [...] want to make this ban, CCW or APL ban, as inclusive and as broad as possible. So what we had the people in our acquisition and technology community do, was go through that definition with our lawyers, take the results of CCW and say to which systems could this definition be stretched if someone chose to do that [...] And the answer was horrifying even to us. Not only do they capture our four or five land mines that we expected, it caught a total of 35 systems, some as far a field as ATTACKMs and various types of bombs and many munitions that have nothing to do with land mines [...]
>
> That could knock out a number of systems that we really do need – some of our runway and island munitions and that sort of thing, and that's what we're concerned about. We want to be sure that if we're talking a land mine ban, we're talking land mines. That is what we're trying to do here.

In order to avoid being trapped in a wide encompassing agreement by those 'groups and institutions out there', during the negotiation of the APM Convention US representatives proposed an APM be defined as 'a mine *primarily* designed to be exploded by the presence, proximity or contact of a person...'. The insertion of such a purpose based qualification would have reintroduced a distinction that was included within Protocol II of the CCW (see Chapter 7). Yet, one of the main justifications given for the unacceptability of Protocol II was that it implied a 'mine not primarily designed to incapacitate, injury, or kill persons is not subject to agreed restrictions, even if its secondary purpose was to do so'.[28] *If* interpreted in this way in practice, the terms of the APM Convention proposed by the US would have required establishing the primary purpose of APMs (e.g. to incapacitate, injure or kill versus to mark out territory) before knowing whether the APM Convention ruled it out.

As described earlier, the debate about whether cluster munitions are permissible under the APM Convention has involved questioning whether the particular example of 'cluster bombs' should be included within the boundary of APM. Much of discussion noted earlier has centred on what basis mines or mine-like objects should be classified as APMs; whether that be according to their effects, design or a combination of design and primary intent. Yet, the distinction between these different aspects can be undermined. One possible counter against claims that cluster bombs are designed to explode on or near ground impact and as such un-APM-like *vis-à-vis* the APM Convention would be to shift from conceiving of design in terms of intended purpose to the foreseeable effects of technology. If the design of cluster sub-munitions is such that many of them can reasonably be expected to fail to explode, then even according to the design definition under the APM Convention it could be argued that they should be banned. Some governments have been said to support a 'ban by effect' interpretation of the design-based prohibition for anti-vehicle mines with anti-handling devices, an interpretation which could be extended to failed cluster sub-munitions.[29] Much would likely depend on the rate and predictability of clusters dud versus other forms of UXOs. As noted earlier by US Major General Ward, other weapons fail to explode as designed (artillery shells, grenades, conventional bombs, etc.). Yet should it be deemed that cluster bombs are somehow distinct from other UXOs – say on the basis of the rate of failure, the feasibility of technical modifications or the consequences of such failures in terms of casualties or fear – then it could be argued they constitute a special case which makes them more APM-like than other forms of UXO.[30]

The preceding discussion has indicated something of how cluster bombs are varyingly defined as APM-like in their design or effects. Yet in doing so it has taken for granted what counts as an 'APM'. As noted in Chapter 7, the US government has challenged totalizing definitions of APMs. Instead, it has distinguished between 'dumb' and 'smart' landmines, the latter containing self-destruction and self-deactivation mechanisms. This distinction has been central to its public justification for not signing the APM Convention.[31] Rejecting attempts to classify all APMs together, it has retained the right to use smart APMs in armed conflict.[32] According to this reasoning, dumb (or persistent) APMs are the real exemplar of indiscriminate mines than should be banned.[33] The effects of this policy extend outside of the US because its military forces jointly operate with forces that are signatories to the APM Convention. In its implementing legislation for the APM Convention, the *UK Landmine Bill* contains a clause enabling British forces to plan operations with US forces employing APMs so long as British ones are not actually engaged in laying mines.[34] Such an exemption has itself brought accusations that the policies of the UK and others have significantly undermined the APM Convention.[35]

In the debates about cluster bombs then, competing claims can and are put forward regarding what is like what for the purpose of assessing the applicability of the APM Convention. In alternative determinations of the boundaries and essences of the categories employed, alternative factors are identified as relevant. Depending on how one conceives of design, for instance, the likely failure rate of cluster sub-munitions or other UXOs may or may not be germane. In practical terms, such questions may be just the start. For organizations assessing what and how to campaign about cluster bombs, other considerations can come into play that in turn can lead to arguments about the arguments made about categories and particulars.[36] In *The Campaign Against Cluster Bombs*, for instance, MAC asked whether attempts to campaign for failed cluster bomblets to be covered by the APM Convention would amount to changing the essence of the treaty or merely ensuring it covered what it was meant to cover. So it asked both whether NGOs such as MAC would be characterized as 'dishonest by insisting on an inclusive interpretation of International Humanitarian Law as it relates to the mine ban treaty definition' as well as whether 'the norm being established against the effect of victim-activated weapons [through the APM Convention] ... is put at risk if APM ban campaigners do not ensure that weapons that have the same effect as landmines (at least when they operate as *de facto* landmines) are not also banned'.[37]

Other tensions can be suggested for campaigning organizations considering how to categorize sub-munitions. On the one hand, the APM Convention might not be considered a useful venue because seeking to include cluster bombs within it might provide a convenient opportunity for certain State Parties to withdraw. On the other hand, this venue might be considered extremely useful because few State Parties would withdraw from such a politically high profile agreement. The APM Convention might not be regarded as an appropriate venue because major militaries powers (China, Russia, US) are not in it, or this might itself be regarded a reason for pursuing restrictions on cluster bombs since a precedent could be set without having to (initially) involve those major states with known objections to cluster restrictions. While it might be argued failed cluster bombs should be included within the APM Convention because they represent an especially dangerous case of UXOs, their very uniqueness might be said to require a specific prohibition agreement.

Citing concerns about the potential negative impact on the universality of the APM Convention from attempts to achieve an inclusive definition of APMs, MAC's *The Campaign Against Cluster Bombs* recommended against using the APM Convention to address cluster bombs. For MAC and most other NGOs, the CCW has become the major international avenue for seeking controls. Since 2001 government expert meetings have been convened under this convention to discuss ERW, including unexploded cluster bombs. With the conclusion of a generic

Protocol in 2003 for the clearing, destruction, recording and prevention of ERW (explicitly excluding mines[38]), at the time of writing these government expert meetings are considering whether a Protocol specific to cluster bombs is required. Progress in agreeing to a protocol has been slow, as some countries have rejected any focus on cluster sub-munitions, regarding this as inconsistent with the ERW Protocol that does not differentiate between types of munitions.

What and where is the problem?

The previous section suggested attempts to pin down 'what is like what?' are open for questioning; what counts as relevant to making characterizations and what such characterizations count for are multiply conceived. Discussions about what kinds of restrictions are needed and whether cluster bombs should be regarded a special case of ERW turn, in part, on empirical assessments regarding the problems posed by their use and the reasons for this. If the rate of sub-munition failure is attributed to choices made about how and where they are used, then arguments about the failure of 'cluster bombs' *per se* are inappropriate. Many of the general claims offered in the last sub-section have been unpacked and questioned in recent debates. Although the preceding discussion about categorizations spiralled off into many directions, specifically asking the wherefores of 'the problem' with cluster bombs requires marshalling and contrasting further detailed arguments that in turn raise arguments that spread out along various tangents.

As suggested earlier, much of the humanitarian concern today about cluster bombs centres on the rate they initially fail to explode 'as designed'.[39] Dispute has taken place regarding the percentage of failures and the appropriateness of generalizations about failures across munition types and combat settings. When the UK government was asked in 2000 to estimate the percentage of unexploded ordnance resulting from cluster bombs dropped at various heights, a defence minister replied that: 'Approximately 5 per cent of the bomblets within a Cluster Bomb fail to detonate when they impact. Regardless of the height from which they are dropped, this figure does not vary.'[40] An estimate of roughly 5 per cent has been offered elsewhere by defenders of this technology.[41] As noted previously, those making more critical assessments have argued that in practice the failure rate is much higher, over 10 per cent and sometimes as high as 30 per cent.[42] In such appraisals a variety of practical considerations have been offered to explain why expectations about a low dud rate has proved so wrong; this including considerations associated with the manufacture, storage, loading, airspeed, wind conditions, terrain of impact, angle of sub-munition impact and drop height.[43]

While empirical data about failure rates and the effects of unexploded sub-munitions might be identified by many as key, arguably limited detailed, systematic and authoritative post-conflict assessments exist. As an indication of this, when questioned about cluster bombs in the Iraq war, while Lord Bach was able to say that the UK forces had used some 66 RBL 755 cluster bombs as of

4 July 2003, he also added that 'We have no means of knowing the number of unexploded cluster bombs there are in Iraq' and 'We have no means of knowing the number of people who have been killed or injured by cluster bombs since the end of the war.'[44] By May 2004 a government defence minister stated that some 5,800 sub-munitions had been cleared from the British led South East Area of Operations in Iraq, but as there was no further details collected about the type or origins of those sub-munitions, it was 'not possible to quantify the number of unexploded cluster bombs and bomblets that remain in Iraq having been dropped by British military operations'.[45] When Joan Ruddock MP asked the Secretary for Defense 'what reviews have been undertaken by his Department regarding the civilian casualty figures caused by unexploded cluster submunitions in the post-conflict regions of (a) the Gulf, (b) Kosovo and (c) Afghanistan; and what assessment [has been] made of the impact of these bomblets on Iraqi civilians in the future' a defence minister responded that 'No such reviews and assessments have been undertaken by the Ministry of Defence.'[46]

In many of the conflicts during the 1990s and early part of the twenty-first century, much debate has taken place regarding the failure rate of cluster sub-munitions. Campaigning organizations have maintained that what information is available puts the failure rate much higher than 5 per cent. With this questions have been asked regarding the specific reasons in each case for the higher than expected rates – whether that derived from how or which weapon were used. King's review of the use of cluster bombs in recent wars prior to 2000 concluded that in practice an over-all failure rate of 5–15 per cent was normal with some types having rates above 25 per cent.[47] In the case of the 1991 Gulf War, for instance, he estimated the most commonly air-dropped type of sub-munition (the M118 'Rockeye') might have not initially exploded 20–40 per cent of the time due to an insufficient drop height and its impact on soft sand.[48] A report by Human Rights Watch (HRW) suggested that by February 2003, 1,600 civilians had been killed and 2,500 injured in Kuwait and Iraq (60 per cent of victims under 15-years old) because of ground and air based cluster weapons.[49] The group, however, was unable to establish reliability figures for the US-led war in Afghanistan beginning in October 2001.[50] In Kosovo, HRW cited figures compiled by the UN Mine Action Co-ordination Center that the dud rate established for particular combat areas was between 7 and 11 per cent. McGrath accused the British government and NATO of 'criminal negligence' in Kosovo for deploying cluster bomblets such as the BLU 97/B and variants of the BL-755 which were said to produce high failure rates, the former especially when it is used from high altitudes (as often done in Kosovo) and the latter when it strikes the ground on an angle or lands on soft terrain.[51] Some of those offering critical evaluations of cluster bombs have gone back to their use in Laos by American forces during the 1960s and 1970s to substantiate the persistent problems of unexploded sub-munitions.[52]

With competing claims about the rate of initial failure have come further ones about why these sub-munitions might later subsequently explode. While the comments here by US Major General Ward contend that proximity is not enough to set off bomblets (so they are not 'mine-like'), others have disagreed.[53] McGrath cites a US document from 1997 APM Convention discussions regarding the BLU 97/B that says when it 'fails to operate as designed and remains unexploded (it) can be detonated or exploded by the presence, proximity or contact of a person. And, when detonated or exploded, produces an effect similar to a traditional anti-personnel landmine'.[54] Others have stressed the importance of breaking down different sorts of fusing mechanisms employed in determining the likelihood and reason for setting them off.[55] It is not just the technical characteristics of the weapons that are said to matter, their small size and bright colours entices children to pick up or otherwise disturb them.[56]

The discussion suggested something of the problems associated with pinning down the threats posed by 'cluster bombs'. Substantiating questions regarding the relation between failed unexploded sub-munitions and APMs or UXOs requires marshalling comparative figures about reliability rates or other matters. Such information is not easily obtained. Yet however hard fought to gain, any such data can be queried regarding its credibility and robustness. General statements to the effect that 'X does Y because of Z' have been questioned as the Xs, Ys and Zs cited are unpacked. The legitimacy of general statements are often cast into doubt as the range of possible issues at stake are elaborated. Just what claims should count as credible facts are also ripe for dispute.[57]

Are cluster bombs permissible under International Humanitarian Law?

Contentions about the source of the problems posed by cluster bombs enter into evaluations of whether their after-effects make them consistent with the provisions of International Humanitarian Law and thus legally permissible. As in other instances though regarding the meaning of rules and compliance with them, just what it means to follow the provisions in this area of law is not somehow determined in advance. Article 48 of the 1977 Additional Protocols to the Geneva Conventions sets out a basic rule for wars: 'the Parties to the conflict shall at all times distinguish between the civilian population and combatants and between civilian objects and military objectives and accordingly shall direct their operations only against military objectives'. Those concerned with the after-effects of cluster munitions often have queried this class of technology in relation to this basic rule and its elaborating codified articles.

With regard to concerns about the proportionality of cluster bombs, Article 51(5)(b) of the Additional Protocol I bans an indiscriminate attack which it defines as one:

> which may be expected to cause incidental loss of civilian life, injury to civilians, damage to civilian objects, or a combination thereof, which would be excessive in relation to the concrete and direct military advantage anticipated.

With this have come questions about the meaning of terms such as 'attack', 'excessive' civilian loss of life and damage, and 'concrete and direct military advantage'. Wiebe argues the official US position has been one of interpreting military advantage in a broad fashion to include both advantages to the war strategy as whole as well as those gained in particular tactical encounters. The ICRC and many NGOs have called for a much more narrow definition to include only short-term tactical advantages. By contrast, when it comes to determining civilian loss of life and damage the overall situation is reversed with those groups voicing concerns about clusters bombs pointing to their long term effects and those deploying them principally concerned with the immediate risks.[58]

An illustration of how certain formulations of what counts can be marshalled as to suggest the appropriateness of clusters is given in a news briefing during the 2001 Kosovo war when it was put to Major General Wald that some complaints had been made that unexploded cluster bomblets appear as . . .

REPORTER: 'Small, attractive, bright colored packages' that children find intriguing, and they pick them up and the thing goes off. Is there any reason to change that?

MAJOR GENERAL WALD: I hope that doesn't happen, but I would certainly say that the sooner we have the Serb/MUP forces leave Kosovo, and we can have the Kosovar Albanians get back to a normal life, there are probably going to be a lot more children survive because of that than they would picking up some small object accidentally out in the trees.[59]

Herein the contribution of cluster bombs to the speed of the overall war effort (i.e. getting Serb/MUP force to leave Kosovo) is said to outweigh concerns about the humanitarian effects on children, if there are any from said accidental encounters with unexploded munitions. Others may object to this line of reasoning by arguing it could undermine nearly any attempt to limit the means of war and it, in effect, amounts to the argument that the ends justify the means.[60]

At stake in these disagreements about proportionality are not only the interpretation of terms but just how determinations of adherence or deviations to the principle of proportionality can be made. To conceive of military advantage in terms of a campaign as whole makes it quite hard for those not centrally involved in planning operations (e.g. campaigning NGOs) to argue about the relative merits of an attack, whereas treating military advantage in most immediate terms makes the difficulties with weighing of gains more manageable. The call to factor in long-term civilian deaths not only demands that parties to a conflict take steps to review and assess causalities (something, from the previous quotes, the UK would appear not to have done in recent conflicts) but opens the possibility that they might be called to account in the future for attacks on the basis of that information.

A further complicating factor cited in claims about the proportionality of cluster bombs is the question of what alternative methods of force would have been used if cluster bombs had not. As the UK Ministry of Defence stated during the 2003 Iraq war:

> I can confirm that British forces have used cluster bombs, which, as I have told the House before, are the most suitable weapons for dealing with wide-area targets. If we did not use such weapons on appropriate occasions, we would put our own and coalition forces at greater risk.[61]

Not only has it been argued that troops would be in greater danger but so might civilians because the other weapons used will also fail to detonate and therefore result in casualties (see last sub-section).[62] Determining the proportionality of cluster bombs *vis-à-vis* questions about after-effects requires calculating the relative dud rates and employment tactics for different types of munitions.

Such an approach to the issues at stake has consequences for how determinations of adherence or deviation from the principle of proportionality are conducted. In a legal analysis for the UK government of ERW under International Humanitarian Law delivered as part of the CCW expert meetings, in relation to questions about the alternative means force that might be used, Christopher Greenwood QC stated:

> What is required, in other words, is to examine the whole picture. By concentrating on the problem of ERW to the exclusion of other effects of particular weapons, it may be that the protection of the civilian population is diminished rather than enhanced. I am not in a position to assess whether that would in fact be the case but the question requires careful consideration.[63]

Adopting this line of thinking entails delaying questions about the acceptability of cluster bombs until each attack rather than ruling them out or in from the start. Then, the 'whole picture' must be examined. In relation to the last sentence by Greenwood, it can be asked just who could be in a position to assess the varied issues at stake. While those calling for limitations on cluster in relation to International Humanitarian Law have sought to assess both the weapon's post-conflict costs (in contrast to the UK Ministry of Defence) and relative 'military advantages',[64] they are often in a position of disadvantage in doing so by generally not being privy to key elements of what those planning military force might cite as 'the whole picture'.

Besides these issues about the proportionality, the effects of cluster sub-munitions have been questioned by reference to 51(4)(b) of the Additional Protocol I which forbids State Parties to 'employ a method or means of combat which cannot be directed at specific targets'. As with APMs, the manner in which unexploded bomblets affect civilians and combatants without distinction is said by some to make them 'inherently indiscriminate'.[65] Yet, as noted earlier, no munition has a 100 per cent detonation rate and the resulting UXOs can then be set off by civilians and combatants alike. International Humanitarian Law, however, does not ban any weapon that might become UXOs. In practice, 'indiscriminateness' is not treated as an absolute property, but one evaluated relative to others means of force. So with regard to cluster sub-munitions, much debate has taken place regarding whether they are better understood as APM-like or merely like any other UXOs.[66] Just what basis might be used to make such a classification is not established in International Humanitarian Law. Criteria marshalled in past analysis have included comparative dud rates across varied domains, the number of unexploded munitions left remaining post-conflict,[67] the overall effects on civilians, the rate of fatalities and severe injuries from activating them, the ease of activation and the ability to locate munitions for future clearance operations.[68]

Specifying what constitutes an 'acceptable' or at least a comparatively similar dud rate for cluster sub-munitions is not uncomplicated. Questions can be asked about the adequacy of standards set by other munitions and whether reasonable efforts have been made to lower dud rates. So, though the US government has proposed to reduce the failure rate of its *new* cluster sub-munitions to 1 per cent by 2005 in line with (unstated) other munitions,[69] the Vietnam Veterans of America Foundation has argued a failure rate between 0.1 and 0.3 per cent is achievable through existing technologies.[70] As noted at the start of this chapter, some have placed significant stay in 'technical fixes' to alleviate many of the problems identified with cluster munitions. The possibility of achieving this though has been contested by those pointing to considerations such as the failure to reduce dud rates of cluster bombs as promised in the past, the deficiencies of certain self-destruct mechanisms in landmines, the potential for self-deactivated sub-munitions to restrict land access, and the prohibitive costs of retrofitting and purchasing modified weapons.[71]

Concerns voiced about the indiscriminateness of cluster bombs and their human-itarian consequences also relate to their immediate effects. The wide 'footprint' across which sub-munitions disperse combined with imprecision in their targeting has led to questions about when and whether cluster bombs can be said to be a discriminate means of force. Article 51(5)(a) of the Additional Protocol I forbids:

> an attack by bombardment by any methods or means which treats as a single military objective a number of clearly separated and distinct military objectives located in a city, town, village or other area containing a similar concentration of civilians or civilian objects.

Evaluations of cluster bombs thus turn on the interpretation given to the terms of prohibitions; such as the meaning of phrases 'clearly separated and distinct' and 'similar concentration' as well as their relevance for a given circumstance. Criticisms of the use of these devices in Indo-China by the US military in the 1960s and 1970s centred on the appropriateness of such 'area weapons', their likelihood to cause civilian casualties and whether civilians were being deliber-ately (and repeatedly) put at risk because of them.[72] In the 1999 Kosovo War the NATO practice of dropping bombs at high altitude to avoid anti-aircraft fire was said to enlarge the spread area of sub-munitions. In the 2003 Iraq war, HRW heavily criticized the number of attacks with cluster munitions in civilian areas by US and UK forces.[73] While noting the use of air-delivered cluster 'bomblets' in populated areas had decreased in comparison to past wars, the group stated ground-launched cluster 'grenades' had been fired extensively in populated areas and this had resulted in hundreds of civilian casualties. HRW further noted that various modifications comparatively reduced the threat to civilians from the immediate consequences of air-delivered cluster bombs. This included employing guided cluster bombs, sub-munitions fitted with stabilizing chutes and infrared guided anti-armour sub-munitions.[74]

So what?

In examining claims about what and where the problem is with 'cluster bombs', the previous section maintained efforts to fix down a sense of these matters are readily contested. Alternative boundaries, meanings and essences are marshalled to suggest what the 'this' is under discussion and how much information would we have to know about 'it'. Attempts to offer some feature of cluster munitions or the way they are used as a significant source of concern are questioned by others who contend that this aspect is itself contingent on further features. So proposals to define the issues at stake in terms of narrow design criteria can be undermined by asking about the foreseeable effects of certain designs. Notions of expected effects themselves can be related to matters of choice and purpose regarding the intensity of efforts to modify cluster weapons. A further consideration in establishing the problem with these weapons is that efforts to define a sense of the context ('the whole picture', 'the history') and the technology in question are bound together in the way relations of similarity and dissimilarity are attributed. Determining what and where the problem is depends on securing simultaneous concord about many related issues.

In this process much disputation centres on the generality of claims offered. Attempts to forward wide ranging claims in the form that 'cluster bombs have Y effects because of Z' that might underlie broad commendations or condemnations are open to criticism. Just what sub-munitions, used in just what conditions and against what targets are all possible topics for questioning generalizations. Yet, simply putting forward claims that in some particular instance a certain form of sub-munition used in a specific way had a certain effect does little to help determine what might need doing in the future. This section considers the recommendations offered by prominent states and NGOs in 2003–04 with a particular view to asking how such proposals have addressed the matter of generality. Few organizations or governments have called for either banning all cluster bombs altogether or carrying on without change, but just what measures would be 'good enough' in between these options is not widely agreed.

Citing their high dud rate, Norway has destroyed its old stocks of air-delivered cluster bombs and requires the Ministry of Defense to approve the future use of cluster weapons.[75] In contrast, the US policy combines a variety of measures including pursuing technical modifications to achieve a greater field reliability for new ground and air delivered sub-munitions (99 per cent or higher) by 2005,[76] undertaking evaluations of the need for retrofitting for specific existing sub-munitions (e.g. M864 DPICM[77]), destroying certain stockpiles, acquiring new sub-munitions[78] and reviewing use and targeting practices. On occasion other initiatives have been undertaken. After a number of civilian deaths in Nis and near Doganovic during the 1999 Kosovo war, President Clinton was said to order a temporary directive against the further use of cluster bombs.[79] Despite this, as in the 2003 Iraq war, the US retains the right to use cluster munitions in populated areas; in part justified through arguments that forbidding this would provide further encouragement for enemy combatants to locate themselves within populated areas. As such, the official policy as of 2004 is not one of supporting an additional Protocol under the CCW or incorporating cluster bombs within the APM Convention. Rather the aim is to apply existing provisions under International Humanitarian Law, a position broadly supported by other countries.[80]

As indicated at the start of this chapter, many states have taken the improvement of reliability rates as a central plank of reform. The Swiss government has proposed establishing international standards for reliability of at least 98 per cent. The logic of this basic approach has been challenged elsewhere. McGrath contends that any overall rate risks neglecting the manner in which large numbers of unexploded sub-munitions will be grouped together in some areas, the large number of resulting duds left that will still create dangers even with a substantially lower failure rate, and the problems posed by these duds for post-conflict clearance.[81]

Numerous questions can and have been asked of unilateral or multilateral efforts to set reliability standards: Who should assess whether adherence has been achieved or what level should be established in the first place? Should it be limited to 'government experts to decide such matters, taking account of both technical and operational limitations of the weapons systems and the desired humanitarian goals'?[82] If the rates refer to actual wartime usage to respond to past objections about the suitability of practice tests, then how will the acceptability of particular cluster types become established given the past dearth of specific information about the after effects of cluster munitions? Will it be necessary to wait until after a conflict in which a particular type of sub-munition is used to properly assess it? What, if any, exceptions might be made for higher dud rates because of 'non-standard' environmental or conflict conditions? Would these conditional factors themselves be uniform across sub-munitions types or as the French government advocated, must reliability rates 'be defined for standard use conditions [that] are peculiar to each type of submunition, depending on its life profile'.[83] How will post-conflict assessments of reliability during one attack (operation, war, etc.) be balanced against others? If reliability rate were to be improved might this inadvertently make cluster munitions more acceptable and thus more prevalent force options (thereby nullifying humanitarian gains)? In the push for general criteria, as China and Russia objected, might 'technical specifications...in effect limit or deprive most developing countries of their legitimate right for self-defence'[84] given the additional costs and technical requirements. Should exemptions to standards be made for those that cannot afford retrofitting or the acquisition of new weapons? With each attempt to devise 'flexible provisions'[85] questions can be asked whether any reliability rates could serve as relatively straightforward guides for evaluation.

As part of a call for the enforcement of the existing provision of International Humanitarian Law, in 2000 the ICRC made a number of specific recommendations for cluster bombs. Along with the general need for greater responsibility by user countries in clearing ERW, providing technical advice on what munitions were used in conflict, and warning civilian populations about ERW dangers, it proposed that:

- The use of cluster bombs and other types of sub-munitions against military objectives in populated areas should be prohibited, as is currently the case with incendiary weapons (another weapon causing area-wide effects) under Protocol III of the 1980 UN Convention on CCWs.
- In order to reduce the risk to civilians in future conflicts, cluster bomb and other sub-munitions should be fitted with mechanisms which will ensure their self-destruction immediately after the device fails to explode upon impact as designed.
- The use of cluster bombs should be suspended until an international agreement on their use and clearance has been achieved.[86]

So while agreeing with many governments on the need for technical measures to improve reliability in general, the ICRC defined cluster bombs as incendiary device-like in relation to their area-wide effects, a characteristic which made them inappropriate for civilian areas. Moreover until agreement was reached on matters surrounding their use and clearance, these weapons should not be employed. Whereas the US position of retaining the option for ground commanders to use cluster munitions in populated areas where it can prevent or respond to enemy fire as well as in pre-planned air strikes is open to accusations that in practice it allows for a wide range of strikes, the ICRC position of no-use in populated areas is open to the criticism that it relies on unsubstantiated generalizations about effects that pay no heed to the 'unrivalled efficiency'[87] of cluster bombs. For instance, the French government has differentiated the humanitarian impact of sub-munitions on the basis of their purpose, which it defines in terms of whether the munitions are 'precision weapons (aerial cluster bombs having an effective guidance system and intended for the destruction of ground infrastructures such as airport runways) and area weapons'.[88] While that latter have 'saturation' effects that might liken them to 'incendiary weapon-like' in relation to Protocol III of the CCW, for the former this cannot hold.

As governments have taken a range of positions on the necessary steps, so too have human rights and peace organizations. In 2004 at a government expert meeting of the CCW, HRW called for a new binding protocol under the CCW that would regulate, 'but not completely prohibit' cluster munitions by clarifying and extending the provisions of IHL for the 'specific character of this type of munition'.[89] While the harm done to civilians by cluster munitions was identified as unique, the organization acknowledged the need to counterbalance this with their military utility. Citing conflicting interpretations and uncertainty expressed regarding the meaning of the principle of proportionality (e.g. what counts as 'reasonably foreseeable' effects), the processes for weighing civilian harm against military necessity, and what measures are required to prevent munitions from becoming ERW under Protocol V of the CCW, it called for a clarification of the provisions of IHL.[90]

For the group a new CCW protocol could address topics such as the need to prohibit 'strikes with non-precision guided submunitions in populated areas as well as attacks in environments that increase the number of duds. It could set guidelines or standards for accuracy and dud rates. It could also supplement post-conflict remedial measures by refining Protocol V's requirements for cluster munitions in particular.'[91] While HRW's call for elucidation and extending of ongoing disputes contained little in the way of preferred recommended do's and don'ts, in relation to strikes on populated areas it argued 'a cluster munition strike on a populated area should be considered indiscriminate under the law, unless the military, which should bear the burden of proof, could show the military advantage of a particular strike outweighed the civilian harm'.[92]

In contrast to this call to strengthen the provisions for regulating cluster bombs, the Mennonite Central Committee has contended they should be banned outright.[93] Lessons from past experience are said to justify this position: the mine field effects of unexploded sub-munitions, the impossibility of using them safely as far as civilian deaths are concerned and their indiscriminate track record.[94] Where HRW states that is 'unaware of any conflict where cluster munitions have been used uniformly in a manner fully consistent'[95] with IHL so as to substantiate a call to clarify the rules in place, Mennonite Central Committee cite the track record of cluster bombs (such as in Laos) as proof of these weapons have clear indiscriminate effects. No tinkering with the design or the operational deployment will due as 'Whether dropped from the air, blasted from cannons, or "delivered" by cruise missiles, the characteristics of cluster munitions are so abhorrent, so inherently indiscriminate, and so likely to cause unnecessary suffering, that they should be banned.'[96] As a Christian relief and peace agency, this categorical position avoids the call for more accurate or more reliable weapons, both of which might be seen as, in effect, calling for more deadly weapons. Yet, engaging in arguments about the relative appropriateness of cluster bombs is not presented as without its moral difficulties:

> As Mennonites committed to peace and opposed to the execution of war in any form, we have been loathe to walk into these discussions of the law of war, with its gruesome calculus between 'military necessity' and 'collateral

damage'. We enter those discussions not because we have abandoned our commitment to peace, but because we have seen and heard too many stories like the one of the family from Nong Oh.[97] Farmers around the world must every day walk into dangerous fields, risking injury from unexploded cluster bombs to feed their families. We owe it to them to walk into the dangerous fields of international diplomacy and 'war talk' to call on the nations of the world to halt their use of these weapons.[98]

As a further contrasting position, in 2004 MAC argued for a mixed approach of banning certain sub-munitions while calling for restrictions in the way others are used.[99] So, it argued governments should consider banning those sub-munitions with the following characteristics: overly complex fusing and arming system (that might fail to trigger an explosion as designed), excessive age (that might decrease reliability), the lack of a self-destruct mechanism, the presence of ribbon or other external device (that might break the descend of sub-munitions), or that are fired from inaccurate delivery systems such as artillery. In addition, other operational restrictions were asked for including:

No use of cluster munitions in or near populated areas.
Timely information provided to civilian population and/or humanitarian deminers.
Appropriate drop or launch altitude.
Proper analysis of type of weather and terrain in target area.
Destruction, not transfer of obsolete submunitions.[100]

These three NGO campaigns identify different primary sources of concern with and therefore what needs to be done, which themselves are underpinned by alternative assessments of the severity of the problem. With each, tensions exist in the generality of recommendations made. The identification of specific sub-munitions to be banned (as suggested by HRW elsewhere[101]) or characteristics of sub-munitions to be forbidden (as suggested by MAC[102]) on the one hand might be seen as prudent measures that would attempt to remove the 'worst offenders'. By eliminating them from the arsenals of militaries, such campaigns could have definite positive impacts. On the other hand, a practical consequence of eliminating specific types might be bringing greater legitimacy to the rest, an outcome more or less prudent depending on assessments made of the relative acceptability of what remains. Attempts to identify specific sub-munitions or characteristics that might justify a ban are open to question regarding the feasibility of possible modifications to their use or design that might make them relatively acceptable.

The advisability of calling for a blanket ban or a more differentiated approach are likely to turn on assessments of the expected foreseeable consequences of different types of sub-munitions and whether some are disproportionally 'disproportional' in their effects. If certain types inflict the lion's share of civilian damage then removing them would have a substantial benefit. Yet, whether adequate detailed information is available to substantiate such evaluation is open to question, not least because many cluster munitions have not been used in combat. Further questions can be asked about just what factual basis would be adequate for making credible claims about the predictable consequences of certain sub-munitions. Whereas precise information might be needed in calls for a ban on particular types, the relevance of such information for the whole category of cluster bombs would no doubt be queried by user governments. Comparatively general knowledge about the effects of this type of weapon overall might be marshalled as part of a wide ranging call for a ban, though such evidence would likely be criticized as glossing over the potential for specific munitions to be used in a fashion permissible under international law. What relevance data gained about past experience would have for future innovations in a weapon's design or modifications to their use is yet still other matter for thought.

Despite the differences between the recommendations made by HRW, Mennonite Central Committee and MAC, arguably all provide limited elaborations regarding the mechanisms whereby prohibitions would be established and policed. While both HRW and MAC called for a new protocol under the CCW, just how notions about what constitutes an adequate drop altitude, an appropriate reliability rate, a populated area, an excessively old munition or any other provisions should be established remain unspecified. Even for the Mennonite Central Committee which calls for a sweeping ban, the bounds of the category of 'cluster bombs' would not be a minor matter.

Conclusion

The previous sections of this chapter proposed some of the ethical and analytical difficulties associated with specifying the humanitarian consequences of cluster munitions for the purpose of considering the necessity of prohibitions. Translating claims about what is going on into justifications for certain courses of action is a fraught and problematic process, not least because the ever present potential for questioning presumptions about the source of 'the problem' with these weapons. What counts as a relevant consideration, a justifiable comparison, compelling empirical data or a good enough generalization are multiply conceived. Why a focus is given to some things (e.g. ERW, cluster bombs, certain sub-munition types) rather than others or why certain relations of similarly or dissimilarly are drawn turn on pragmatic assessments of what needs doing that are made in conditions of uncertainty. As suggested, just whether and what problems are specific to cluster munitions (as opposed to other weapons) is a long running topic of commentary.

Adopting a discursive orientation to accounts, this book has resisted adjudicating on the empirical accuracy of competing claims in favour of considering what is accomplished through the arguments and counter-arguments made regarding what is appropriate. In doing so though, it has also contended that choices are made about what arguments are presented, what lines of questioning are pursued and where context ends. All accounts of cluster bombs are managed descriptions that suggest explanations for what is wrong with them as well as what does and does not need to be done with them.

If the definition of cluster bombs, their resemblance to other weapons, the source of the any problems with them and the generality of claims made about them are topics of contestation, then consideration is needed regarding how debates proceed. Chapter 4 proposes possible strategies for those seeking to reduce the humanitarian consequences from the use of cluster bombs; more specifically strategies for questioning the practices of user governments. These derive from the analysis given in the next chapter regarding the importance of attending to the movement and disposal of contestation in controversies. A case will be made for shifting focus from attempts to establish definitive lists and do's and don'ts informed by empirical evidence to attending to how uncertainties, ambiguities and binds are distributed.

Chapter 10

Dealing with unfinished business

A treaty is a disagreement reduced to writing.

(British Foreign Office adage[1])

Previous chapters discussed some of the vexed and vital problems of characterizing the world so as to ascribe place and purpose to things and acts. As maintained, attempts to offer persuasive arguments about the relative acceptability of the employment of weaponry face persistent challenges which evade easy resolution. Accounts of what should be done by way of prohibitions must find credible ways of reconciling or at least managing various predicaments associated with issues such as making categorizations of objects and acts; specifying how they should be understood in relation to 'their context', and ensuring statements and rules with general relevance can be responsive to specific instances. Closure on these is a contingent accomplishment.

In considering such issues, previous chapters also argued that in many respects the problems of characterizing the world should be regarded as ineradicable; in potential if not in practice depictions can be challenged. All of the loose ends associated with demarking what is 'acceptable' from 'unacceptable', 'appropriate' from 'inappropriate' and 'permissible' from 'not permissible' cannot be tied up. Competing attempts to establish controls on the basis of a weapon's capabilities, its users or its uses are not exclusive of one another. Because categorizations are bound up with particularizations and what is deemed a general claim can be regarded as specific in relation to a different set of issues, characterizations are readily open to question. In addition, the wider context of relevance and the cases being discussed do not stand apart; rather they are in many respects mutually defined. Much scope exists for a troubled movement between what is general and specific, a categorization and a particularization, and technology and its context.

Moreover, while what counts as 'good enough' contextualizations, generalizations and categorizations are 'good enough' for some practical purpose, often little agreement exists on what that purpose should be. Various examples illustrated how those partaking in discussions about prohibitions are highly adept in assuming lines of argumentation that challenge attempts to resolve questions about what is taking place, what issues are at stake and therefore what needs doing. Rules, standards and agreements can attempt to structure discussions about how lines should be drawn between the permissible and the inexcusable but they themselves are in need of interpretation and negotiation. While it might be assumed that rules would regularly seek to impose clear and viable do's and don'ts in the case of weapon prohibitions, this way of thinking both underestimates the possible import of abstract rules and overestimates the ability of precise rules to specify what counts as appropriate behaviour in specific cases. While a workable unanimity can be reached regarding the meaning prohibitions, this must be worked for.

I do not simply wish to contend that debates are characterized by claims and counter claims that shift around in an uneasy manner. However intractable the problems encountered, individuals and organizations find ways of 'getting along'. A key question therein is how the difficulties of specifying what is and is not acceptable are managed. How then can relatively workable and persuasive prohibitions be established given the scope for questioning at each turn? For despite whatever problems are recognized in cutting up and classifying the world, prohibitions do this all the same. Unless one simply abandons the search for humanitarian limits in the development and use of weaponry, then the matter of how to 'go on' is an important one.

This chapter considers some of the strategies employed as well as what is accomplished through such strategies. As will be argued, when faced with fundamental difficulties associated with providing a definitive resolution to the problems of establishing a sense of order and coordinating behaviour, an important phenomenon for consideration is how commentators engage in various strategies to deny, defer, deter, delay and deflect having to resolve the difficult issues involved. The manner in which tensions are 'moved on' helps to constitute a sense of where responsibility should rest for handling the tension-ridden issues associated with determining what is acceptable. In keeping with previous chapters, this one maintains symmetry in its treatment of 'actors' and 'analysts' accounts by suggesting the argument presented in this book exemplifies the dynamics it attributes elsewhere.

This is done by undertaking an iterative and interpretivist process of 'reading back' on what has been discussed in the chapters so far. This chapter seeks to offer a further understanding of what is taking place and what gets accomplished in debates about the acceptability of weaponry.

Disposal strategies

The manner in which analysis must strike a balance between offering general and specific claims about the world has been a recurring theme. The argument of this book has inevitably engaged in both commenting about the specific topic of weapon prohibitions but also alluded to the general nature of debates about controversial technologies. In keeping with this effort to strike an appropriate level of generality, this chapter proposes the notion of 'disposal strategies' as a useful way to characterize the various ways of managing the difficulties of demarcation and classification.

'Disposal' is an apt guiding concept in a number of ways. First, if there is no final, definitive, in principle resolution to the difficulties outlined, then a key question is how actors 'rid themselves' (or attempt to rid themselves) of the need for resolution. Second, 'disposal' also points to the active ordering, adjustment, bestowing, attributing and regulating that takes place. Each of the partial and provisional 'resolutions' considered later is inextricably bound up with determinations of who or what is the determinant of causality, the bearer of responsibility or the source of blame. But more than that, the strategies are also highly suggestive of what counts as relevant to the discussion. Different elements of socio-technical systems come into view and alternative lines of authority are drawn, notions of agency and expertise shift, and a sense of the scene transforms as certain strategies are engaged in. As such, the strategies are co-constituting of both identity and technology. Third, characterizations of what is going on and why they are meant to persuade (or dispose) others to accept certain ways of seeing what needs to be done. Finally, the strategies are offered as contingent resources, in relation to specific situations, and thus are themselves occasioned and disposable.[2]

Disposing of the problems of ordering

By retracing earlier arguments, this section examines a variety of inter-related disposal strategies. Of central importance is how the uncertainties, difficulties and dilemmas associated with characterizing the world are made manageable. In this, sometimes individuals seek to specify what is really going on despite the contestability of any determinations while elsewhere the issues involved might be left unspecified or unelaborated despite the importance of doing so. Making problems 'manageable' is the operative description because the strategies do not provide a definitive resolution the problems faced.

Problem, what problem?

So how do commentators attempt to manage the problems of ordering and what is accomplished in such practices? One of the bluntest ways for 'coping' with the inter-relatedness of technology-context, general-specific and categories-particulars is to *deny* the pertinence of such this. Calls for outright bans on or unquestioning acceptance of certain weapons are often based on general claims and wide-ranging categorizations that give no heed to context, that make no allowance for weapons in specific situations and that give little indication of any possible contingencies. In short, denial is about asserting that there are no substantial difficulties with devising classifications and evaluations. Amnesty International's (AI) position that it 'opposes the use, possession, production and transfer of nuclear weapons, given their indiscriminate nature' is an example of such a strategy. With such a comprehensive condemnation, complicated security assessments need not be undertaken to determine the way forward; nuclear weapons are simply deplorable, full stop.

As argued earlier, such sweeping claims are open to challenge in theory and often challenged in practice. Prohibitions establishing outright bans are rarely agreed upon, and the actual import of such prohibitions is generally negotiated. Justifying such an outright ban requires being able to convincingly argue that irrespective of the how, by who or when a weapon is used that the outcome will be unacceptable.[3] Such a position follows on logically from a pacifist stance on force,[4] but not so easily from other positions. As suggested in the International Court of Justice (ICJ) ruling in Chapter 7, categorical condemnations are often found wanting. In this case, questions were asked about counts as an instance of nuclear weapon (e.g. are tactical nuclear weapons really 'nuclear weapons'), the effects of such weapons in certain 'ideal' situations (e.g. in the high seas or against WMD underground bunkers) and the necessity of using them in certain situation (i.e. as a means of self-defence where the very existence of a state is at stake) to question the advisability of unqualified statements. Whereas calls for outright bans suggest no need to go beyond the weapon in question, counters to that position search out for the varied technical and use-related issues that might be deemed pertinent.

Consider another area. Despite the widespread condemnation of chemical and biological weapons in many policy circles today, the analysis of biodefence and non-lethal weapons in the previous chapters have indicated the way in which sweeping condemnations have been challenged. In a similar manner, Zanders argued that historically the constraints against chemical warfare (CW) and biological warfare (BW) have never been absolute.[5] International law consists of many competing doctrines (e.g. the right to self defence and the need to limit the methods of war), laws have been written or applied in such a way as to exclude some countries from their scope and technological innovations have constantly challenged the classification of weapons. The history of efforts to secure a norm against chemical and biological weapons has not been one of reference to objective and persevering criteria about what counts as inherently unacceptable. Rather such an evaluation has had to be repeatedly secured in response to changing situations.

In many cases the problems of offering broad, all encompassing characterizations are recognized as part of prohibitions even as they specify wide ranging do's and don'ts. As mentioned in Chapter 1, the UN Standard Minimum Rules for the Treatment of Prisoners states that 'irons' should not be used as restraints. This unconditional standard like all the others UN Minimum Rules makes exceptions for 'experiment and practices' that might depart from individual rules so long as they are consistent with the overall spirit of the Rules (whatever that is). Such qualifications are rife. In response the horrors of the use of incendiary devices in the Second World War against Tokyo and other cities, the UN Convention on Certain Conventional Weapons (CCW) prohibited the use of weapons *'primarily* designed to set fire to objects or to cause burn injury' (emphasis added) against *certain* targets in *particular* situations. The US Department of Defense has held out against signing even this limited prohibition unless it can ensure it has the ability to employ incendiary weapons in instances where it determines these options might be preferable from a humanitarian perspective.

This last point about incendiary weapons raises the issue of exactly who determines the acceptability of weaponry and the need for prohibitions. Attempts to establish sweeping condemnations or endorsements, as well as the counters to such appraisals, often take their legitimacy from mobilizing a certain kind of expertise that is supposed to outrank others. For instance, in Chapter 5 contrasting categorical and contingent appraisals of napalm were justified through marshalling alternative claims as to what counted as the relevant expertise for making appraisals. The success of attempts to suppress questions about context or boundaries in no small part depends on the status accorded to particular forms of expertise.

Chapter 7 examined the International Committee of the Red Cross's (ICRC) attempts to promote definitions of which conventional weapons cause unnecessary suffering and superfluous injury. The criteria sought to offer objective generalized, use-independent guidelines specifying what was relevant for making evaluations. Potential contingencies associated with weapons were suppressed in favour of universal guidelines that spoke to all conflict scenarios. The possibility of formulating a universal scheme despite the complexities associated with diverse employments of force was said to rest with medical professionals' ability to make objective determinations about what counts as superfluous injury or unnecessary suffering. In this sense, the criteria denied certain contingencies through a proposed *deference* to medical expertise derived from the practices of collecting casualty figures, measuring wounds and treating patients. With the standards of acceptability clear and defined, fault for causing unnecessary suffering in the future would rest with designers, procurers and others who turn a blind eye to the foreseeable design dependent consequences of weaponry. While the status of medical experts might provide some general cache of credibility, in this case it proved insufficient to fend off criticism. Critics countered by suggesting that the criteria relied on various assumptions that could not be justified. US representatives marshalled field surgeons and others of their own with knowledge of the medical consequences of war to suggest the casualties rates set out were not applicable to modern conflict and to highlight various contingencies.

Deference though need not even be limited to an identified community or individual. For instance, in Chapter 9, a legal adviser to the UK government counselled against 'concentrating on the problem of ERW to the exclusion of other effects of particular weapons [because] it may be that the protection of the civilian population is diminished rather than enhanced'.[6] What would be needed in the case of evaluating cluster munitions versus other force options that might result in explosive remnants of war (ERW) following this logic would be for some unidentified decision maker to consider 'the whole picture' of the relative advantages and harms from certain options. Even ignoring the scope for questioning about what constitutes 'the whole picture', it is not at all clear from the discussion in Chapter 9 that anyone could or would even claim to be in a position to make such an assessment.

In the main this subsection has considered denial in terms of forwarding sweeping and universal claims about the status of weaponry. Denial as a strategy is much more prevalent though. There is always something left unsaid in accounts. Because at some stage the questioning of the relevant context, the meaning of terms and applicability of claims must end, the denial of contingencies and questions is widespread. As argued previously, language itself entails a process of typification and approximation. The practice of offering accounts of the world inevitably entails leaving elaborations unfinished and leaving certain issues aside. How this is done and by who are key. In certain situations the term 'weapons of mass destruction' might be taken as relatively unambiguous in meaning, whereas in others it is actively unpacked. While questioning how categories such as leg-iron, landmine and biological weapons are established, this analysis has unavoid-ably employed these and other such terms at times in an unproblematic fashion as standing for definite things. Just when and how the inter-relatedness of technology-context, general-specific and categories-particulars can reasonably be suppressed to offer certain statements about the world are matters of much possible dispute.

Saving agreement for another time and place

This book has argued that the problems of specifying the acceptability of weaponry and the need for prohibitions – what have been treated as problems of imposing order – are not easily resolved. Often, though, policies do not set out to definitively resolve what should be done. Nor, on some occasions, do they even attempt to specify what might be relevant to making decisions. Rather, the strategies adopted are those of *temporal delay* and *organizational deferral*.[7]

In many respects, the UK government policy covering applications for incorpo-ration component parts examined in Chapter 5 postpones the task of specifying just what is and is not relevant to making decisions about the appropriateness of export controls. At issue in this case was how to reconcile the stated desire for clear national export controls reflecting concerns about the end use of exports with attention to the impact of such controls on British defence production rela-tions; and, in turn, what these concerns meant for the categorization of technol-ogy. While the Consolidated EU and National Arms Export Licensing Criteria and the 'incorporation component' policy articulated by Jack Straw ostensibly set out clear criteria to guide export decisions, the meaning of the criteria was said to be in need of determination on case-by-case basis depending on the understand-ing of the situation and the export. Any attempt to treat the criteria as 'hewn in tablets of stone'[8] was steadfastly rejected as have been efforts to specify their meaning in advance of any export decision. No lasting interpretation was offered for the meaning of the end-use considerations, though they were said to be of central importance to adequacy of the export policy.

In short, rather than ministers trying to lay down decrees, under the incorporation part policy officials privately consulting with one another decide which applications fall under the heading of 'incorporation component', what constitutes an extenuating circumstance and how general rules should be applied in specific situations. How this is done is bound up with the how the equipment under question is understood. Components might be alternatively (or even simultaneously) treated as isolated pieces of hardware that on their own are fairly insignificant financially and militarily, or they might be deemed an essential part of a global production process. According to the policy elaborations given by members of the government, just how the export technology ought to be conceived is not something that should be fixed in advance and neither should the range of possible considerations be delimited. In this respect, the 'materiality and significance' of the UK-origin components has no necessary bearing on how it will be regarded for the purposes of making decisions. The import of an export is something that needs to be re-worked for each occasion. So when asked by the Parliamentary Committees on Strategic Export Controls to describe in detail how future decisions would be taken for various types of spare parts, government ministers responded that:

> Licenses to export spare parts for existing UK-supplied main equipment are considered on a case-by-case basis against the Consolidated EU and National Arms Export Licensing Criteria and the guidelines published by the Government in July 2000, whether the export is direct but indirect but unincorporated. We cannot comment on a theoretical case, and in deciding whether to issue an export licence we would, as ever, take account of all relevant circumstances against the announced policies.[9]

The *general* policy then is that officials will decide upon and justify the appropriateness of future exports for each specific case.[10]

Assessments of the appropriateness of the HUDs transfer took either a major or a minor shift (depending on one's categorizations of past practices) in July 2002, when an F-16 jet dropped a guided bomb on an apartment complex where Sheikh Salah Shahada was located and in doing so killed fifteen civilians. The widespread international condemnation of the bombing reportedly gave the Foreign Office pause to reconsider the transfer of F-16 components. Government officials assured apprehensive parties that the existing rules would be more strictly implemented in the future.[11] Here as elsewhere though, just what counts as a strict interpretation of the rules remains to be established through future decisions. The balance being sought by officials in the policies examined is how both to devise rules that facilitate discretion (so as to maintain much lauded flexibility) and to impose definite limitations (so as to convince sceptics that strict controls are indeed in place).

With regard to cluster sub-munitions, Chapter 10 argued the meaning of key notions such as 'military advantage' and 'excessive' civilian loss of life in the calculation of proportionality are matters-yet-to-be-decided. Variable time frames have been proposed, each of which has implications for who is likely to be in a position to make determinations about whether an attack is proportional. Moreover, calls to factor in possible ERW-related casualties from other munitions used in lieu of cluster munitions counter suggestions to make definitive, pre-conflict statements about the appropriateness of cluster bombs, by advocating instead each deployment be considered on its individual merits. This in turn means that only those privy to the detailed, case-specific deliberations about force options are in a position to judge the merits of using cluster munitions.

The resort to strategies of delay and deferral could be characterized in a number of ways, as: sensible responses to future contingencies, pragmatic political positions, pervasive aspects of establishing rules or some combination of these. With regard to the first, British officials have stressed the contingencies associated with making determinations of the acceptability of future exports. Echoing the themes discussed in Chapter 4, defenders of deferral might well ask how one can know in advance whether a transfer might escalate conflict or act as a prudent means for self-defence. Should not each transfer be treated on its own merits rather than by fiat in advance? If criteria for exports offer conflicting advice, then should not they be weighed against each other in terms of the case in question?

Alternatively, a strategy of deferral might be characterized as a convenient and pragmatic political response to competing demands. As elsewhere, in relation to prohibitions 'vague language may be adopted as a deliberate strategy to facilitate compromise, allowing all sides of the dispute to retain hope that their interpretations will be embraced'[12] at a later date. Instead of seeking clarity and agreement, the approach is what the former US State Department Spokesperson James Rubin called 'kicking the can down the road'.[13] Argument about the meaning of potential contentious terms and provisions is left to another day in the hope that this situation might prove more conducive. Harper makes this argument in suggesting the terms 'riot control agent' and 'method of warfare' were deliberately left ambiguous and ill-defined in the negotiation of the Chemical Weapons Convention (CWC) so as to reach a compromise.[14] Many of the agreements discussed in this book likewise have relied on seemingly straightforward terms whose exact meaning is far from clear.

While strategy of deferral might be evaluated as a prudent orientation to contingent circumstances or a pragmatic ploy, previous chapters have argued that deferral is a pervasive feature of the application of rules. The content of rules or even their past interpretation does not dictate how they will be applied in the future. What counts as 'in the spirit' of a prohibition is something that must be worked out anew for each case. Even when the meaning of a rule is deemed clear, whether it applies is another matter. New contexts (the post-9–11 security environment) or a new understanding of a long-existing context (the globalization of the production of defence equipment) have been cited as reasons for forgoing past practices or set new precedents. In practice, determinations of what prohibitions mean, whether they have been violated, or whether they are relevant depends on situated judgements regarding how an understanding of the issue in question is formulated.

Although the act of deferring entails postponing any final resolution of uncertainties, difficulties and dilemmas, how it is done can be part of the transforming of subsequent decision making. Consider again the ICJ decision regarding the legality of the use or threat of use of nuclear weapons. The judges ruled that:

> the threat or use of nuclear weapons would generally be contrary to the rules of international law applicable in armed conflict, and in particular the principles and rules of humanitarian law;
> However, in view of the current state of international law, and of the elements of fact at its disposal, the Court cannot conclude definitively whether the threat or use of nuclear weapons would be lawful or unlawful in an extreme circumstance of self-defence, in which the very survival of a State would be at stake.

Just what should count as 'the very survival of a State' was not defined in the ICJ opinion. Overall, while the threat or use of nuclear weapons was regarded as *generally* against international law, the decision did not rule that it *always* would be. As such, the judges deferred making any final determination of the legitimacy or illegality of nuclear weapons. As Falk argues, though, the decision need not be interpreted as a neutral one.[15] In the first instance, the decision can be read as making the use of such weapons illegal except in extreme case of self-defence; and even here the ICJ posed the possibility that their use or threat of use might still be illegal. To the matter of deferral, the ICJ advised that even in extreme self-defence cases nuclear states would be compelled under Article 51 of the UN Charter eventually to seek an international mandate for any such actions. While whether any such state would in retrospect seek such a mandate is a moot point, the ICJ did state a certain process that should be undertaken.[16]

Whose problem?

This last point about the UN Charter raises the matter of whose problem it is to justify claims about the acceptability of weaponry. If there are persistent difficulties in making any final, definitive, in principle resolutions about what counts as 'good enough' contextualizations, generalizations and categorizations, then *deflecting* away responsibility for making resolutions is an important 'disposal' strategy.

In relation to the acceptability of landmines (Chapter 7), for instance, past debates about the merits of alternative prohibition regimes can be viewed as attempts to deflect responsibility for justifying whether general principles are being followed. In relation to this weapon, in the 1980s and 1990s various amendments had been proposed to the UN Certain Conventional Weapons Convention to reduce the threats to civilians from mines. However, policing enforcement to these measures would have required justifying claims about the 'primary' purpose and self-destruction rates of landmines. Any claims forwarded about such matters would have been open to unpacking regarding the ways in which they generalized, categorized and contextualized. Those governments and NGOs who suggested that the provisions of the CCW were unenforceable sought to deflect from themselves the task of trying to make authoritative attributions regarding the real purposes of specific anti-personnel mines (APMs). They did so by agreeing to the APM Convention that banned the category of APMs outright. In the APM Convention, matters of intent, purpose or competence have no place.

Yet even for those that have ratified the APM Convention, this has not settled all disputes about the acceptability of mines. Instead, efforts to treat a particular type of weapon as categorically unacceptable have led to disputes about the nature of that category; such as the boundary between 'anti-vehicle' and 'anti-personnel' mines.[17] While NGOs and others concerned about the humanitarian consequences of mines and the possibility of holding would-be users and developers to account have deflected from themselves the need to authoritatively determine the tactical purpose of specific mines (e.g. whether they were meant to inflict casualties or restrict military movements), they now have to examine the boundary between APMs or anti-vehicle mines[18] as well as contend with the relevance of the prohibition for other weapons such as unexploded cluster munitions. The efforts by some states not party to the APM Convention to develop anti-vehicle mines with self-destruct mechanisms or sensors for discriminating between the types of target raises the further questions of who should have the burden of demonstrating the reliability of such measures (e.g. producers, governments, NGOs), how this should be done (e.g. in terms of transparency) and what institutions should be involved in making determinations (e.g. the UN or each state on their own).

As stated earlier, in seeking to provide a credible and persuasive reading of the contentious issues at stake in making appraisals of weaponry, this book has employed the argumentative strategies used elsewhere. To refer to decision making regarding export controls (Chapter 5) or the nature of biodefence R&D (Chapter 6) as non-transparent, *deflects* responsibility away from me as author to further elaborate how general principles are applied in particular situations. Analysis need not continue because it cannot.

To elaborate, in relation to both of these cases, the governing organizations in question have suggested that consistent rationales have been employed to decide upon the appropriateness of exports and projects. In relation to various controversies discussed in this book, policy makers have contended that if only those commenting on cases could see the 'big picture' (one, regrettably, often limited to a few), then they would understand that criteria are being consistently followed, that core principles are in place, etc. By citing various considerations, this analysis has questioned the likelihood of such rationales for some cases. Yet, as also argued in this book, when viewed in relation to an alternative understanding of the relevant context, events and decisions once seen as distinct can be viewed as similar. No matter what the detail presented, this analysis could have provided even yet further analysis meant to situate these cases. Instead, the 'fog of uncertainty' attributed to many decisions was said to function to *deter* challenges to the legitimacy of how general rules are applied to specific situations, how categorizations are made of 'component parts', and how the context of the new 'modern reality' is drawn upon for making decisions about weapons applications.

As criteria and rules don't apply themselves, it has been maintained that in conditions of secrecy, knowing what it means to say that decisions are taken in some spirit is quite difficult. Examples in previous chapters, such as the controls on leg-irons or the frequency of casualties from cluster sub-munitions, suggested that the limits on the availability of knowledge have severely curtailed attempts to challenge policy decisions. In the former, only sustained investigative efforts have enabled awkward questions to be posed. While conditions of secrecy might limit the amount of contention by making it difficult for would-be critics to substantiate arguments that a government went against its stated principles when making particular export decisions, it also leads questions whether any ethical grounding exists. Despite the focus mentioned, the secrecy entailed with the justifications for some decisions should not simply be characterized in a negative fashion as limiting information. The 'concealment' of some information is also highly productive in manner identities and characterizations are formed.[19] After having examined the publicly accessible information about the US biodefence programme, Piller and Yamamoto concluded it was not possible to conclusively determine its offensive qualities, though the confrontational political posturing of US administrations was enough for them to deem the biodefence programme 'provocative and strongly suggestive of offensive goals'.

In relation to the last two paragraphs and the strategy of deflection, a key question for any analysis is 'When is enough enough?'. While the process of contextualizing might not have an in principle end and alternative categorizations might always be offered of actions and objects, in my account the said limitations on evidence provides a convenient stopping point for questioning the appropriateness of characterizations. To maintain decisions about the export of weapon components and biodefence R&D activities are at some level non-transparent, and therefore practically unknowable, deflects the task from analysts the task of having to give further substantiations of their claims. Instead the failure of officials to provide adequate specification or explanation of their decisions indicates where the responsibility lies: with the very officials themselves who are able, but unwilling, to act in a fashion required.

Shifting around the problems of ordering

Building on from previous chapters, this one has sought to ask how individuals try to secure agreement about the wisdom and meaning of prohibitions and what is accomplished in such efforts. The notion of 'disposal strategies' was offered as a characterization of the techniques for managing the persistent, and perhaps irresolvable, difficulties associated with determining the acceptability of weaponry. The focus was on the directed movement or displacement of contested problems. Key concerns in this process of shifting around problems are question of *who* is responsible for and able to determine what counts as acceptable by way of the use of weaponry and *when* such decisions must be made. The management and distribution of difficulties is central to shoring up perceptions of the legitimacy of rules restricting technology, what counts as relevant to a debate, as well as constituting an understanding of what technology is, what it is for and what it does.

Part IV

Future agendas

Chapter 11

Troubles with humanitarian prohibitions

> War experience is nothing if not a transgression of categories. In providing bridges across the boundaries between the visible and the invisible, the known and the unknown, the human and the inhuman, war offered numerous occasions for the shattering of distinctions that were central to orderly thought, communicable experience, and normal human relations. Much of the bewilderment, stupefaction, or sense of growing strangeness to which combatants testified can be attributed to those realities of war that broke down what Mary Douglas calls 'our cherished classifications'.
>
> (Eric Leed *No Man's Land*[1])

The transgression of the distinctions and classifications of everyday life has been a recurring theme in the study of war. Instead of examining this, following the wording of the 1868 Declaration of St. Petersburg, this book has considered the creation of classifications and the interpretation and application of rules so as to set 'limits at which the necessities of war ought to yield to the requirements of humanity'.[2] It has sought to develop a greater appreciation of the intellectual and ethical issues, discomforts and unease in attempts to establish formal limits on weaponry; to find a ground between 'anything goes' and 'nothing goes' when it comes to inflicting violence. Such efforts entail their own sense of strangeness and are bedevilled by problems of specifying just what is taking place, why, and how it should be evaluated. In the 'calculus between "military necessity" and "collateral damage"'[3] much is bewildering.

The problems of setting limits have been conceived of as problems of ordering. Forwarding particular prohibitions requires cutting through heterogeneous relations so as to capture a persuasive characterization of just what is taking place and why. The world becomes divided along certain lines where some things are deemed permissible while others are ruled out. How definitions of the effects of technologies, the identity of users or the circumstances of use are interpreted and sustained through this cutting up process are key concerns. While any situation involving force might be acknowledged as complex, abstract prohibitions almost always depend on simplified accounts of what is happening. Enforcing prohibitions or 'merely' describing the state of the world are acts that inevitably involve suspending questions about what might well be questioned so as to say what is going on, to whom and why. Designating certain weapons or employments of them as 'indiscriminate', 'concentrated' or 'repugnant' entails equating actions or objects in a manner that is inevitably contingent and thereby contestable. Why, how and who makes certain comparisons, cites certain contexts or offers up particular issues for consideration in defining whether and what problem exists can be queried.

If an orderly situation is one where agreement exists about how to go on, then in relation to disputes about the prohibition of weaponry examined in this book, what is happening is not so much the imposition of order as ongoing conflicting attempts at ordering. Working consensus about the rights of wrongs of force – what counts as the problem, the facts, an agreement, the aims of prohibitions, an adequate justification as well as who can and should make up the relevant community to make such judgments – is ongoing achievement. In relation to just who or what is the principal source of the problem, numerous agents might be identified: the direct users of weapons, the organizations that deploy them, the manufacturers, etc. Pointing responsibility in one direction typically entails moving it from elsewhere.

To develop an appreciation of what is at stake in the ordering of world, this analysis has not taken as its main preoccupation what limits should be drawn or why certain limits have been agreed, but instead attended to what takes place in the setting of formal limits. In doing so, description rather than explanation has been the initial aim and remaining in rather than transcending the difficulties faced the persisting agenda. Its utility derives not from its purported ability to authoritatively resolve or even characterize disputes, but in fostering certain ways of thinking about the prohibition of weaponry. As contended, attempts to offer prohibitions involve managing pervasive predicaments with making general claims responsive to specific situations, defining what counts as relevant versus peripheral, situating events in context and offering convincing categorizations. As a result, arms control agreements setting out ethical standards for force are potentially contestable. While they may not always be challenged in practice, specifications of just what is at stake and why are characterized by a persistent fragility. Ready-made classifications rarely prove of lasting adequacy, not least because counter-actions are taken in response to the imposing of particular classifications.

In Part I argued that analyses of controversies could be usefully structured by attending to three questions: 'What is like what?', 'What and where is the problem?' and 'So what?'. Responses to these are bound up in the practices of categorization, contextualization and generalization and they are consequential for how agency and expertise are defined. The disputes examined entailed competing arguments regarding what counted as good-enough-for-the-practical-purposes-sought characterizations of technologies and events. In the questioning of arguments made about the appropriateness of weaponry in the use of force, characterizations of what is taking place and why can usefully be thought of as attempts to secure 'temporary resting places constructed for specific utilitarian ends... [Offered] because some particular social practice needs to block the road of inquiry, halt the regress of interpretations, in order to get something done'.[4] But as analytical notions, the relevancy of categorizations, contextualizations and generalizations are contestable by those that do not seek to get something done or seek to get something else done. Further, determinations about what constitutes a good enough understanding are made in conditions of graded authority.

The characterizations of what is going on and why have been orientated to as situated accounts. In the mix of claim and counter-claim, it is not simply the case that those holding certain beliefs about the ethics of conflict will advance widely applicable categories that cover a range of contexts whereas those opposed will offer highly particularized and specific claims. Rather whether some statement is regarded as general or specific, entails a categorization or a particularization or puts the discussion 'in context' are often the very topics on which the debate turns. Although in some particular argument certain individuals might assert that decisions should be made on a case-by-case basis while others will suggest the need for steadfast principles, these logics are not an inevitable reflection of maintaining certain partisan beliefs.

As argued, while isolating elements of the complex socio-technical systems associated with modern warfare might widely be recognized as a limited way of addressing humanitarian concerns, attempts to establish prohibitions often aim to do just that. In making this argument, the focus has not been to show that characterizations of world are 'emergent and constructed (rather than fixed and natural), contested and polymorphic (rather than unitary and singular), and interactive and process-like (rather than static and essence-like)'.[5] Instead it has asked how accounts move back and forth or simultaneously treat the world as emergent and fixed, contested and unitary, and interactive and static, etc. as some elements are questioned while others are not. Moreover, I have made the case for a symmetrical orientation to analysts' and actors' accounts. While attention has been drawn to the performative aspects of language-as-action in contemporary debates, so too has this analysis made use of language as a form of representation. As an analysis it has moved between the knower and the known, the unpacking of categories and the use of them and the reliance on facts as well as their querying.

Through exploring these matters, this book has sought to develop an appreciation for the contingencies and contradictions associated with formalizing standards regarding the acceptability of force. The argument has aimed for exemplification rather than just description. As maintained, a greater appreciation of the issues at hand and the commitments of commentary can derive from lingering in difficulties instead of seeking authoritative escapes. This way of thinking impinges on the status of the claims offered. Rather than reaching for authoritative understanding of why certain prohibitions are agreed or why they mean what they mean in practice, this book has concerned itself with what is done in attempts to grasp the world. In this, while generalizations have been forwarded, they have been treated as 'contingent generalizations',[6] where what even counts as a generalization was open to questioning. While the notion of disposal strategy was proposed in

Chapter 9 as a way of making sense of how uncertainties and indeterminacies are managed in disputes, those strategies themselves were regarded as contingent and disposable ways of ordering in and the ordering of the world.

What is to be done?

While this book has sought to develop an understanding of what is entailed in establishing and enforcing weapons prohibitions, the question can be asked of just what it suggests for the future crafting of prohibitions as well as for further analysis. If the search for definitive demarcations is as problematic as it is vital, the matter of how best to go on is not an easy one. This section revisits the types of responsive strategies mentioned in Chapter 8 – seeking to impose ever tighter rules, attempting to explain why certain limitations are or are not adhered to and asking what is accomplished in accounts of weapons. Following previous chapters, the emphasis will be with the last option wherein, paraphrasing the philosopher John Dewey, the proposal is made to shift from the search for certitude in classifications to greater imagination in the way they are handled.

Clearer lines, tighter rules and better enforcement

One widespread response to the lack of finality and definitiveness afforded by prohibitions is to seek ever more precise rules regarding what is and is not permissible by way of technologies, their uses or the intent of users. Ambiguous terms, vague definitions or poorly elaborated criteria can be changed to more clearly demark what is and is not allowed. Much of the campaigning efforts of the NGOs mentioned in this book have been dedicated to documenting and decrying the political failure of governments to agree more precise controls than those currently established.

Where limitations are deemed necessary, much can be said overall for such a strategy of 'tightening down'. At the time of writing in 2004, for instance, the European Commission is considering adopting restrictions 'concerning trade in certain equipment and products which could be used for capital punishment, torture or other cruel, inhuman or degrading treatment or punishment'.[7] Among those technologies considered for cruel, inhuman or degrading treatment or punishment include leg-irons. Instead of adopting any of the previous vague classifications for leg-irons and ordinary handcuffs employed in the UK that provided the basis for so much of the past controversy (see Chapter 1), the Commission's list of equipment requiring detailed pre-export approval scrutiny and possible licence refusal define ordinary handcuffs as

> handcuffs which have an overall dimension including chain, measured from the outer edge of one cuff to the outer edge of the other cuff, between 150 mm and 280 mm when locked and have not been modified to cause physical pain or suffering.[8]

Also included on the list are individual cuffs and shackle bracelets. This remit should reduce (though certainly not eliminate) the feasibility of exporting leg-irons from the EU through labelling them as 'handcuffs'. Likewise, one could imagine certain practical benefits deriving from definitively stating what counts as 'superfluous injury', how to calculate 'proportionality' or establishing what is significant about an 'incorporation part'.

As suggested in the previous chapters though, the pursuit of precision faces numerous limitations. One practical barrier is that little exists in the way of international institutions authorized with creating, interpreting and enforcing prohibitions.[9] International law, and international humanitarian law in particular, is largely the result of agreements between sovereign states that can be withdrawn from or selectively adhere to if states so choose to do so (though – for some – penalties might follow). Even in relation to domestic rules and regulations, as in the case of export controls, the criteria and codes in place are rarely legally binding outside of official embargoes. In addition, as suggested in controversies about 'napalm bombs', tactical nuclear weapons or 'non-lethal' chemical–biological weapons, technical innovations can be offered to challenge or circumvent one time settlements about the meaning of prohibitions. For those overall supportive of agreements such as the Chemical Weapons Convention (CWC) or the Treaty on the Non-proliferation of Nuclear Weapons (NPT), constantly subjecting them to major redrafting in order to keep them up to date with technical and security developments would not be entered into lightly for fear that such undertakings would jeopardize what fragile agreement does exist regarding the status of the treaties. The search for further precision in relation to these agreements might be regarded as undermining what agreement does exist.

Discretion as well, is widely sought in how rules are to be interpreted. At least when the rules apply to their own actions, governments regularly and explicitly seek to devise 'flexible' and 'responsive' controls in which in some unspecified manner attempt to bring all-things-under-consideration in the 'modern reality'[10] that is continuingly unfolding. The British Consolidated EU and National Arms Export Licensing Criteria was offered as a case in point in Chapter 5. Consider another. As previously mentioned, at the time of writing the European Commission is in the process of adopting restrictions on the trade of equipment which could be used for capital punishment, torture or other cruel, inhuman or degrading treatment. While a relatively sophisticated definition of leg-irons has been adopted in the criteria for this category of products, the UK government has opposed efforts to make the criteria legally binding because 'it is more appropriate that the exercise of discretion is carried out by the licensing authority, taking into account all the circumstances that might be apparent to it'[11] – whatever, it might be commented, would count as 'all the circumstances'. It is not only governments that can resist moves towards precision though. Human rights or peace groups can favour ambiguity and imprecision in key words so as to help co-ordinate efforts and to provide future flexibility. Since those devising rules cannot foresee all possible future challenges to them, ensuring some discretion in their future application is important in preventing the formation of loopholes.

This analysis though has forwarded a more underlining difficultly with establishing clear definitions, categories and classifications than those mentioned earlier: the accomplished status of rule following. In the cases examined, multiple and competing versions were offered of what following a rule should entail. Just what background information is required to know what a rule means, what to do in the case of conflicting rules, what other rules are relevant to the application of a given rule are all topics for contention. Seeking to define the central concepts of prohibitions (e.g. terms such as 'concentration of civilians', 'military objective', 'feasible precautions') to facilitate their application and conformity often shifts dispute to the definitions of the terms in the definition. To argue that rules will or should be applied in a similar way for similar cases is no guarantor of what action follows. The provisions set out in prohibitions have been approached as resources for channelling arguments rather than specifying what counts as appropriate action.

While in many areas of life the indeterminacy underlying just what it means to follow a rule might not be subject to relentless questioning, the same cannot often be said when it comes to adhering to rules about the appropriateness of the use of force. Rather than the 'quiet agreement'[12] that make rules intelligible and their meaning recognizable, 'noisy disagreement' and 'quiet discord' are more typical. While a small group of government officials working together might reach unanimity regarding what counts as napalm or the spirit of some text, when the practical judgements for certain decisions are aired more widely disagreement often ensues. Opposing characterizations are routinely offered regarding what is taking place with the threat or use of violence. The 'plain case' or the 'just-so' description of acts and contexts that could provide the foundation for the unproblematic and durable application of rules is arguably rare in relation to the use force and certainly has been so for the controversies considered in this book. The formality of agreements is no indicator of interactional closure.[13]

An additional complication associated with the application of normative prohibitions is that often the question at hand is not how to apply a rule in an agreed domain, but whether the standards for appropriate conduct set out in one area should apply elsewhere. Debate can centre on whether one weapon system regarded as inhumane or permissible is sufficiently similar to another. So in the case of cluster munitions considered in Chapter 9, the extent of and basis for their resemblance to banned anti-personnel landmines is central to alternative evaluations of the former's permissibility under international humanitarian law. Here as elsewhere, there is not consensus on how conventions about what is acceptable by the way of weaponry should be extended.

Of course, none of these problems are absolute barriers to devising clearer lines for demarking what is or is not permissible. It might well be maintained that exactly what is needed is to build international institutions or generate the required political will to lay down such lines. For those nations bound by it, and where it is deemed relevant, the newly formed International Criminal Court will act to shore up the meaning of the laws of war and the boundaries of customary international humanitarian law. Just whether the Court will comment on the legality of whole classes of weapons rather than just the legality of certain acts of force remains much less clear. Yet, as with International Court of Justice (ICJ) ruling considered in Chapter 7, despite the scope for greater legal review in some areas, in practice the import of many national and international prohibitions will be readily disputed and considerable scope will exist for once agreed interpretations to be overturned. Attempts to tie down meaning are never complete. A key question therefore, and one taken up below, is how to address the scope for contestation about formal rules.

Promulgating norms

Rather than seeking ever more precise formal standards so as to co-ordinate behaviour, as noted in previous chapters, in recent years much attention has been given to the role of social norms in fostering shared expectations for what is right and wrong in international conduct. While norms might be codified in formal text, this need not be the case and written rules rarely capture the breadth of issues that norms might. Tannenwald[14] and Price[15], for instance, argue that the use of nuclear weapons and the development of chemical weapons have become stigmatized in such a matter that very few governments today that could undertake such actions would consider doing so. The logic at work in such decisions need not simply derive from a cost-benefit analysis of breaking with relevant prohibitions or an assessment that the combat effects of certain weapons would be somehow qualitatively more severe than other forms of force. Rather it can be the belief that some acts simply are not appropriate for modern, 'civilized' nations.[16] As such, norms can help constitute a sense of identity as well as provide prescriptions or proscriptions for behaviour.

In this line of thinking, norms can underpin wide-ranging condemnations that certain weapons or acts are unacceptable, whatever the particular circumstances. Even in many cases where norms are not fully 'internalized', social actors often comply with them nonetheless.[17] As may well be argued, while the US has not signed up to the anti-personnel mines (APM) Convention, it is highly unlikely it would employ such landmines in active combat because of what might be called the 'collective international consensus' established that these weapons are indiscriminate and unacceptable. While norms about warfare might be based on explicit arms control agreements (such as the APM Convention or the Biological and Toxin Weapons Convention (BTWC)) or become established parts of customary law, this need not be the case and their import is not limited by the terms of formal agreements.

Ascribing an importance to social norms in establishing standards regarding the acceptability of force, many scholars in the field of international relations have turned their attention to explaining how certain normative prescriptions and proscriptions are formed and made to matter. This line of work has challenged highly pessimistic appraisals of prospects for arms control such as Gray's *House of Cards*.[18] Some have further taken up a practical concern with how norms might be spread or challenged. Various schools of thinking have developed for understanding how particular norms become institutionalized and constrain behaviour.[19] For instance, some analysts suggest that while the existence of norms does not determine conduct in any straightforward manner, some norms have characteristics that make them more likely to influence behaviour than others (e.g. their longevity, detail[20]). Essential in securing norms is getting to a stage of 'agreement among a critical mass of actors on some emergent norm [to] create a tipping point after which agreement becomes widespread'.[21] Other scholars have examined the conditions that impinge upon success or failure and concluded that 'an important factor in norm development is how well the norm resonates with already existing norms'.[22] So in the case of anti-personnel landmines, Price argues that concerned governments and NGOs were able to secure widespread international accord on their special status as deplorable weapons by grafting them onto the existing categorization of nuclear, biological chemical weapons as abhorrent and indiscriminate 'weapons of mass destruction'.[23]

If attempts to delineate and define formal rules for force are ultimately limited, then establishing norms might have a significant role to play in reaching workable agreement about what prohibitions mean. The theoretical orientation adopted in this book, however, would be at odds many of the assumptions underlining academic analysis that treat norms as *explanations* for action. Rather than regarding norm adherence as something that does or does not take place, following the particular discursive orientation outlined in previous chapters, this would be better thought of as a situated phenomenon-in-the-making. As with the rules given so much attention in this book, adhering to a norm is a practical and an interactional accomplishment wherein the meaning of norms, actions and contexts are negotiated and mutually defined. So, as in the case of cluster munitions and the relevance of the norm against landmines, just what the latter might means for the former depends on contingent definitions of what actions are about, determinations which would have consequences within situations. Identifying an awareness of norms (e.g. that many say 'biological weapons are abhorrent') is only the initial step in understanding how they are used as resources in accounting for and giving meaning to actions and their settings.

Attending to movements

Whatever the potential for tightening down or fostering norms, it has been argued here that the meaning of rules and norms is something that must be worked out, often in situations of contestation. If the adage 'a treaty is a disagreement reduced to writing' captures a modicum of the dynamics of prohibitions, then how to deal with situations of disagreement, uncertainty and change should be given some attention. So while not dismissing attempts to devise institutional frameworks and norms, this analysis has been preoccupied with other issues. As was contended in previous chapters, the analytical and ethical difficulties associated with specifying the appropriateness of force has not led to practical paralysis. Chapter 10 examined some of the strategies for negotiating various difficulties and dilemmas. By way of offering an analysis of general relevance, it was argued that when faced with difficulties associated with offering determinations of where unacceptability rests, individuals and organizations engage in various strategies to deny, delay, defer, deter and deflect making specifications about the issues at stake. Such disposal strategies seek to make manageable, rather than definitively resolve, problems of ordering.

The remainder of the book takes up the practical import of this analysis. In moving analytical attention away from locking down a sense of order to attending to how ordering is conducted, I likewise want to shift the emphasis in many discussions about prohibitions. In doing so, the hope is to further stimulate thinking and questioning along some lines and to highlight certain orientations to the problems with classification. The goal is not to completely abandon efforts to lock down meaning, but to reconsider how and what is at stake in the movement between agreement and disagreement, certitude and doubt, and determinacy and indeterminacy.

This is done through reconsidering the prohibition of cluster munitions. Chapter 9 took up themes from previous chapters to structure a discussion about the major humanitarian and military issues associated with these weapons. In doing so it suggested how relations of relevancy are made, sources of agency and culpability are identified, boundaries are drawn and specialized expertise is marshalled in contemporary debates about cluster munitions. Following from this, the remainder of the chapter suggests some workable strategies for engaging the problems of ordering, ones not intended to resolve disputes, but rather offering lines of argument to turn them in particular directions.

In moving from questions of interpretation and analysis to practical strategies, some points of caution need to be made. The previous analysis has spoken to the partial and situated status of accounts about the use of force. When considering what counts as a good-enough-for-all-practical-purpose categorization, classification, characterization or contextualization, the questions of just who the 'we' is that something is good enough for and what is being sought must be addressed. It is not the intent in the remainder of this book to consider strategies relating to all possible positions in debates about the merits of cluster munitions. As argued in Chapter 10, because of the practices of what could be termed information enclosure[24] and of sheer resource availability, those in human rights and peace campaigning groups raising humanitarian concerns with these munitions face significant obstacles. In situations such as this, analysts striving to promote a 'competition of ideas', so as to sharpen and further decision making, have good reason to offer analyses responsive to the agendas of such organizations. In any case, my engagement with the aforementioned issues is not simply a distant one. During 2003–04, I represented Amnesty International (AI) (UK) at meetings of the Cluster Munitions Coalition and partook in subsequent discussions about the prohibition of cluster munitions. For these reasons, the analysis given asks what orientations might be useful from those in civil society organizations seeking to promote awareness and action regarding the humanitarian consequences of these weapons.

As another set of qualifications, at the time of writing, international debates about the merits of cluster bombs are rapidly developing. Any analysis that seeks to specify what should be done by way of future efforts risks being deemed outdated or irrelevant before it is printed. Assessments of the appropriateness of strategies are formed in relation to a sense of the relevant issues of the day and efforts by campaigning organizations are made within a history of dialogues, demands, actions and responses. Looming large at the time of writing is the stalled status of negotiations under the Certain Conventional Weapons Convention (CCW). Bearing in mind these points, the following analysis is not offered as a definitive answer to what should be done for all times and situations, but an attempt to evoke a sense of the possibilities and primary questions that might inform action at a certain point in time.

As well, in asking how the overall argument in this book relates to the 'specific' case of cluster munitions, the following commentary is squarely situated within questions about the appropriateness of generalizations. Further, prescriptions for the future, even prescriptions about how to think about problems, necessarily make use of contingent categories and characterizations. Because of such considerations, the following section is not an effort to end questioning but one located squarely in the middle of it.

The disposing of cluster munitions

Chapter 9 characterized international prohibitions discussions regarding clusters munitions as full of disagreement about many of the 'facts' associated with the military advantage and humanitarian costs of certain options,[25] uncertainty about the ultimate consequences of actions or inactions with certain force options and contention about what counts as expert knowledge. As further maintained, those outside of government agencies concerned about the consequences of these weapons face asymmetrical information conditions that deter them from substantiating many claims about the 'costs' and 'advantages' associated with these weapons. While humanitarian groups are not lacking in examples of civilians injured or killed, efforts to offer conclusive demonstrations of the disproportionality of cluster munitions and their categorical illegality have proven difficult as weapon proponents within governments and militaries point to various operational facts and factors to which they alone are privy. Attempting to convincingly demonstrate what has happened and why places substantial demands on those organizations concerned about humanitarian consequences.

The question of what to do given this understanding is a pressing one. As argued previously, alternative characterizations of the issues entail alternative ways of defining and moving where and with whom the burden of proof for substantiating claims rests regarding what is and is not acceptable. As already discussed in Chapter 10, one set of responses would involve NGOs seeking to marshal more evidence about when, where and to what effects specific cluster munitions have been employed so as to provide the basis for differentiating the acceptable from the unacceptable, say in relation to the reliability rates of different sub-munition types, their design or in what conditions they are used. Lists could be derived on such bases. Procedures for weighing military advantage and civilian harm could be formalized.

An approach in line with the thinking in this book would counsel a somewhat different course; one attentive to the problems of ordering and what is done through characterizations. What follows from this is the need to find ways of moving forward that do not take solace in the supposed determinacy of rules and classifications.

Consider one intervention along these lines. For the Group of Governmental Experts CCW talks in November 2004, the author and Richard Moyes produced a paper for State Party representatives and some concerned NGOs (see Box 11.1).[26] The aim was to challenge the framing of discussions at the time. The title 'Stop killing civilians, start taking responsibility' speaks to the basic problems associated with cluster munitions: the continuing deaths to civilians identified by international organizations as well as the continuing failure of user governments to undertake adequate action to alleviate these despite discussing cluster munitions over thirty years in formal international discussions. In terms of defining the more specific problems with cluster munitions though, rather than seeking to forward an authoritative understanding of these, the paper acknowledges the variety of settings of use and technologies over time as well as the multiple and indeterminate sources of any problems. It is because of this diversity and the continuing civilian deaths that undertaking measures to prohibit these weapons is such a necessity.

The long-standing attention and continuing civilian deaths provide an initial sense of how the responses undertaken by user governments with cluster should be approached. While it is possible to ask many questions about the specific reasons for deaths or what cluster munitions resemble, as contended in the document, these should not distract attention from the unacceptability of the humanitarian consequences. Although some evidence regarding civilian deaths can be marshalled, the exact understanding of these consequences in recent wars is acknowledged as limited – this in part because of the choices made by user governments not to undertake basic steps. Such failings make it difficult to assess the possible results of undertaking specific recommendations currently being proposed by states. Approached in this manner, it can be said that the uncertainties and unknowns faced by NGOs and others concerned with humanitarian consequences are in many respects the products of user governments. Initial doubt is cast on the potential of the states' proposed measures given the complex issues involved, past experience with promises regarding the technical modifications of unexploded sub-munitions and the unpredictability of future practices.

The argument presented in the initial pages discussing the repeated problems with cluster munitions and the past failures of governments to take sufficient

The problem

Cluster munitions are still killing and injuring civilians

It is thirty years since humanitarian concern regarding cluster munitions was first sighted in formal international discussions as grounds for these weapons being subject to specific controls or being banned. The 1974 Conference of Government Experts at Lucerne and the 1976 Conference of Government Experts at Lugano both discussed problems associated with these weapons. At the time, opposition to cluster munitions was focused on their 'area-effects', in particular the likelihood that their large 'footprint' and reliance on 'pre-formed fragmentation' made them indiscriminate and led to unacceptable civilian casualties.

Since then the number of countries possessing, using and affected by cluster munitions has steadily grown whilst no specific international controls over these munitions have been introduced. Despite reported modifications in the design and use of cluster munitions, the humanitarian problems persist – as we have seen most recently in Kosovo, Chechnya and Afghanistan.

In addition to the problem of civilian casualties at the time of use, persistent and severe post-conflict problems with cluster munitions have also been documented. Sub-munitions have been identified as suffering from particularly high failure rates, and thus they present with greater frequency in the post-conflict environment in proportion to the numbers used. The potential for submunition failure to be linked to a broader failure within the system can result in more problematic forms of dense contamination.[a]

It has generally fallen to international organizations to attempt to document and highlight these post-conflict impacts.[b]

The response

A continuing failure by user governments to address the problem

Against three decades of known humanitarian problems, proponents of cluster munitions have failed to adequately investigate and establish the main sources of these problems let alone to initiate reforms that deal with their consequences. While some governments have acknowledged the problems cluster munitions cause both as a result of inaccuracy and legacy of unexploded sub-munitions,[c] the dominate official government response has been one of the denial of a problem and evasion of overall responsibility. User states have been forceful in distinguishing failed cluster sub-munitions from anti-personnel landmines,[d] restating claims about the relatively low failure rate of cluster munitions[e] and denying the importance of certain factors in leading to unexploded sub-munitions[f] so as to avoid giving credence to calls for additional international prohibitions. Meanwhile the humanitarian consequences for civilians continue.

During and after conflicts in Afghanistan, Chechnya, Iraq, Kosovo and Kuwait, insufficient efforts have been made by user governments to establish the full extent of casualties from cluster munitions or the causes for such humanitarian problems. Accurate and reliable information regarding targeting, failure-rates and the possible long-term impact of cluster munition use has not been gathered by the bodies who are responsible for that use.[g] This makes it difficult to evaluate the relative importance of design or use factors in leading to humanitarian problems or the likely impact of possible modifications. Failure to undertake such evaluations amounts to a failure to take satisfactory precautions to assure that civilians are receiving sufficient protection.

While indiscriminate attacks are prohibited under International Humanitarian Law (IHL),[h] the meaning of terms such as 'attack', 'excessive' civilian loss of life and damage, and 'concrete and direct military advantage' are not at all clear. While those employing cluster munitions have spoken about military advantage in a broad fashion, including advantages to the war strategy as whole and advantages gained in particular tactical encounters, when it comes to determining proportionality there have been moves to see humanitarian impact only in relation to immediate effects.[i]

States have relied on abstract justifications that using alternatives to cluster munitions would either:

- expose their forces to greater risk[j]

or

- increase the likely civilian casualties at the time of the attack through the requirement to use a greater number of munitions containing a greater quantity of explosives.[k]

This latter point has been utilized for some thirty years now. However, the burden of responsibility should be to show that, whichever weapons system is chosen, the impact on civilians is proportional to the concrete military advantage. If it breaches IHL to use cluster munitions in a certain situation, such a breach is not made acceptable by the possibility that using an alternative weapon system would have breached IHL even more.

Various technical and operational modifications are reported as being ongoing. The US policy combines the pursuit of technical modifications to achieve a greater reliability for ground and air delivered sub-munitions

(99 per cent or higher) by 2005,[1] undertaking evaluations of the need for retrofitting for specific existing sub-munitions,[m] destroying certain stockpiles, acquiring new sub-munitions,[n] and reviewing use and targeting practices. Many others have taken the improvement of reliability rates as a central plank of reform. The Swiss government, for example, has proposed establishing international standards for reliability at least 98 per cent.[o]

It is not clear that such initiatives will reduce the negative humanitarian impact of cluster munitions. For example: many past announcements regarding improvements in submunition reliability have proven of dubious worth as indicators of subsequent performance in combat.[p] Reliability is only one factor contributing to the presence of dangerous ordnance. The actual quantity of unexploded ordnance is dependent upon reliability and the total quantity of munitions used. As we have noted – unexploded submunitions are only part of the overall humanitarian problem of cluster munitions.

Issues to answer for

Given the established and continuing humanitarian problems, the uncertainty surrounding the full extent of the problem and its causes, the past failure of attempts to alleviate them, and concerns about future usage, the onus for justifying the continued possession and use of cluster munitions rests with user governments

As minimum part of justifying why and how these weapons are acceptable, governments should be able to answer and provide evidence in relation to some basic questions:

Who bears the burden of risk in conflict?

- How are decisions taken and documented regarding whether or not the civilian cost from cluster munition use would be excessive in relation to the concrete and direct military advantage anticipated? What is the minimum level of information required about the target area in order to make such a decision? How recent must this data be in order to be considered a reliable basis for decision making? Who are the specific individuals responsible for deciding how this balance is made and whether sufficient evidence exists to make an appropriate decision?
- If military advantages are calculated regarding advantages to the war strategy as whole, in addition to advantages expected in particular tactical encounters, how can the decisions taken be assessed by outsiders to the military? If they cannot, how can confidence be established regarding the appropriateness of such decision making?

- How are the assessments made in relation to the two points given made differently with respect to different forms of weaponry? How is the area affect of cluster munitions and possible inaccuracy, factored into the assessment of the target area?
- Most of the recent use of cluster munitions in war has taken place in situations where those using cluster munitions have had a considerable air and ground superiority. How do such asymmetrical capabilities affect decision making? How do expectations regarding military losses relate to the burden of risk borne by civilians?[q]

The number of unexploded submunitions is unacceptably high:

- How can appropriate, accurate, realistic and measurable failure rates be determined? How can we measure the composite failure rate of the whole delivery system – rather than only individual munitions?
- In evaluating adherence to any self-imposed failure-rate regime or evaluating the claims of manufacturers, how would states evaluate failure rates? What would be the sample frame within which failure rates were determined and how would the uneven distribution of failures within that sample frame be evaluated? How can states build confidence in the transparency and accountability of such processes?
- What, if any, exceptions might be made for higher failure-rates due to 'non-standard' environmental or other conditions? If such conditions could be established as excusing increased failure rates, and such failure-rates had been determined to afford humanitarian protection, how does employment of cluster munitions in such conditions reflect on commitment to protection of civilians?
- If practical reliability rates were improved how would states ensure that cluster munition use does not proliferate and increase such unacceptable casualities at the time of use and the number of unexploded submunitions are actually increased?
- Given the continuing problems posed by cluster munitions despite previous attempts to modify their use and design, by what criteria and standards will states in the future determine whether the current reforms have been adequate? If these cannot be specified, what is to prevent yet further forestalling of the introducing specific international controls over these munitions in the future (as has taken place in the past)?

Conclusions

After thirty years without significant progress towards addressing the concerns raised by civil society regarding cluster munitions, states need to stop killing civilians and start taking responsibility. The first step in this process should be to explain in detail the actual mechanisms by which user states ensure the protection of civilians as required by IHL. In addition they should lay out how a realistic, appropriate and measurable regime could be established for evaluating cluster munitions failure rates in real combat situations. States undertaking such processes also need to consider the requirement to build confidence through related mechanisms of transparency and accountability. Such processes are required in order to determine whether there are any grounds to believe cluster munitions can be used in anything other than an irresponsible manner.

* Discussion paper by Dr Brian Rappert and Richard Moyes, November 2004. B.Rappert@exeter.ac.uk and Richard.Moyes@biscituk.biz
a Landmine Action. 2002. *Explosive Remnants of War: Unexploded Ordnance and Post-conflict Communities*, London.
b See for example, ICRC. 2000. *Explosive Remnants of War: A Study on Submunitions and Other Unexploded Ordnance*, Geneva, Human Rights Watch. 2002. *Fatally Flawed: Cluster Bombs and Their Use by the US in Afghanistan*, Washington DC, Landmine Action. 2002. *Explosive Remnants of War: Unexploded Ordnance and Post-conflict Communities*, London and The UK Working Group on Landmines. 2000. *Cluster Bombs: The military Effectiveness and Impact on Civilians of Cluster Munitions*, London.
c Norway, 2003 (CCW/GGE/VI/WG.1/WP.3) noted that 'all air-delivered cluster bombs previously in Norwegian stock have been destroyed, because of their low level of precision and high dud rate'. It is important to note that this source is cited as evidence that some states have accepted the existence of problems. It is not accepted that the Norwegian distinction between air-dropped and ground-launched is an adequate basis for protecting civilians.
d For instance, during a news briefing on 21 April 2003, US Secretary of Defense Donald Rumsfeld and General Richard Myers of the Joint Chiefs of Staff were asked:

Q: Mr. Secretary, prior to the conflict, human rights groups complained about the use of cluster bombs by the United States. Now that the major combat phase is over, we're seeing the evidence that this, in fact, is a weapon that can continue to kill after the hostilities are over. There've been a small but significant number of people maimed or killed, including some children and some American forces as well. Would you consider limiting the use of cluster bombs in the future, or perhaps even eliminating them from the U.S. arsenal in response to this kind of – type of criticism?
MYERS: I think it gets back to – well, first of all, cluster bombs are not like mines, completely different subject. Cluster bombs are set to go off when they strike their target or whatever they do, so they're not like a mine that lies there until it's activated. I have not heard of injuries due to cluster bombs, but we'll look into it. It's possible, of course, but we'll have to look into it. And…
Q: Well, we've been seeing pictures of unexploded sub-munitions in various residential areas…
MYERS: We'll have to find out who's they are, and do all that sort of thing. I just – I have not seen those pictures, but I'll…

e As opposed to repeated claims by user governments that cluster munitions fail at a rate 5 per cent, estimations made post-conflict have consistently placed the over figure over 10 per cent and often much higher. See for example, UK Working Group on Landmines. 2000. *Cluster Bombs: The Military Effectiveness and Impact on Civilians of Cluster Munitions*.

f A UK defence minister reported that: 'Approximately 5 per cent of the bomblets within a Cluster Bomb fail to detonate when they impact. Regardless of the height from which they are dropped, this figure does not vary' (Spellar in *UK House of Commons Hansard*, 24 January 2000, Column 59). Later in the year, when asked about the government's assessment NATO cluster munition failure rates in Kosovo, Spellar stated that 'The cluster munitions used by the UK have a manufacturer's estimated failure rate of approximately 5 per cent. The failure rate of other nations' cluster munitions (which have different specifications) may vary, but any assessment is a matter for these nations. We are not aware of any agreed NATO estimate of the failure rate of cluster munitions used by Allies in Kosovo' (*UK House of Commons Hansard*, 24 November 2000, Column 337W). The following excerpts from the 21 June 2000, UK Parliament Select Committee on Defence, Minutes of Evidence are also pertinent:

> 1220. [...] Are you telling me that the failure rate is no different from 30,000 feet to under 15,000 feet? [...] You have admitted that the MoD have done no tests on that, that you relied on the manufacturer's own assessment of the failure rate. Why did you do no tests on that? Why did you use it without doing any tests on it?
> (*Mr Hoon*) The failure rate of the cluster bomb concerns the bomblets that are released at the time.
>
> 1221. Absolutely.
> (*Mr Hoon*) I am not a technical expert on munitions but my understanding is that the failure rate would still be the same whatever height the bomb was dropped. It does not make any difference whether you drop it from 20,000 feet or from 200 feet.
>
> 1222. Is it likely to land on the target, for example, at a higher level? What is the likelihood of it differing from its target?
> (*Mr Hoon*) That has not actually been the difficulty as far as cluster bombs are concerned. The criticism has been that some of the bomblets – 5 per cent – have not exploded. Now they have been left on the ground and I recognise that there have been civilian casualties as a result. I am not saying to you that those decisions were taken lightly; they were not. This is an extremely effective weapon and had we not used that extremely effective weapon we would have put our forces at greater risk.

Such statements are interesting because the actual incidence of unexploded sub-munitions does not relate solely to the submunition but relates to the whole system of delivery (within which delivery altitude may be a significant factor). In fact there was also criticism of the potential inaccuracy of the weapons, although this is denied here. As we go on to note in footnote 19, the 'greater risk' to British forces needs to be understood in the context that 'there were no casualties amongst allied forces in the course of the actual campaign' in Kosovo.

g For instance, when the UK Secretary for Defence was asked 'what reviews have been undertaken by his Department regarding the civilian casualty figures caused by unexploded cluster submunitions in the post-conflict regions of (a) the Gulf, (b) Kosovo and (c) Afghanistan; and what assessment [has been] made of the impact of these bomblets on Iraqi civilians in the future' a defence minister responded that 'No such reviews and assessments have been undertaken by the Ministry of Defence' (*UK House of Commons Hansard*, 15 July 2003, Column 191W).

h Article 51(5)(b) of the Additional Protocol I (amongst other Protocols) bans an indiscriminate attack which it defines in part as one:

> which may be expected to cause incidental loss of civilian life, injury to civilians, damage to civilian objects or a combination thereof, which would be excessive in relation to the concrete and direct military advantage anticipated.

i Wiebe, Virgil. 2000. 'Footprints of death: cluster bombs as indiscriminate weapons under International humanitarian law' *Michigan Journal of International Law* 22(1): 100–5. See also, how a narrow determination is given of humanitarian consequences even by a country apparently relatively supportive of further controls (Norway. 2003. *National Interpretation and Implementation of International Humanitarian Law with Regard to the Risk of Explosive Remnants of War* CCW/GGE/VI/WG.1/WP.3, 24 November 2003). This in turn draws upon Greenwood, Chris. 2002. *Legal Issues Regarding Explosive Remnants of War*, CCW/GGE/I/WP.10, 23rd May 2002.

j For example, the Dutch Government responded to a parliamentary question of 10 April 2003, that, " 'The government considers cluster munitions developed to combat armoured and non-armoured military targets on a given surface to be a legitimate weapon, for which, moreover, no effective alternative is available. Use of other weapons in situations like this would also entail unnecessary risks for pilots, as they would have to carry out a greater number of sorties to achieve the desired effect. Quoted in an ABM AMRO bank memo at: http://www. abnamro.com/com/about/data/Insys_memoEN.pdf

k For example, in a letter to The Rt Hon. Sir George Young MP (28 February 2002) the British government stated that:

> There could be serious implications of using other weapons against such targets. In most cases, this would mean using large unitary bombs, which would risk far greater damage than cluster bombs at the time of the attack.

This argument was one of the first formulated in support of cluster munitions. Erik Prokosch. 1995. *The Technology of Killing*, p. 151, reports an American government delegate at the 1974 conference in Lucerne as saying:

> In the CBU flak suppression role, they drive crews from their weapons into shelters' [...] 'The pellets [pre-formed fragmentation] don't have a strong penetration capacity, so the crews are protected. So are civilians if they take cover, as they almost always do. The choice would be general-purpose bombs which would result in increased casualties.

Prokosch goes on (p. 154) goes on to report a British government delegate saying:

> The implication for this conference is that a far greater weight of HE [high explosive] must be delivered into an area to achieve the same probability of destroying tanks when using blast bombs rather than BL755.

The arguments against charges that cluster munitions are indiscriminate at the time of use have barely changed in 30 years, and yet no strong evidence has been presented to support these arguments or to lay out the mechanisms by which the balance of risk to civilians is evaluated during the process of targeting.

l Cohen, William. 2001. *Memorandum for the Secretaries of the Military Departments: Department of Defense Policy on Submunition Reliability* 10 January 2001, and Melita, A. *Munitions Insights/Initiatives* at http://www.dtic. mil/ndia/2001munitions/melita.pdf

m Human Rights Watch Briefing Paper. 2003. *Cluster Munitions: A Foreseeable Hazard in Iraq March* (New York: Human Rights Watch).

n See Human Rights Watch. 2003. *Cluster Munitions: Measures to Prevent ERW and Protect Civilian Populations* (New York: Human Rights Watch).

o Various country positions as of mid-2003 are presented in Handicap International. 2003. *Cluster Munition Systems* (Lyon: Handicap International).

p For a review of official claims and counterclaims about reliability rates see UK Working Group on Landmines. 2000. *Cluster Bombs: The Military Effectiveness and Impact of Cluster Munitions*.

q   The following excerpts from the 21 June 2000, UK Parliament Select Committee on
Defence, Minutes of Evidence provide a remarkable example:

> 1215. How many refugees and innocent civilians is a pilot worth?
> (*Mr Hoon*) I do not think it is proper for me to try and deal with that.
>
> 1216. In your assessment?
> (*Mr Hoon*) Judgments are made. Military campaigns inevitably involve risk both for
> the armed forces of this country and, indeed, for civilians of other countries. That is
> something which is taken into account which is why we take account of relevant
> principles of international law both in terms of the targets that we select and, indeed,
> in terms of the equipment that we utilise.
> late....
>
> 1219. Was there not a report recently of children killed by a [submunition] left from
> a cluster bomb in dreadful circumstances? Have there not been other deaths as a
> result of those failed cluster bomb munitions?
> (*Mr Hoon*) To repeat: in a military campaign there will be casualties. We were
> remarkably fortunate that there were no casualties amongst allied forces in the
> course of the actual campaign. We all regret that there are civilian casualties in a
> military campaign but if you want to preserve human rights, if you want to preserve
> democracy, there are times when it is necessary to use force. That was what we did.

action builds up to the conclusion giving (p. 187) the importance of locating the
onus for justifying the use of cluster munitions with those seeking to employ them.
If concerned groups are deterred in various ways from being able to offer
convincing evidence regarding disproportionality or to establish the exact reason
for unexploded ordnance, then compelling users to make the case for continued
use is one way ahead. In this way, the document extends the Cluster Munition
Coalition's central demand 'No use, production or trade of cluster munitions until
the humanitarian problems associated with the weapons have been resolved', by
furthering it along the lines that the responsibility for specifying and demonstrating
when the problems have been 'resolved' should rest with proponents rather than
detractors. So instead of NGOs and others deriving a list of possible recommendations regarding what constitutes appropriate fusing and arming systems, self-
destruct mechanisms and or drop altitudes that might lead to many difficult and
divisive questions about what (explicitly or implicitly) makes for 'appropriate'
force, those justifications should be made by users.

Through this approach, the attempt is made to move governments on from
abstract arguments about 'military necessity' and 'difficult decisions'. Rather
than supposing it is enough that 'judgments are made' and 'there will be casualties'
as British Defence Minister Geoff Hoon does (see Box 11.1 reference 17), attention
is directed towards the processes whereby decisions are taken. A key question in
this is 'Who bears the burden of risk in conflict?'. The sub-section with this title
makes various demands that stress the importance of not adopting an attitude
of deference regarding decision making, not accepting the forever deferral of

responsibility in organizations, requiring the basis for judgements be open to wider scrutiny, and questioning the basis on which similarities and dissimilarities are draw between weapon systems. The expectation in posing such questions is not that the information provided could or would simply resolve disputes, but rather through asking them key points of contention and ways of arguing could be brought to the fore.

Consider in particular this in relation to last bullet point under 'Who bears the burden of risk in conflict?':

*   Most of the recent use of cluster munitions in war has taken place in situations where those using cluster munitions have had a considerable air and ground superiority. How do such asymmetrical capabilities affect decision making? How do expectations regarding military losses relate to the burden of risk borne by civilians?

It is sometimes said there is much overlap between the concerns of user governments and humanitarian groups regarding the after-effects of unexploded sub-munitions since such remnants are not desirable from a military or a human-itarian point of view.[27] While that might be the case in certain respects, it breaks down in how risks are distributed. As generally large area weapons, cluster muni-tions might provide military advantages over other options in certain situations. The high altitude bombing of ill-defined targets thought to be spread out over an area might expose pilots to less danger than the multiple attacks with unitary munitions. Yet even accepting this basic characterization of the situation, in such rationalizations risks to civilians from the immediate attack and the later remain-ing unexploded sub-munitions are being traded-off against the safety of military personnel. With the considerable military superiority of the users of cluster munitions in most recent wars (e.g. Kosovo, Chechnya, Afghanistan, Iraq) the dynamic herein is one of avoiding a marginal increase in risk to users through the employment of cluster weapons to shift significant risks to civilians. While quantifying that shift would no doubt be problematic, those governments advo-cating the continuing use of cluster munitions should be compelled to recognize the issues at stake and to explicitly justify how decisions are made (see Box 11.1 reference 17 referring to the Kosovo war).

'Stop Killing Civilians, Start Taking Responsibility' document (sub-section 'The number of unexploded submunitions is unacceptably high') turns to matters asso-ciated with the failure rate of unexploded sub-munitions. A number of demands are made for user governments to provide basic factual information that hitherto has not been collected or made public. Again this is not done with the intention of simply establishing the facts of the matter so as to resolve disputes. Rather the call is for the onus of justification to be with user governments in light of the possibilities for creatively negotiating standards and their past collective failure to respond in an adequate fashion. In short, tying up the loose ends associated with demonstrating failure rates should be the problem of users. So as a minimum, given the questionable status of past claims that humanitarian problems are being corrected, states should be able to specify how it is that they will determine the success or failure of current initiatives. If they cannot do so in a plausible fashion, then past experience would give many reasons why those concerned with humanitarian consequences should regard current reforms promising 'things will be better tomorrow' as part of the long running and unacceptable deferral by states of their responsibilities. The document also raises concerns about future usage; in particular how the gains made from decreasing the dud rate might be lost because of greater usage of 'new and improved' munitions.

The lines of questioning given in the 'Stop Killing Civilians, Start Taking Responsibility' document do not merely list a series of important questions in their own right, but express an orientation to the issues associated with cluster munitions. This approach has as its starting point two premises: (a) the unacceptability of the repeated civilian deaths killed from these weapons both when they explode as intended and when they fail to do so and (b) the past failure of user states to adequately address these concerns through unilateral or multilateral action. What is needed then is a way to halt the forever delaying of addressing humanitarian concerns. This 'searching questions' approach does not attempt to specify the ultimate socio-technical reasons for certain consequences with cluster munitions. Rather, with the continuing problems and the unwillingness or inability of user governments to undertake sufficient action (e.g. in forum such as the CCW), then the default position should be that of no use of cluster munitions. If certain types of munitions in certain types of situations are by some calculation determined to be necessary and the most appropriate option, then this is a matter for users to publicly substantiate (something which previously they have been markedly unwilling to do).

The main practical roles for NGOs that follow from this way of thinking are to document as best as possible the consequences from cluster munitions and to hold government to account for their actions and failures. That might be done in forum such as the CCW, but it is in no way limited to this. The initial uncertainties and difficulties associated with substantiating claims about what needs doing and where such actions will lead should be deflected away from NGOs who typically struggle to know the particulars of operational deployments in comparison to users but who are often just as knowledgeable regarding the civilian consequences of conflict. The overall approach expressed in 'Stop Killing Civilians, Start Taking Responsibility' is sufficiently open-ended to provide an umbrella under which diverse campaigning organizations can unite, this in comparison to proposing explicit problematic ethical positions regarding what is and is not required by the way of next modifications to the use of cluster munitions.

Given the previous arguments in the book, such a strategy should not be regarded as way of escaping from the dilemmas and difficulties associated with determining what is prudent by way of formal prohibitions. The effort to deflect problems onto users would only be an initial move in a series of responses and counter-responses. For instance, should user governments introduce new measures and provide information about targeting procedures or design processes, concerned NGOs might well be asked to comment on their adequacy. Such demands might be responded to with a further questioning of the basis of claims made or evaluations of the measures undertaken. This sort of questioning could turn more accusatory should questionable practice continue. In any such actions, the categorizations, contextualizations and generalizations offered would be opening for unpacking in the manner these have throughout this book. As ever these are matters for future debate which cannot be fully determined here, where consideration needs to be given to how choices must be made about what sort of situation is faced and what sort of cases are being considered. In the process it is prudent to constantly question how meaning is attributed to the world and a place given to prohibitions in securing peace.

Notes

I The chains that bind?

1 See, for example, M. van Creveld, *Technology and War*, London: MacMillan, 1991; S. Rosen, *Winning the Next War*, Ithaca, NY: Cornell University Press, 1994; and S. Croft, *Strategies of Arm Control*, Manchester: Manchester University Press, 1996, Chapter 1.

2 Amnesty International (UK), *Repression Trade (UK) Limited*, London: Amnesty International (UK), 1992.

3 N. Tebbit, *Hansard*, 28 March, London: HMSO, 1984.

4 T. Sainsbury, *Hansard*, 17 October, London: HMSO, 1991.

5 Amnesty International (UK), *Leg-Irons*, London: Amnesty International (UK), n.d. Available http://www.amnesty.org.uk/action/camp/arms/cases/irons.shtml (accessed on 2 November 2004).

6 Amnesty International (UK), *Repression Trade (UK) Limited*, p. 33.

7 Ibid., p. 9.

8 United Nations, *United Nations' Standard Minimum Rules for the Treatment of Prisoners* Geneva: United Nations, 1955. Available http://www.unhchr.ch/html/menu3/b/h_comp34.htm (accessed on 22 November 2004).

9 Amnesty International, *Aim Higher*, Available www.amnesty.org.uk/action/camp/arms/cases/irons.shtml (accessed on 2 November 2004).

10 In 2003, 43 American firms were reported manufacturing leg irons, shackles or thumb-cuffs with a further 10 companies in Western Europe, see Steve Wright, 'Civilising the torture trade', *The Guardian*, 13 March 2003.

11 See United Nations, 1995. *United Nations' Standard Minimum Rules for the Treatment of Prisoners*, Geneva: United Nations Congress on the Prevention of Crime and the Treatment of Offenders.

12 F. Abrams and E. Helmore, 'Best of British leg irons on sale in America', *The Independent*, 16 November 1999.

13 D. Chidgey, *Hansard*, 22 November, London: HMSO, 1999, Column 425.

14 P. Hain, *Hansard*, 15 February 2000: Column 491W.

15 J. Burke and B. Johnson-Thomas, 'British firms trade in torture', *The Observer*, 10 September 2000.

16 See as well Anon., 'Una empresa vasca exporta grilletes para presos que España no permite por vejatorios', *El Pais*, 2 October 2000.

17 C. Wheeler, 'Torture shackles made in Brum' *Sunday Mercury*, 15 December 2002, pp. 1–7.

18 Foreign Affairs, *Second Joint Report*, 6 May, London: HMSO, 2003. Available http://www.parliament.the-stationery-office.co.uk/pa/cm200203/cmselect/cmfaff/474/47402.htm#evidence (accessed on 22 October 2004).

19 European Parliament, *Resolution on the Second Annual Review of the EU Code of Conduct on the Export or Transfer of Arms*, 3 October 2001.

20 Foreign Affairs, *Second Joint Report*, 2003.

21 Such as those in Amnesty International (UK), *UK Foreign and Asylum Policy: Human Rights Audit 2000*, London: Amnesty International [UK], 2001 and E. Mitchell, *UK Arms Exports to Zimbabwe*, London: Campaign Against the Arms Trade, 2001.

2 Striving for order

1 F. Nietzsche, *The Will to Power*, New York: Vintage Books, 1968.

2 To paraphrase L. Wittgenstein. *Zettel*, Oxford: Blackwell, 1967, §446.

3 International Court of Justice, *Legality of the Threat or Use of Nuclear Weapons*, The Hague: ICJ, 1996. Available http://www.dfat.gov.au/intorgs/icj_nuc/unan5a_b.html (accessed on 20 November 2004).

4 Ibid.

5 Z. Bauman, *Modernity and Ambivalence*, Cambridge: Polity, 1991.

6 Ibid., 3.

7 For a discussion of these matters see K. Grint and S. Woolgar, *The Machine at Work*. Cambridge: Polity Press, 1999.

8 Y. Sandoz, 'Preface', in E. Prokosch (ed.) *The Technology of Killing*, London: Zed, 1995.

9 As has been argued about the ICRC SIrUS project, see J. Piachaud, 'Arms limitations or a tacit way of accepting their use?', *Medicine, Conflict, and Survival* 1998, 14, 243–49. For a more general discussion see F. Terry *Condemned to Repeat?*, Ithaca, NY: Cornell University Press, 2002, p. xi.

10 Ibid., p. xiii.

11 Ibid.

12 For a consideration of some of the former see T. Smith, 'The new law of war: legitimizing hi-tech and infrastructural violence', *International Studies Quarterly*, 2002, 46, 355–74.

13 Cluster Munitions Coalation, *CMC International Launch Conference*, 12–13 November 2003, The Hague.

14 W. Cohen, *Memorandum for the Secretaries of the Military Departments: Departmnet of Defense Policy on Submunition Reliability*, 10 January, Washington, DC: Department of Denfense, 2001.

15 As alleged was undertaken by British troops employing the new L20A1 artillery munition in the 2003 Iraq war. See Human Rights Watch, *Off Target*, New York: Human Rights Watch, 2003, pp. 96–7.

16 As in the 7 September 2003 speech by G.W. Bush. Available http://news.bbc.co.uk/1/hi/world/americas/3088936.stm (accessed on 8 September 2003).

17 That is those cluster munitions not employing precision targeting technology. See Human Rights Watch, *Off Target*.

18 D. Markow, 'The Russians and their nukes', *Air Force Magazine*, February 1997, 41. Taken from C. Dunlop, 'Technology: recomplicating moral life for the nation's defenders', *Parameters*, 1999, Autumn, 24–53.

19 R. Falk, 'The challenges of biological weaponry', in Susan Wright (ed.) *Biological Warfare and Disarmament*, London: Rowman & Littlefield, 2001, p. 29.

20 J.K. Jacobsen, 'Duelling constructivism', *Review of International Studies*, 2003, 29, 36–60.

21 S.Woolgar and D. Pawluch, 'Ontological gerry-mandering', *Social Problems*, 1985, 32, 214–27.

22 M. Mulkay, 'Don Quixote's double', in S. Woolgar (ed.) *Knowledge and Reflexivity*, London: Sage, 1988, p. 81–100.

23 K. Bonner, 'Reflexivity and interpretive sociology', *Human Studies*, 2001, 24, 267–92.

24 See Croft, *Strategies of Arm Control*.
25 P. Scranton, 'Determinism and indeterminacy in the history of technology', *Technology and Culture*, 1995, 36(2), S31–S53.
26 HLA Hart, *The Concept of Law*, 2nd Edition Oxford: Oxford Clarendon Press, 1994.
27 As inspired by Malcolm Ashmore, see Mulkay, 'Don Quixote's double'.

3 Forceful arguments

1 J. Potter and M. Wetherell, *Discourse and Social Psychology*, London: Sage, 1987, 110–3.
2 N. Chomsky, 'One Man's World', *News Statesman*, 17 November 2003. Available http://www.newstatesman.co.uk/ (accessed on 22 November 2004).
3 D. Edwards, *Discourse and Cognition*, London: Sage, 1997.
4 G. Kitching, *Marxism and Science: An Analysis of an Obsession*, University Park, PA: Pennsylvania State University, 1994, p. 98.
5 J. Potter, *Representing Reality*, London: Sage, 1997 and Potter and Wetherell, *Discourse and Social Psychology*.
6 J. Austin, *How to do Things with Words*, Cambridge, MA: Harvard University Press, 1962, p. 12.
7 Edwards, *Discourse and Cognition*, p. 14.
8 Ibid., p. 16
9 J. Potter, 'Discourse analysis as a way of analyzing naturally occurring talk', in Silverman, David (ed.) *Qualitative Research*, London: Sage Publications, 2004, 200–21.
10 K. McKenzie, 'Facts and narratives of war', *Human Sciences*, 2001, 24, 187–209.
11 From M. Lynch and D. Bogen, *The Spectacle of History*, Durham, NC: Duke University Press, 1996.
12 British Broadcasting Corporation. 'Iraq stand-off in "final phase"', *BBC News*, 21 February 2003. Available http://news.bbc.co.uk/1/hi/uk_politics/2786131.stm (accessed on 21 February 2001).
13 In some interactional settings, for instance, previous misconduct and deception by individuals might be taken (by some anyway) as a sign of their present trustworthiness. For instance, as illustrated in the claims given by Oliver North in Congressional hearing regarding the Iran–Contra affair. See Lynch and Bogen, *The Spectacle of History*.
14 As inspired by N. Pleasants, 'A Wittgensteinian social theory?', *Philosophy of the Social Sciences*, 1996, 26(3), 397–416 and Kitching, *Marxism and Science*.

4 The technologies of conflict and the conflicts about technology

1 Taking these topics from K. Grint and S. Woolgar, *The Machine at Work*, Cambridge: Polity Press, 1999.
2 Here following for instance, K. Grint and S. Woolgar, 'Computers, guns and roses: what's social about being shot', *Science, Technology, and Human Values*, 1992, 17, 366–80 and S. Woolgar and G. Cooper, 'Do artefacts have ambivalence?: Moses' bridges, winner's bridges and other urban legends in S&TS', *Social Studies of Science*, 1999, 29, 433–45.
3 Human Rights Watch, *Civilian Death in the NATO Air Campaign*, Washington, DC: Human Rights Watch, 2000 (accessed on 21 February 2003).
4 See J. Webb 'Iraqi civilian deaths "avoidable"', *BBC News*, 12 December 2003. Available http://news.bbc.co.uk/1/hi/world/middle_east/3312295.stm (accessed on 12 December 2003).

5 E. Prokosch, *The Technology of Killing*, London: Zed, 1995.
6 Van Creveld, *On Future War*, London: Brassey's, 1990.
7 See, J.C. Swearengen and E.J. Woodhouse, 'Cultural risks of technological innovation', *IEEE Technology and Society Magazine*, 2001, Spring, 15–28 and L. Winner, *Autonomous Technology*, Cambridge, MA: MIT Press, 1977.
8 Winner, ibid., 302.
9 See D. Stone, 'Causal stories and the formation of policy agendas', *Political Science Quarterly*, 1989, 104(2), 281–300 and B. Wynne, 'Unruly technology: practical rules, impractical discourses and public understanding', *Social Studies of Science*, 1998, 18(1), 147–67.
10 B'Tselem, *Death Foretold*, Jerusalem: B'Tselem, 1998 and A. Mahajna, N. Aboud, I. Harbaji, A. Agbaria, Z. Lankovsky, M. Michaelson, D. Fisher, M. Krausz, 'Blunt and penetrating injuries caused by rubber bullets during the Israeli–Arab conflict in October, 2000', *The Lancet* 2002, 359, 1795–1800.
11 B'Tselem, *Death Foretold*, 10.
12 See A. McGill, 'Responsibility judgments and the causal background', in D. Messick and A. Tenbrunsel (eds) *Codes of Conduct*, New York: Russell Sage Foundation, 1997, p. 240.
13 G. Friedman and M. Friedman, *The Future of War*, New York: Crown, 1996, p. xi. Quoted from Dunlop, 'Technology: recomplicating moral life for the nation's defenders', *Parameters*, 1999, Autumn, 24.
14 See, for example, N. Sims, 'Morality and biological warfare', *Arms Control*, 1991, 8, 5–23. Of course, means and motive often become inseparable in justifications for force.
15 See Medical Foundation for the Care of Victims of Torture, *Staying Alive by Accident: Torture Survivors from Turkey in the UK*, London: Medical Foundation, 1999.
16 For a historical analysis of debates about the abhorrence of chemical weapons see R. Price, *The Chemical Weapons Taboo*, Ithaca, NY: Cornell University Press, 1997.
17 R. Malcolmson, *Nuclear Fallacies*, Kingston: McGill-Queen's University 1995, pp. 10–1.
18 Ibid., 104.
19 M. Hanson, 'Nuclear weapons as obstacles to international security', *International Relations*, 2002, 16(3), 361. See as well J. Rotbalt (ed.), *Nuclear Weapons: The Road to Zero*, Basingstoke: Macmillan, 1998.
20 Motto quoted from D. Jenkins, *The Final Frontier*, London: Verso, 2002.
21 Foreign and Commonwealth Office, *Strengthening the Biological and Toxin Weapons Convention*, London: HMSO, 2002.
22 M. van Creveld, 'Technology and World War II', in C. Townshend (ed.) *The Oxford Illustrated History of Modern War*, Oxford: Oxford University Press, 1997.
23 See Creveld, *Technology and War* and Dunlop, 'Technology'.
24 See J. Stone, 'Politics, technology and the revolution in military affairs', *Journal of Strategic Studies*, 2004, 27(3), 408–27.
25 Jonathan Glover, for instance, cites the deaths caused to civilians during the sinking of a ferry transporting the German supply of heavy water for German atomic programme by Norwegian operatives during the Second World War as instance where such deaths are defensible because of the possible consequences of inaction. See J. Glover, *Humanity*, London: Pimlico, 2001.
26 Dunlop, 'Technology'.
27 *The Guardian*, 'Which path back from the brink?', *The Guardian*, 18 October 1982.
28 As another counter, in relation to protracted conflicts in Southeast Asia Khan has argued the presence of nuclear capabilities may well have only further protracted the tensions between Pakistan and India by decreasing the willingness of these states to seek forms of conflict resolution. S. Khan, 'A nuclear south Asia', *International Relations*, 2001, 15(4), 61–77.

29 See N. Brown, B. Rappert and A. Webster (eds), *Contested Futures*, Aldershot: Ashgate, 2000.

30 J. Alexander, *Future War*, New York: St. Martin's Press, 1999.

31 H. Collins and T. Pinch, *The Golem at Large*, Cambridge: Cambridge University Press, 1998.

32 T. Farrell, *Weapons Without a Cause*, London: Macmillan, 1996.

33 As observed though, to say that certain weapons have little strategic value does not mean they have no value at all. For instance, weapons acquisition can be embroiled in the international and domestic politics of arms controls, where technologies become bargaining chips in negotiations.

34 Dando, *A New Form of Warfare*, Chapter 5.

35 As another example, Human Rights Watch argued that US fascination with the ability to track satellite phone transmission by Iraqi leaders in the 2003 Iraqi lead to a misplaced reliance on it as a basis for aerial attacks. Human Rights Watch. *Off Target*, New York: Human Rights Watch, 2003.

36 As argued in A.J. Bacevich and L. Kaplan, 'The Clinton Doctrine', *The Weekly Standard*, 30 September 1996, 16–20.

37 B. Hatch Rosenberg, 'Anthrax attacks pushed open an ominous door', *Los Angeles Times*, 22 September 2002. Available http://www.fas.org/bwc/news/anthraxreport.htm (accessed on 22 September 2002).

38 M. Leitenberg, *Biological Weapons in the Twentieth Century: A Review and Analysis*, Washington, DC: FAS, 2001. Available http://www.fas.org/bwc/papers/21centurybw.htm (accessed on 14 April 2004) and K. Nixdorff and W. Bender, 'Ethics of university research, biotechnology and potential military spin-off' *Minerva* 2002, 40, 15–35.

39 This prospect came to the fore in 2001 when Australian researchers announced they created a particularly powerful strain of the mousepox virus as part of attempts to develop a mouse contraceptive. Similar types of manipulations to human smallpox could make it resistant to current vaccines. See R. Jackson, A. Ramsay, C. Christensen, S. Beaton, D. Hall and I. Ramshaw, 'Expression of mouse interleukin-4 by a recombinant ectromelia virus suppresses cytolytic lymphocyte responses and overcomes genetic resistance to mousepox', *Journal of Virology*, 2001, 75, 1205–10.

40 R. Zilinskas (ed.), *The Microbiologist and Biological Defense Research*, New York: New York Academy of Science, 1992.

41 United States Department of State, 'Bush strategy to defend against bioterrorism', US Department of State Fact Sheet. 5 February 2002.

42 See M. Leitenberg, J. Leonard and R. Spertzel, 'Biodefense crossing the line', *Politics Life Sciences*, 2003, 22, 1–2.

43 Price, *The Chemical Weapons Taboo*.

44 M. Billig, *Arguing and Thinking*, Cambridge: Cambridge University Press, 1996 and M. Billig, S. Condo, D. Edwards, M. Gane, D. Middleton and A. Radley, *Ideological Dilemmas*, London: Sage, 1989.

45 These activities are referred to 'research' rather than 'development' so as they do not fall foul of the BTWC.

46 See The Sunshine Project, 'US military operating a secret chemical weapons program', Sunshine Project News Release 24 September 2002. For a general overview of technical possibilities see M. Dando, *The New Biological Weapons*, London: Lynee Rienner, 2001 and for a technical analysis see E. Kagan, 'Bioregulators as instruments of terror', *Clinics in Laboratory Medicine*, 2001, 21, 607–18.

47 See B. Rappert, *Non-Lethal Weapons as Legitimizing Forces?: Technology, Politics and The Management of Conflict*, London: Frank Cass, 2003. During its introduction into policing and military operations at the start of the twentieth century, for instance, 'tear gas' was alternatively portrayed as more or less humanitarian than other forms

of force and as similar or dissimilar to 'chemical warfare'. See D. Jones, 1978, 'From military to civilian technology', *Technology and Culture*, 19(2), 151–68.

48 See, for instance, Amnesty International, *Cruelty in Control? The Stun Belt and Other Electro-shock Equipment in Law Enforcement*, Report AMR 51/54/99 London: Amnesty International, 1999 and Omega Foundation, *Crowd Control Technologies*, Report to the Scientific and Technological Options Assessment of the European Parliament. PE 168.394 Luxembourg: European Parliament, 2000.
49 See Rappert, *Non-Lethal Weapons as Legitimizing Forces*, Chapter 4.
50 Grint and Woolgar, *The Machine at Work*, 32.

5 Weapons: what are they?

1 J. Crawley, 'Officials confirm dropping firebombs on Iraqi troops', *San Diego Union-Tribune*, 5 August 2003.
2 M. Savidge, 'Protecting Iraq's oil supply', *CNN*, 22 March 2003.
3 L. Murdoch, 'Dead bodies everywhere', *Australian Sydney Morning Herald*, 22 March 2003.
4 Commentary by Jeff Davis, US Navy, Office of the Assistant Secretary of Defense, see ibid.
5 Murdoch, 'Dead bodies everywhere'.
6 Associated Press. 'Marines dropped devices similar to napalm on Iraqi troops'. Available http://www.mercurynews.com/mld/mercurynews/news/local/6465972.htm (accessed on 3 June 2003).
7 J. Synder in 'Heavy reproaches against US Pentagon: napalm bombs in the Iraq war'. Available http://www.informationclearinghouse.info/article4395.htm (accessed on 13 November 2004).
8 MONITOR, 'Schwere Vorwürfe gegen US-Pentagon: Napalm-bomben im Irak-Krieg', Nr. 507 Aired 7 August 2003. Available http://www.wdr.de/tv/monitor/beitragsuebersicht.phtml (accessed on 13 November 2004).
9 Potter, *Representing Reality*.
10 Of napalm, Michael Blecker of Swords to Plowshares reportedly said 'Napalm is a push-button word...Everything you think about Vietnam and the insanity of that war, and there are certain terms for it – Agent Orange, Tet, Khe Sanh, My Lai and napalm.' See M. Taylor, 'Military Says Goodbye to Napalm', *San Francisco Chronicle*, 4 April 2001.
11 J. Crawley 'Officials confirm dropping firebombs on Iraqi troops', *San Diego Union-Tribune*, 5 August 2003. Likewise a US Marine Corps jet pilot questioned about the use of the bombs in Iraq commented: 'We really don't pay much attention to it, to us it is a very dangerous thing. You know I really cannot speak for the effects, obviously I have not been on the receiving end of it, but I would venture to say its got lethal effects which is why it is useful, but it is no more no more less lethal than many of the other weapons we use'. See MONITOR. 2003. 'Schwere vorwürfe gegen US-Pentagon'.
12 See GlobalSecurity.org. 'Incendiary weapons'. Available http://www.globalsecurity.org/military/systems/munitions/incendiary.htm (accessed on 2 January 2005).
13 US Department of Defense Office of Arms Control Implementation and Compliance *Article-by-Article Analysis of the Protocol on Prohibitions or Restrictions on the Use of Incendiary Weapons*, Washington, DC: DoD, n.d. Available http://www.defenselink.mil/acq/acic/treaties/ccwapl/ccw_p3art.htm (accessed on 12 December 2004).
14 Here I am 'following' Mulkay, 'Don Quixote's double'.
15 N. Goodman, *Problems and Projects*, New York: Bobbs-Merrill Company, 1972.

16 B. Barnes, 'Concept application as social activity', *Crítica*, 1987, XIX, 19–46, 24.
17 B. Barnes, *T.S. Kuhn and Social Science*, London: Macmillan, 1982, 30.
18 See as well P. Westen, 'The empty idea of equality', *Harvard Law Review*, 95, 537–96.
19 Barnes, 'Concept application as social activity', 34.
20 Hart, *The Concept of Law*, 126.
21 W. Sharrock and G. Button, 'Do the right thing!', *Human Studies*, 1999, 22, 193–210 and M. Lynch, 'Extending Wittgenstein', in Andrew Pickering (ed.) *Science as Practice and Culture*, Chicago, IL: University of Chicago Press, 1992.
22 See, for example, B. Mariani, and A. Urquhart, *Transparency and Accountability in European Arms Export Controls*, London: Saferworld, 2000.
23 Amnesty International, 'Italy and small arms', *The Terror Trade Time*, June 2001.
24 Amnesty International, *Imported Arms used in Israel and the Occupied Territories with Excessive Force Resulting in Unlawful Killings and Unwarranted Injuries*, London: Amnesty International, 2000.
25 R. Cook, 'Export controls', *House of Commons Hansard*, 28 July, London: HMSO, 1997.
26 N. Krau, 'France and Germany stop arms sales to Israel', *Ha-aretz*, 17 December 2000, 1.
27 Anon. 'UK violates own ban on arms sales to Israel', *MENA Business Reports – Asia Africa Intelligence Wire*, 7 July 2002.
28 R. Norton-Taylor, 'UK equipment being used in Israeli attacks', *The Guardian*, 29 May 2002.
29 HMSO, *House of Commons Hansard*, 26 October 2000, Columns 199–203W.
30 The Council for the Advancement of Arab–British Understanding, *LAW condemns UK Arms Deal*, 9 July 2002.
31 R. Cook, *Point of Departure*, London: Simon & Schuster, 2003.
32 M. White and R. Norton-Taylor, 'Straw provokes row over arms for Israel', *The Guardian*, 9 July 2002, 10.
33 Foreign Affairs, *Second Joint Report*, 6 May, London: HMSO, 2003. Available http://www.parliament.the-stationery-office.co.uk/pa/cm200203/cmselect/cmfaff/474/47402.htm#evidence (accessed on 9 June 2003).
34 Oral evidence by Jack Straw. Ibid., paragraph 21.
35 Saferworld, *Submission to the Quadripartite Select Committee: New Guidance issued by the Government – July 2002*, London: Saferworld, 2002.
36 Oral evidence by Straw, *Second Joint Report*, paragraph 21.
37 Saferworld, *Submission to the Quadripartite Select Committee: New Guidance issued by the Government – July 2002*.
38 Oral evidence by Straw, *Second Joint Report*, paragraph 23.
39 Ibid., 21.
40 As in BBC News, 'Straw defends arms sales change', *BBC News*, 9 July 2002.
41 See, for example, Sir R. Scott, *Report of the Inquiry into the Export of Defence Equipment and Dual-Use Goods to Iraq and Related Prosecutions* (HC 115: vols I–VI), London: HMSO, 1996 and Amnesty International, *Repression Trade Limited*, London: Amnesty International, 1992.
42 Oral evidence by Straw, *Second Joint Report*.
43 Ibid., paragraph 27.
44 HMSO, *House of Commons Hansard*, 23 July 2002, Column 841.
45 Oral evidence by Straw, *Second Joint Report*, paragraph 28.
46 B. Barnes and D. Edge, *Science in Context*, Cambridge, MA: MIT Press, 1982, 70.
47 Interview with E. Sneh, *BBC News 24*, Aired 23 July 2002.
48 10 Downing Street, 'Export licences/arms sales', *Media Brief*, 8 July 2002. Available http://www.number-10.gov.uk/output/page2456.asp (accessed on 26 July 2002).

49 10 Downing Street, 'Export licences/arms sales', *Media Brief*, 8 July 2002. Available http://www.number-10.gov.uk/output/page2456.asp (accessed on 26 July 2002).
50 Foreign Affairs, *Second Joint Report*, paragraph 137.
51 HMSO, *Response of the Secretaries of State for Defence, Foreign and Commonwealth Affairs, International Development and Trade and Industry to the Strategic Export Controls: Annual Report for 2001*, Licensing Policy and Parliamentary Scrutiny, London: HSMO 2003, 14.
52 Nor was the meaning of the contention by Foreign Office officials after the bombing in Gaza City on 22 July 2002 bombing that existing rules will be more strictly implemented, as reported in BBC News, 'UK tightens Israel arms exports', *BBC News*, 27 August 2002. Available http://news.bbc.co.uk/1/hi/uk_politics/2218599.stm (accessed on 30 August 2002).
53 BBC News, 'Arm scandal shocks settlers', *BBC News*, 19 July 2002. Available http://news.bbc.co.uk/1/hi/world/middle_east/2138155.stm (accessed on 30 August 2002).
54 Billig, *Arguing and Thinking*.
55 10 Downing Street, 'Export licences/arms sales'.
56 C. Adams, 'Israel to benefit from arms export reforms', *Financial Times*, 9 July 2002, 6.
57 BBC News, 'Arms sales to Israel', *BBC News*, 8 July 2002. Available http://news.bbc.co.uk/1/hi/programmes/world_at_one/2116155.stm (accessed on 1 September 2002).
58 P. Dunne and S. Perlo Freeman, *Bigger than the Sum of its Parts: Components and the Impact of a Responsible Arms Control Policy on the UK Economy*, March, Oxford: Oxfam, 2003.
59 Ibid., 8.
60 Defence, Foreign Affairs, International Development and Trade and Industry Committees, *Third, Second, Third Fourth Reports*, 2 February London: HMSO, 2000.
61 E. MacAskill, 'Britain's ethical foreign policy: keeping the Hawk jets in action', *The Guardian*, 20 January 2000, p. 1 and Mitchell, *UK Arms Exports to Zimbabwe*.
62 See House of Commons Select Committee on Defence, *Third Report*, 6 March. London: HMSO, 2001. Available www.publications.parliament.uk/pa/cm200001/cmselect/cmdfence/212/212def02.htm (accessed on 24 April 2001).
63 Ibid.
64 British Broadcasting Company, 'A Newsnight investigation into arms sales'. Available http://news.bbc.co.uk/hi/english/events/newsnight/newsid_1211000/1211849.stm (accessed on 4 March 2001).
65 As, for example, in Amnesty International UK, *UK Foreign Policy and Asylum Policy: Human Right Audit 1999*, London: AIUK, 1999; Amnesty International UK, *UK Foreign Policy and Asylum Policy: Human Right Audit 2000*, London: AIUK, 2000; and Amnesty International UK and Oxfam GB, *Destination Unknown*, London: AIUK, 2000.
66 Billig, *Arguing and Thinking*, 186.
67 Goodman, *Problems and Projects*, 444.

6 Weapons: what are they for?

1 J. Miller, S. Engelberg and W. Broad, 'U.S. germ warfare research pushes treaty limits', *New York Times*, 4 September 2001.
2 Ibid.
3 For background to this project see J. Miller, S. Engelberg and W. Broad, *Germs*, New York: Simon & Schuster, 2001.
4 See as well J. Miller, 'When is bomb not a bomb? Germ experts confront US', *New York Times*, 5 September 2001.
5 M. Wheelis and M. Dando, 'Back to bioweapons?', *Bulletin of the Atomic Scientists*, 2003, 59(1), 40–6.

6 V. Clarke, *Department of Defense News Briefing*, 4 September 2001.
7 B. Hatch Rosenberg and M. Leitenberg, 'Who's afraid of a germ warfare treaty', *LA Times*, 6 September 2001. See also J.R. Bolton, *Beyond the Axis of Evil: Additional Threats from Weapons of Mass Destruction*, Heritage Lecture No. 743, Washington. DC: Heritage Foundation, 2002.
8 See R. Sinsheimer, 'Scientists and research', in Susan Wright (ed.) *Preventing a Biological Arms Race*, Cambridge, MA: MIT Press, 1990, 71–7. Even for some of those supporting the BTWC, the validity of the claims regarding the absolute moral repugnance of biological weapons are seen as conditional. See as well the special issue of *Arms Control*, 8(1).
9 The CWC, however, does contain three schedules of chemicals and precursors that identifies those which are subject to verification measures.
10 Rosenberg and Leitenberg, 'Who's afraid of a germ warfare treaty'.
11 D. Huxsoll, 'Narrowing the zone of uncertainty', in Raymond Zilinskas (ed.) *The Microbiologist and Biological Defence Research*, New York: New York Academy of Science, 1992.
12 Leitenberg, *Biological Weapons in the Twentieth Century*.
13 See as well L. Cole, *The Eleventh Plague*, New York: WH Freeman and Company, 1997 and K. Alibek and C. Baily, 'BioShield or biogap?', *Biosecurity and Bioterrorism* 2004, 2(2), 132–3.
14 J. King and H. Strauss, 'The hazards of defensive biological warfare programmes', in Susan Wright (ed.) *Preventing a Biological Arms Race*, Cambridge, MA: MIT Press, 1990, 120–32.
15 G. Cassell, L. Miller and R. Rest 'Biological warfare: role of scientific societies', in R. Zilinskas (ed.) *The Microbiologist and Biological Defence Research*, New York: New York Academy of Science, 1994, 233.
16 L. Wells, 'Policies and prospects', Presented at Meeting on National Security and Research in the Life Sciences National Academies and the Center for Strategic and International Studies (Washington, DC), 9 January 2003.
17 Leitenberg, *Biological Weapons in the Twentieth Century*.
18 Ibid.
19 C. Piller and K. Yamamoto, *Gene Wars*, New York: Beech Tree Books, 1988.
20 S. Wright and S. Ketcham, 'The problem of interpreting the US biological defense program', in Susan Wright (ed.) *Preventing a Biological Arms Race*, Cambridge, MA: MIT Press, 1990, 169–96.
21 Ibid., 191.
22 A point also made by Leitenberg, *Biological Weapons in the Twentieth Century*.
23 Huxsoll, 'Narrowing the Zone of Uncertainty', 185.
24 See, for example, B. Smith, T. Inglesby and T. O'Toole, 'Biodefence R&D', *Biosecurity and Bioterrorism*, 2003, 1(3), 193–202.
25 See G. Brumfiel and J. Knight, 'In the shadow of war', *Nature*, 2003, 426, 748–9 and Mae-Wan Ho, *Is Unregulated GE Research on Vaccines & Disease a Public Health Threat?*, Washington, DC: Organic Consumers Association, 2001. Available http://www.organicconsumers.org/patent/gevaccines120301.cfm (accessed on 29 December 2004); B. Hatch Rosenberg, 'Defending against biodefence: the need for limits', *Disarmament Diplomacy*, February/March 2003, 1–6 and E. Choffnes, 'Bioweapons: new labs, more terror?', *Bulletin of the Atomic Scientists*, September/October, 2002, 29–32.
26 M. Williams, 'The coming threat: bioweapons are much more prevalent and virulent than most of us realise. And we have little defense', *Acumen*, 2003, 1, 40–50.
27 BBC News, 'Interview with Brian Iddon', *The World at One*, 8 July 2002. Available http://news.bbc.co.uk/1/hi/programmes/world_at_one/2116155.stm (accessed on 14 November 2004).

28 See Cole, *The Eleventh Plague*.
29 Ben-Ami Scharfstein, *The Dilemma of Context*, London: New York University Press, 1989.
30 Of course, that sentence itself displays the 'same' reliance on similarity and difference. And so does the previous one. And so....
31 Grossberg, *We Gotta Get Out of this Place*, p. 397 in Jacobsen, 'Duelling Constructivism', 36–60.
32 As paralleling the intellectual exercises of Alfred Schultz.
33 Including the Naval Research Laboratory (Washington, DC) and the Armstrong Laboratory (Brooks Air Force Base, San Antonio, TX). See The Sunshine Project. 2002. *US Special Forces Seek Genetically Engineered Bioweapons*. 12 August (Austin, TX: Sunshine Project).
34 Harper, 'A call for a definition of method of warfare in relation to the Chemical Weapons Convention', *Naval Law Review*, 2001, XLVIII, 132–60.
35 Editorial, 'New technologies and the loophole in the Convention', *Chemical Weapons Convention Bulletin*, 1994, 23, 1–2.
36 See, for example, Sunshine Project, *Pentagon Program Promotes Psychopharmacological Warfare*, 1 July, Austin, TX: Sunshine Project, 2002 and Sunshine Project, *US Army Patents Biological Weapons Delivery System Violates Bioweapons Convention*, 8 May, Austin, TX: Sunshine Project, 2003.
37 Sunshine Project, *The Destabilizing Danger of 'Non-Lethal' Chemical and Biological Weapons in the War on Terrorism*, 19 September, Austin, TX: Sunshine Project, 2001.
38 Sunshine Project, *The Return of ARCAD*, 6 January, Austin, TX: Sunshine Project, 2004.
39 Sunshine Project, *US Plans for Use of Gas in Iraq*, 7 February, Austin, TX: Sunshine Project, 2003.
40 See 'Iraq weapons inspector David Kay's congressional testimony', *The Guardian*, 3 October 2003. Available www.guardian.co.uk (accessed on 11 July 2004).
41 See, for example, BBC News, 'Iraq report "proves case for war"', *BBC News*, 3 October 2003. Available http://news.bbc.co.uk/1/hi/uk_politics/3159366.stm (accessed on 4 October 2003).
42 It might be said that a similar importance is attached to context in what British Secretary of Defence Geoff Hoon said when interviewed for the BBC *Today Programme* on 5 February 2004:

JOHN HUMPHRYS: The new leader of that survey group, the man who resigned from leading that survey group a couple of weeks ago and the previous leader of that survey group, not one of those people believed that Saddam had those weapons – not just has but had those weapons of mass destruction – all three of them.

GEOFF HOON: What is actually important is what those of us responsible for taking those decisions believed and on the basis of a long history of intelligence material certainly provided to me I judged not on the basis of a snapshot provided to me in September 2002 but over many years of seeing week by week the relevant intelligence I judged and I still judge Saddam had access to weapons of mass destruction.

43 For instance, consider the following exchange between Prime Minister Blair and Donald Anderson MP during oral evidence given to the House of Commons Liaison Committee:

DONALD ANDERSON: Prime Minister, that is some way ahead surely, but it was clear on the evidence of David Kay to the Senate Committee that the inspection process of the UN inspectors had been remarkably successful. In short, the containment policy of President Clinton, which you had rejected, was working. Do you admit you were wrong?

MR BLAIR: I do not accept that is, Donald, if I can say this with respect, a proper description of what David Kay actually said.

DONALD ANDERSON: Let me quote what he says. He says in effect that all the consensus of those who were the weapons inspectors was that they had achieved a great deal. I think somewhere I have the quote.

MR BLAIR: I think what he actually says is that he pays tribute to their work and he says that they did achieve a great deal, but I actually have his quotes here and I thought I would bring them in because I thought you....

DONALD ANDERSON: Let me give you the quote. 'It turned out that we were better than we thought we were in terms of the Iraqis feared that we had capabilities. The UN inspection process achieved quite a bit'.

MR BLAIR: Yes, I do not dispute that, but that is not to say....

DONALD ANDERSON: That is, they had contained the weapons programme of Saddam Hussein and you were saying that the containment process had failed.

MR BLAIR: With respect, it is a different thing to say that they had achieved quite a bit than for him to say that the containment programme was working. If I could actually quote to you, he says this in fact in respect of the question put to him by Senator Warner: 'Senator Warner, I think the world is far safer with the disappearance and removal of Saddam Hussein. I have said I actually think this may be one of these cases where it was even more dangerous than we thought. I think when we have the complete record, you are going to discover that after 1988 it became a regime that was totally corrupt, individuals were out for their own protection and in a world where we know others are seeking WMD, the likelihood at some point in the future of a seller and a buyer meeting up would have made that a far more dangerous country than even we anticipated'.

DONALD ANDERSON: But that was surely some time in the future. He was saying that you had said consistently that the containment policy of your friend President Clinton had failed and, therefore, there needed to be a change of policy.

MR BLAIR: Exactly and if I can then read what he also says, and incidentally this may be of help to the Committee and I hope it will be of help to Parliament tomorrow, that I have asked the permission of Senator Warner to put in the Library of the House of Commons the full evidence of David Kay to the Senate Intelligence Committee, and I really ask people and I ask our media particularly to read the whole of that evidence because the idea that this is a man saying that weapons of mass destruction and Saddam Hussein were a load of boloney and nothing really existed, he is saying precisely the opposite of that. If I could just read this because it is important, and he says this....

DONALD ANDERSON: But briefly.

MR BLAIR: Well, I just think it is important that we deal with the point. 'In my judgment, based on the work that has been done to this point of the Iraq Survey Group, Iraq was in clear violation of the terms of Resolution 1441. Resolution 1441 requires that Iraq report all its activities, one last chance to come clean about what it had. We have discovered hundreds of cases based both on documents, physical evidence and the testimony of Iraqis....

DONALD ANDERSON: But it is not concluding that he was an imminent threat.

MR BLAIR: Well, I have not got this exact quote, and I will look it up, but he does in fact go on to say that he does perceive it as a threat. The point I am telling you, and, with respect, I think this is clear, what is true about David Kay's evidence, and this is something I have to accept and it is one of the reasons why I think we now need a further inquiry, it is true, David Kay is saying, that we have not found large stockpiles of actual weapons. What is untrue is to say that he is saying that there was no weapons of mass destruction programme or capability and that Saddam was not a threat.

HMSO. *House of Commons Hansard*, Minutes of evidence before the Liaison Committee, London: HMSO, 2003.

44 Ibid.

45 Following the quote by Tony Blair as part of oral evidence given to the House of Commons Liaison Committee in 2004, the exchange below took place where Blair's conclusion was thrown in doubt by other MPs:

> TONY WRIGHT: This matters because the legal basis for war that you were quite clear in advancing was the fact of weapons of mass destruction. Last July you told us, 'The truth is that to take action we had to have the proper legal basis and that was through the weapons of mass destruction issue. I accept entirely the legal basis for action was through weapons of mass destruction.' In the absence of weapons of mass destruction what happened to the legal basis for war?
>
> MR BLAIR: The legal basis is the breach of the UN Resolutions, that is the whole issue to do with weapons of mass destruction. If Saddam was continuing to develop weapons of mass destruction capability in breach of UN Resolutions then there is no doubt at all of the legal justification.
>
> MR BEITH: But the UN Resolutions were based on your having persuaded other countries in the UN of the reliability of our intelligence.
>
> MR BLAIR: It was not simply that, with respect, the question was whether there had been a breach of the UN Resolutions and the UN Resolutions were to do with the development of weapons of mass destruction and also to do with making full declarations to the UN inspectors, they were also to do with weapons of mass destruction programmes and they were to do with weapons of mass destruction capability. I have been honest enough to come along and say – and this is the reason for having a fresh inquiry – that I have to accept that Dr Kay, the head of the Iraq Survey Group, has said he has not found large stockpiles of weapons, I have admitted that, but the critics must also admit the rest of what he has said, which is that he has also said he has found evidence of weapons of mass destruction programmes, capability, Saddam's intention to develop those weapons and the breaches of the UN Resolution that that entails. So the legal basis of the action, with respect, if Dr Kay is right, is entirely secure because if you go through the UN Resolutions – and I have not got 1441 and 687 in front of me – there is a whole series of things that he was supposed to do and as Dr Kay says, the breaches of the UN Resolutions he has probably breached eight or ten times.
>
> TONY WRIGHT: Let us just try this another way because this gets a bit confusing, does it not?
>
> MR BLAIR: I think it is simple.

46 Interview with S. Ritter. BBC News, *Hardtalk*, 6 October 2003.

47 See as well A. Coghlan and D. Mackenzie, 'Is Iraq turning camelpox into a biological weapon?', *New Scientist*, 20 April 2002.

48 See, for instance, Grint and Woolgar, 'Computers, guns and roses: what's social about being shot', and especially Grint and Woolgar, *The Machine at Work*.

49 H. Garfinkel, *Studies in Ethnomethodology*, Cambridge: Polity, 1994 [1967], p. 78.

50 J. Heritage, *Garfinkel and Ethnomethodology*, Cambridge: Polity, 1984, p. 149.

51 What is missing from accounts is often just as important as what is included. Various commentators cited in this chapter and the previous one have contended that particular categorizations, classifications and contexts of weapons were forwarded for unmistakably self-interested reasons. Only once this is understood, it was said, could the true purpose of activities be assessed. Wright, for instance, draws on once restricted British and American government documentation to argue that the agreement of the BTWC in late 1960s and the early 1970s had little to do with reinforcing the proclaimed principles against the deliberate spread of disease or the importance of weapons disarmament (see S. Wright, in S. Wright (ed.) *Biological Warfare and*

Disarmament, London: Rowman and Littlewood, 2003, 313–42). Rather the selective focus on biological weapons at the time (instead of considering chemical or nuclear weapons disarmament) was a strategic calculation regarding what was in the national interests of these particular countries. The separation of biological weapons from these other categories of weapons enabled to the US and UK to appear concerned about issues of disarmament but continue activities they thought of military importance to their own nations. Just as the negotiation of prohibitions in the past were limited by publicly unspoken reasons, it could be argued that unstated interest-based considerations are at work today driving the classification and categorization of weapons and the interpretation of prohibitions. By not theorizing about the role of interests and according them a central place in explaining what is going on, some might suggest that this chapter is too abstract or idealist in its orientation to grasp the real issues at stake. As a necessarily partial way of knowing the world, any theory of interests proffered as an explanation for action, however, could itself be situated against a particular background and streams of intellectual explanatory thought.

7   Weapons: what do they do?

1 HMSO, *House of Commons Hansard*, 4 February 2004, Column 772.
2 See J. Guillemin, *Biological Weapons*, London: Columbia Press, 2005, Chapter 9.
3 T. Dupuy, *Numbers, Predictions and War*, New York: Bobbs-Merrill, 1979 and T. Dupuy, *The Evolution of Weapons and Warfare*, New York: Bobbs-Merrill, 1981.
4 R. Coupland and D. Meddings, 'Mortality associated with the use of weapons in armed conflicts, wartime atrocities, and civilian mass shootings', *British Medical Journal*, 1999, 319, 407–10.
5 B. Rappert, 'The distribution and the resolution of the ambiguities associated with technology, or why Bobby cannot spray', *Social Studies of Science*, 2001, 31, 556–67.
6 Office of Technology Assessment, *Proliferation of Weapons of Mass Destruction*, OTA-ISC-559 Washington, DC: OTA, 1993, 53–4.
7 For example, as in A. Cordesman and A. Burke, *Defending America*, Washington, DC: Center for Strategic and International Studies, 2001.
8 M. Leitenberg, 'An assessment of the threat of the use of biological weapons or biological agents', in M. Martellini (ed.) *Biosecurity and Bioterrorism*, Washington, DC: Landau Network Centro Volta, 2000. At the time of writing, for instance, the US government maintains that an American biodefence establishment insider(s) is probably the most plausible instigator of the 2001 anthrax attacks.
9 J.W. Crawford III, 'The law of noncombatant immunity and the targeting of national electrical power systems', *Fletcher Forum of World Affairs*, Summer/Fall 1997, 21, 101. Taken from Dunlop, 'Technology'.
10 A. Schutz, *Collected Papers* (Vol. 1), The Hague: M. Nijhoff, 1962.
11 Lord Hutton, *Report of the Inquiry into the Circumstances Surrounding the Death of Dr. David Kelly CMG*, 28 January 2004, Chapter 6.
12 Its full name being the Convention on Prohibitions or Restrictions on the Use of Certain Conventional Weapons Which May Be Deemed to Be Excessively Injurious or to Have Indiscriminate Effects.
13 International Committee of the Red Cross, *The SIrUS Project*, Geneva: ICRC, 1997, 8.
14 Rappert, *Non-Lethal Weapons as Legitimizing Forces?*.
15 International Committee of the Red Cross, *The SIrUS Project and Reviewing the Legality of New Weapons*, Geneva: ICRC, 1999 and R. Edwards, 'Humane killing', *New Scientist*, December 1999, vol. 164 Issue 2215 14.
16 Billig, *Arguing and Thinking*.
17 J. Goldblat, 'Anti-personnel mines: from mere restrictions to a total ban', *Security Dialogue*, 1999, 30, 9–23.
18 Landmine Action, *Civilian Footsteps*, London: Landmine Action, 2001.

19 German Initiative to Ban Landmines and Landmine Action, *Alternative Anti-Personnel Mines*, London: Landmine Action, 2001.
20 Human Rights Watch, *Human Rights Watch Position Paper on 'Smart' (Self-Destructing) Landmines*, 27 February, Washington, DC: Human Rights Watch, 2004.
21 L. Klotz, M. Furmanski and M. Wheelis, *Beware of the Siren's Song Why 'Non-Lethal' Incapacitating Chemical Weapons are Lethal*, March 2003. Available www.fas.org/bwc/papers/sirens_song.pdf (accessed on 15 April 2003).
22 See R. Reid, *Tongues of Conscience*, London: Constable, 1974, 316.
23 J. Rothschild, *Tomorrow's World*, New York: Mc-Graw Hill, 1964: 43 quoted from Reid, *Tongues of Conscience*.
24 N. Lee, 'The challenge of childhood', *Childhood*, 1999, 6, 455–74.
25 N. Tannenwald, 'The nuclear taboo', *International Organization*, 1999, 53, 433–68.
26 H. Stimson, 'The decision to use the bomb', *Harper's*, February 1947, 98 in Tannenwald, 'The nuclear taboo', 443.
27 P. Feaver, *Guarding the Guardians*, Ithaca, NY: Cornell University Press, 1992, 125 in T. Farrell and H. Lambert, 'Courting controversy', *Review of International Studies*, 2001, 27, 315.
28 Farrell and Lambert, 'Courting controversy', 319.
29 J. Gaddi, *The Long Peace*, Oxford: Oxford University Press, 1983.
30 T. Schelling, *The Strategy of Conflict*, Cambridge, MA: Harvard University Press, 1960.
31 Amnesty International, *Decisions of the 2003 Amnesty International Council Meeting*, August, London: AI-IS, 2003.
32 Ibid.
33 US Defense of Department, *Findings of the Nuclear Posture Review*, 6 January, Washington, DC: DoD, 2002.
34 R. Nelson, 'Lowering the threshold', in Brian Alexander and Alistair Millar (eds) *Tactical Nuclear Weapons*, Washington, DC: Brassey's, 2003; R. Nelson, 'Low-yield earth-penetrating nuclear weapons', *Science and Global Security*, 2002, 10(1), 1–20 and V. Sidel, H. Geiger, Abrams, R. Nelson and J. Loretz, *The Threat of Low-Yield Earth-Penetrating Nuclear Weapons to Civilian Populations: Nuclear 'Bunker Busters' and Their Medical Consequences*, Washington, DC: International Physicians for the Prevention of Nuclear War, 2003.
35 Alexander and A. Millar, *Tactical Nuclear Weapons*.
36 I. Safranchuk, 'Tactical nuclear weapons in the modern world', in B. Alexander and A. Millar (eds) *Tactical Nuclear Weapons*, Washington, DC: Brassey's, 2003.
37 International Court of Justice, *Legality of the Threat or Use of Nuclear Weapons*. The Hague: ICJ, 1996.
38 Ibid., article 36.
39 This in the absence of any specific prohibitions on nuclear weapons *per se*.
40 See International Court of Justice, *Legality of the Threat or Use of Nuclear Weapons*, Article 95 and also 94.
41 International Court of Justice, *Legality of the Threat or Use of Nuclear Weapons – Dissenting Opinion of Judge Koroma*. Available http://www.cornnet.nl/~akmalten/ukoroma.html (accessed on 13 August 2004).
42 International Court of Justice, *Legality of the Threat or Use of Nuclear Weapons*, Article 43.

8 Predicaments with prohibitions

1 See *American Heritage Dictionary of the English Language*, Fourth Edition. Boston, MA: Houghton Mifflin, 2000.
2 F. Nietzsche, *The Will to Power*, London: Weidenfeld & Nicolson, 1968.
3 See Billig, *Arguing and Thinking* and Michael Billig *et al.*, *Ideological Dilemmas*.

4 Sunshine Project, 'The destabilizing danger of "non-lethal chemical and biology weapons'.
5 Goodman, *Problems and Projects*, 444.
6 As was put to the author after raising critical issues about US policy in this area at *Thinking About the Unthinkable: The Impact of the Use of Weapons of Mass Destruction (WMD) – Chemical, Biological, Radiological and Nuclear- upon their International Non-Proliferation Regimes: A US-European Dialogue*, 26–27 June 2003.
7 Such a discussion took place in *The Impact of Use Upon the WMD Regimes – A Food for Thought Paper to Underpin a Discussions at the MCIS-IISS* Workshop, 26–27 June 2003.
8 Scharfstein, *The Dilemma of Context*.
9 10 Downing Street. 'Export Licences/Arms Sales'.
10 For an analysis of the latter, B. Latour, *Aramis*, London: Harvard University Press, 1996, Chapter 4.
11 Lee, 'The challenge of childhood'.
12 Heritage, *Garfinkel and Ethnomethodology*.
13 Edwards, *Discourse and Cognition*, p. 5.
14 See contributions in S. Wright (ed.), *Biological Warfare and Disarmament*, London: Rowman & Littlefield, 2001.
15 R. Price and N. Tannenwald, in P. Katzenstein (ed.) *The Culture of National Security*, New York: Columbia University Press, 1996, pp. 114–52.
16 T. Risse, in I. Katznelson and H. Milner (eds) *Political Science: The State of the Discipline*, London: WW Norton & Company, 2002.
17 Such as T. Farrell and T. Teriff (eds), *The Sources of Military Change*, London: Lynne Rienner, 2002; M. Finnemore, *National Interests and International Security*, Ithaca, NY: Cornell University Press, 1996; M. Finnemore and K. Sikkink, 'International norms dynamics and political change', *International Organization*, 1998, 52(4), 887–917; W. Jepperson and P. Katzenstien, 'Norms, identity and national security', in P. Katzenstein, *The Culture of National Security*, New York: Columbia University Press, 1996, 33–78; and H. Müller, 'Internalization of principles, norms and rules by governments', in V. Rittberger (ed.) *Regime Theory and International Relations*, Oxford: Clarendon Press, 1993.
18 K. Waltz, *Theory of International Relations*, Reading, MA: Addison-Wesley, 1979.
19 For a related discussion of these issues see T. Hopf, *Social Construction of International Politics*, London: Cornell University Press, 2004.
20 Bonner, 'Reflexivity and Interpretive Sociology'.
21 Again as inspired by Malcolm Ashmore, see Mulkay, 'Don Quixote's Double'.

9 Fractured worlds: the case of cluster munitions

1 C. Dickey, M. Dennis, B. Nadeau, A. Bernard and J. Barry, 'Seeds of Carnage: After the war in Kosovo, unexploded cluster bombs continue to kill and maim dozens of victims', *Newsweek International*, 2 August 1999.
2 Geneva Centre for Humanitarian Demining, *Explosive Remnants of War*, Geneva: GICHD, 2002, 3.
3 C. King, *Explosive Remnants of War*, Geneva: International Committee for the Red Cross, 2000.
4 See Landmine Action, *Explosive Remnants of War*, London: Landmine Action, 2002.
5 ICRC, *Explosive Remnants of War*, Geneva: ICRC, 2003.
6 Ibid.: 8.
7 T. McDonnell, 'Cluster bombs over Kosovo', *Arizona Law Review*, 2002, 44(1), 31–130.

8 Handicap International, *Cluster Munitions Systems: Situation and Inventory*, Paris: Handicap International, 2003, 33.

9 M. Hollestelle, *Explosive Ricochet*, 31 August, Utrecht, Pax Christi, 2003.

10 Mines Action Canada. *Mines Action Canada...Ban Landmines Now*. Available http://www.minesactioncanada.com/clusters/index.cfm?fuseaction = Start (accessed on 7 January 2005).

11 See as well V. Weibe, 'Footprints of death', *Michigan Journal of International Law*, 2000, 22(1), 85–167.

12 As reported, the manufacturer was compelled to name the weapons 'cargo ammunition' by the fair organizers because of the sensitivity of 'cluster bombs' in the UK. R. Norton-Taylor, 'Cluster bomb news', *The Guardian*, 9 September 2003.

13 Department of Defense. *DoD News Briefing Secretary Rumsfeld and Gen. Myers*, 21 April 2003.

14 As in Human Rights Watch, *Cluster Munitions: A Foreseeable Hazard in Iraq*, New York: Human Rights Watch, 2003.

15 FAIR, *That's Just the Way Life is in Iraq*, 6 May, Washington, DC: Fairness & Accuracy in Reporting, 2003.

16 Mines Action Canada, *Mines Action Canada...Ban Landmines Now*.

17 Indeed others have maintained cluster sub-munitions are more dangerous than APMs since the former are intended to kill whereas the latter generally maim. See Human Rights Watch, *Fatally Flawed: Cluster Bombs and their Use by the US in Afghanistan*, Washington, DC: Human Rights Watch, 2002.

18 Major T. Herthel, 'On the chopping block', *Air Force Law Review*, 2001, 22, 229–69.

19 See as well D. Kennedy and W. Kincheloe, 'Steel rain: submunitions in the desert', *US Army Journal*, 1993, 43: 24–31.

20 DoD, *DoD News Briefing*, 13 May 1999. Available http://www.defenselink.mil/transcripts/1999/t05131999_t0513asd.html (accessed on 13 June 2004).

21 King, *Explosive Remnants of War*, 36.

22 General Sir H. Beach, *Cluster Bombs: The Case for New Controls*, Brussels: ISIS Europe, 2001, 5.

23 R. Price, 'Reversing the gun sights', *International Organization*, 1998, 52(3), 613–44.

24 A group of NGOs met in Bad Honnef on 23–24 June 1997 and defined a mine as any device which possesses one or more of the following characteristics, it 'may be exploded through contact by, or presence or proximity of, a person or persons, and which is capable of killing, injuring or incapacitating one or more persons, any device or munition which, although its primary purpose or design may be other than specified... above, can be deployed in a manner to achieve such effect without modification or through a specific design feature, any device, including an anti-tank mine, which is fitted with an anti-handling, anti-disturbance or similar mechanism which will cause that device to be exploded through contact by, or presence or proximity of, a person or persons and which is capable of killing, injuring or incapacitating one or more persons'. Available http://www.landmine.de/en.titel/en.search.output/index.html?entry = ed.news.005e4d533f830000 (accessed on 17 December 2004).

25 R. McGrath, 'Clearing the clusters: why activists earlier failed to ban these bombs-and what must be done to stop their use now', *Newsweek International*, 2 August 1999. Available http://www.newsweek.com/nw-srv/printed/int/eur/ov1905_1.htm (accessed on 14 December 2004).

26 Mines Action Canada, *The Campaign Against Cluster Bombs*, Ottawa: MAC, 2001. Available http://www.minesactioncanada.org/documents/ct_cb_7june01.htm (accessed on 17 December 2004).

27 See as well *Guardian*, 6 September 2000 and Ploughshares, *Ploughshares Monitor*, September 1999. Available http://www.ploughshares.ca/content/MONITOR/mons99c.html (accessed on 17 December 2004).

28 J. Goldblat, 'Anti-Personnel mines: from mere restrictions to a total ban', *Security Dialogue*, 1999, 30, 14.
29 Mines Action Canada, *The Campaign Against Cluster Bombs*.
30 The ideas in this paragraph have derived from discussions with individuals debating campaigning strategies for cluster weapons.
31 US State Department, *New United States Policy on Landmines: Reducing Humanitarian Risk and Saving Lives of United States Soldiers*, 27 February, Washington, DC: Bureau of Political-Military Affairs, 2004.
32 See R. Kerber, 'Civilian danger: US is criticized for its plans to use land mines with timers', *Boston Globe*, 20 March 2003.
33 A position rejected by others, see Human Rights Watch, *New U.S. Landmine Policy: Questions and Answers*, 27 February, Washington, DC, Human Rights Watch, 2004.
34 House of Commons, *Research Paper – The Landmines Bill*, 98/74, 9 July, London: HMSO, 1998.
35 R. McGrath, 'A wasteland called peace', UK Campaign for a Transparent & Accountable Arms Trade Discussion Paper, 1999. Available http://www.icbl.org/resources/raejune99.html (accessed on 15 November 2004).
36 Billig, *Arguing and Thinking*.
37 Mines Action Canada, *The Campaign Against Cluster Bombs*.
38 As defined by in Protocol II of the CCW.
39 See Mennonite Central Committee, *Drop Today, Kill Tomorrow*, Akron, PA, Mennonite Central Committee, 1997 and UK Working Group on Landmines, *Cluster Bombs*, London, UK Working Group on Landmines, 2000.
40 Spellar, 'Cluster bombs' *House of Commons Hansard*, 24 January, London: HMSO, 2000, Column 60.
41 See Herthel, 'On the Chopping Block'.
42 R. McGrath, *Cluster Bombs: The Military Effectiveness and Impact on Civilians of Cluster Munitions*, London: Landmine Action, 2000.
43 See Handicap International, *Cluster Munitions Systems: Situation and Inventory*, Paris: Handicap International, 2003; R. McGrath, *Cluster Bombs: The Military Effectiveness on Civilians of Cluster Munitions*, Akron, PA: Mennonite Central Committee and UK Working Group on Landmines, 2000; and King, *Explosive Remnants of War*.
44 Lord Bach, 'Cluster bombs', *House of Lords Hansard*, 8 September, London: HMSO, 2003, Column WA44.
45 A. Ingram, 'Iraq', *House of Commons Hansard*, 5 May, London: HMSO, 2004, Column 1520W.
46 See HMSO, *House of Commons Hansard*, 15 July, London: HMSO, 2003, Column 191W.
47 See as well Wiebe, 'Footprints of death'.
48 See, for example, Ibid. and King, *Explosive Remnants of War*.
49 S. Goose, 'Cluster munitions: Towards a global solution', in *Human Rights Watch World Report*, New York: Human Rights Watch, 2004, 254.
50 See Human Rights Watch, *Fatally Flawed: Cluster Bombs and their Use by the US in Afghanistan*.
51 McGrath, 'A wasteland called peace'.
52 King, *Explosive Remnants of War*.
53 McDonnell, 'Cluster bombs over Kosovo', *Arizona Law Review*, 2002, 44(1), 55.
54 McGrath, 'A wasteland called peace'.
55 King, *Explosive Remnants of War*.
56 As in R. Norton-Taylor, 'Cluster bomb news', *The Guardian*, 9 September 2003. For figures on the comparative rate of injury to children and adults see ICRC, *Explosive Remnants of War*.

57 See G. Hoon, 'Iraq', *House of Commons Hansard*, 1 September, London: HMSO, 2003, 899W.

58 Wiebe, 'Footprints of death: cluster bombs as indiscriminate weapons under international humanitarian law'. See as well, how a narrow determination is given of humanitarian consequences for a country relative supportive of strict controls in Norway, *National Interpretation and Implementation of International Humanitarian Law with Regard to the Risk of Explosive Remnants of War* CCW/GGE/VI/WG.1/WP.3, 24 November 2003.

59 DoD. *DoD News Briefing*, 13 May 1999. Available http://www.defenselink.mil/transcripts/1999/t05131999_t0513asd.html (accessed on 11 May 2004).

60 See Wiebe, 'Footprints of death', 102 (Note 11).

61 G. Hoon, 'Iraq', *House of Commons Hansard*, 3 April 2003, London: HMSO, Column 107.

62 Indeed, in the Vietnam War CBU-24 bombs were said to be introduced for flank suppression as a more conventional, less inhumane, and more highly regarded in world opinion option compared to the proposed alternative of napalm. See M. Krepon, 'Weapons potentially inhumane: the case of cluster bombs', *Foreign Affairs*, 1974, 52(3), 595–611.

63 Christopher Greenwood QC, *Legal Issues Regarding Explosive Remnants of War* Group of Government Experts of States Parties to the Convention on Prohibitions or Restrictions on the Use of Certain Conventional Weapons Which May Be Deemed to Be Excessively Injurious or to Have Indiscriminate Effects CCW/GGE/I/WP.10, 23 May 2002, p. 8.

64 For examples of this see Handicap International, *Cluster Munitions Systems: Situation and Inventory and King, Explosive Remnants of War*.

65 Beach, *Cluster Bombs*, 3.

66 Herthel though has questioned the relevance of attempts to equate APMs with cluster sub-munitions by arguing that under customary international law APMs are not illegal, see Herthel, 'On the Chopping Block', 265.

67 Because of the large number of sub-munitions contained within a single 'cluster bomb', even if these weapons were to have the same failure rate as unitary bombs, they are likely to result in far more UXOs for a given attack.

68 See, for example, P. Leahy, 'Kosovo's deadly legacy', *Congressional Record*, 3 August, Washington, DC: US Congress, 1999, S10070-S10071.

69 Cohen, *Memorandum for the Secretaries of the Military Departments: Department of Defense Policy on Submunition Reliability*, Arlington, VA and Department of Defense.

70 Vietnam Veterans of America Foundation, *Proposed Protocol to Address Explosive Remnants of War*, 25 September 2001, slide 10 Quoted from Human Rights Watch, *Fatally Flawed: Cluster Bombs and their Use by the US in Afghanistan*.

71 McGrath, *Cluster Bombs: The Military Effectiveness on Civilians of Cluster Munitions*; Wiebe, 'Footprints of Death'; and King, *Explosive Remnants of War*.

72 Prokosch, *The Technology of Killing*, Chapter 4.

73 Human Rights Watch, *Off Target*.

74 Ibid., 57–61.

75 Norway *National Interpretation and Implementation of International Humanitarian Law with Regard to the Risk of Explosive Remnants of War*, CCW/GGE/VI/WG.1/WP.3, 24 November 2003.

76 Cohen, *Memorandum for the Secretaries of the Military Departments: Department of Defense Policy on Submunition Reliability* and A. Melita, 'Munitions Insights/Initiatives'. Available http://www.dtic.mil/ndia/2001munitions/melita.pdf (accessed on 3 March 2004).

77 Human Rights Watch, *Cluster Munitions: A Foreseeable Hazard in Iraq March*.

78 See Human Rights Watch, *Cluster Munitions: Measures to Prevent ERW and Protect Civilian Populations*, New York: Human Rights Watch, 2003.

79 Human Rights Watch, *Civilian Deaths in the NATO Air Campaign*.

80 As in J. Birgitte, Presentation to Cluster Munitions Coalition Conference 'Cluster Bombs – Effective Weapons or Humanitarian Foe?', 18 March 2004, Copenhagen.

81 McGrath, *Cluster Bombs: The Military Effectiveness on Civilians of Cluster Munitions*.

82 France, *Technical Improvements to Submunitions*, Group of Government Experts of States Parties to the Convention on Prohibitions or Restrictions on the Use of Certain Conventional Weapons Which May Be Deemed to Be Excessively Injurious or to Have Indiscriminate Effects CCW/GGE/II/WP.6, 10 July 2002, 2.

83 Ibid., 2.

84 China and the Russia Federation, *Technical Improvements to Ammunitions to Prevent and Reduce ERW*, Group of Government Experts of States Parties to the Convention on Prohibitions or Restrictions on the Use of Certain Conventional Weapons Which May Be Deemed to Be Excessively Injurious or to Have Indiscriminate Effects CCW/GGE/II/WP.20, 23 July 2002, 1.

85 As called for in France, *Technical Improvements to Submunitions*, 3.

86 ICRC, *Explosive Remnants of War*, 39.

87 France, *Technical Improvements to Submunitions*, 1.

88 Ibid., 2.

89 Human Rights Watch, *Cluster Munition and International Humanitarian Law*, Prepared for the Convention on Certain Conventional Weapons (CCW) Group of Governmental Experts on Explosive Remnants of War, 5–16 July 2004.

90 The strategy of drawing attention to areas of contention rather than taking a stance on them arguably differentiated the request at the CCW from the position taken in some earlier reports by Human Rights Watch. For instance, in Human Rights Watch, *Fatally Flawed*:

- Cluster bombs should not be used in or near populated or urban areas. The definition of a populated area should include inhabited towns and villages as well as cities…
- Whatever the dud rate, militaries should consider the long-term effects of cluster bombs when choosing targets. They should be particularly careful about using cluster bombs in areas to which civilians may return or in environments that increase the dud rate, such as soft terrain.

91 Ibid., 8.

92 Ibid., 3.

93 For a supporting legal argument to this position see Wiebe, 'Footprints of Death'.

94 T. Peachey, *The Case for a Ban on Cluster Munitions*, December, Akron, PA: Mennonite Central Committee, 2003.

95 Human Rights Watch, *Cluster Munition and International Humanitarian Law*, 4.

96 Mennonite Central Committee, *Clusters of Death*.

97 One of the author's fields notes reads as follows: 'A family in Nong Oh Village, Xieng Khuong province, Laos watched their one son die and their one daughter be injured by a cluster bomb. They were working in the fields when they accidentally hit a bomblet with a digger. The explosion killed the young boy (age 8), and sent shrapnel into the brain of the daughter (age 12). The daughter survived but remains mentally handicapped. The location of the shrapnel makes it impossible to operate'. Ibid.

98 Ibid.

99 Mines Action Canada, 'Reducing the impact of cluster bombs – what can be done?' Geneva Forum Seminar, 8 July 2004.

100 Ibid.

101 Goose, 'Cluster munitions: towards a global solution'.
102 Noting the elements of the classes may not coincide.

10 Dealing with unfinished business

 1 My thanks to Chris Greenwood QC for the source of this quote.
 2 And, of course, those not convinced of the relevance of the concept of 'disposal strategies' might well find it can be thrown away.
 3 The problems with denial also work against claims that the development or use of weapons is inevitably acceptable, though this point is rarely made.
 4 Though, in this regard it should be noted that Amnesty International is not a pacifist organization.
 5 J.P. Zanders, 'International norms against chemical and biological warfare', *Journal of Conflict and Security Law*, 2003, 8(2), 391–410.
 6 Greenwood, *Legal Issues Regarding Explosive Remnants of War*.
 7 On the latter, see Lee, 'The challenge of childhood'.
 8 Oral evidence by Jack Straw, *Second Joint Report*.
 9 HMSO, *Response of the Secretaries of State for Defence, Foreign and Commonwealth Affairs, International Development and Trade and Industry to the Strategic Export Controls: Annual Report for 2001*, Licensing Policy and Parliamentary Scrutiny. London: HSMO, 2003, p. 16–17.
10 This following Lee's work on institutional legitimacy (Lee, 'The challenge of childhood') and Grint and Woolgar's (*The Machine at Work*) post-essentialist theory of technology.
11 BBC News, 'UK tightens Israel arms exports', *BBC News*, 27 August 2002.
12 C. Lindblom and E. Woodhouse, *The Policy Making Process*, 3rd Edition, Englewood Cliffs, NJ: Prentice Hall, 1993, p. 61.
13 BBC News. Interview with James Rubin, *BBC News 24*, 27 March 2003. These comments were made in relation to the vague terms in draft proposals be circulated at the attempts at the time by the US for an UN Security Council Resolution justifying military invasion of Iraq.
14 Harper, 'A call for a definition of method of warfare in relation to the Chemical Weapons Convention'.
15 R. Falk, 'Nuclear weapons, international law and the World Court', *American Journal of International Law*, 1997, 91(1), 64–75.
16 This analysis has itself relied on strategies of deferral and delay, such as in the pervasive use of foot noting and referencing which offer sources for the future validation of my arguments through following the arguments of others.
17 See Actiongroup Landmine.de *Why Anti-Vehicle Mines should also be Banned* Available http://www.landmine.de/en.titel/en.news/en.news.one/index.html?entry= en.news.009732781a360000 (accessed on 23 October 2004).
18 As in German Initiative to Ban Landmines & Landmine Action, *Alternative Anti-Personnel Mines*, London: Landmine Action, 2001.
19 B. Balmer, 'How does and accident become and experiment', *Science as Culture*, 2004, 13(2), 197–225.

11 Troubles with humanitarian prohibitions

 1 E. Leed. *No Man's Land*, Cambridge: Cambridge University Press, 1979, p. 21.
 2 Taken from the 1868, *Declaration of St Petersburg*.
 3 Ibid.
 4 R. Rorty, *Consequences of Pragmatism (Essays 1972–1980)*, Brighton: The Harvester Press, 1982, p. xli.

5 Y. Lapid, 'Culture's ship', in Y. Lapid and F. Kratochwil (eds) *The Return of Culture and Identity in IR Theory*, London: Boulder, 1996, p. 8.
6 C. Rues-Smit, 'Constructivism', in *Theories of International Relations*, 2nd edition, London: Palgrave, 2001.
7 General Secretariat of the Council, *Amended proposal for a Council Regulation concerning trade in certain equipment and products which could be used for capital punishment, torture or other cruel, inhuman or degrading treatment or punishment.* 8 June, Brussels: DG E III, External Economic Relations, 2004.
8 Ibid., Annex II.
9 W.M. Reisman and C. Antoniou, *The Laws of War*, New York: Vintage, 1994.
10 To quote from 10 Downing Street. 'Export Licences/Arms Sales'.
11 D. Briggs, *Minutes of evidence for the House of Lords Select Committee on the European Union – Proposal to Ban Trade in Products Used for Capital Punishment or Torture*, 11 January, London: HMSO, 2005.
12 To paraphrase Wittgenstein discussion of rules.
13 Despite suggestions elsewhere as in R. Iedema, 'Formalizing organizational meaning'. *Discourse and Society*, 1999, 10(1), 49–65.
14 Tannenwald, 'The nuclear taboo'.
15 Price, *The Chemical Weapons Taboo*.
16 For a consideration of such logics see M. Finnemore and K. Sikkink, 'International norms dynamics and political change'.
17 J. Checkel, 'Norms, institutions and national identity in contemporary Europe', *International Studies Quarterly*, 1999, 43, 83–144.
18 C. Gray, *House of Cards: Why Arms Control Must Fail*, Ithaca, NY: Cornell University Press, 1992.
19 C. Reus-Smit, 'Imagining society', *British Journal of Politics and International Relations*, 2002, 4, 487–509 and C. Rues-Smit, 'Constructivism', in *Theories of International Relations*, 2nd edition, London: Palgrave, 2001.
20 As in Finnemore and Sikkink, 'International norms dynamics and political change'.
21 Finnemore and Sikkink, 'International norms dynamics and political change', 93.
22 Price, 'Reversing the gun sights', 628.
23 Ibid.
24 S. Hilgartner, *Science on Stage*, Stanford, CA: Stanford University Press, 2000.
25 Facts that might be needed to substantiate claims about the uniqueness of the effects cluster bombs that would provide the basis for a separate Protocol under the CCW.
26 My thanks to Thomas Nash and Rae McGrath for their comments on earlier drafts of this document.
27 For example, Goose, 'Cluster munitions: towards a global solution'.

Selected bibliography

B. Alexander and A. Millar (eds), *Tactical Nuclear Weapons*, Washington, DC: Brassey's, 2003.

Amnesty International (UK), *Repression Trade (UK) Limited*, London: Amnesty International (UK), 1992.

M. Billig, *Arguing and Thinking*, Cambridge: Cambridge University Press, 1996.

L. Cole, *The Eleventh Plague*, New York: W.H. Freeman and Company, 1997.

H. Collins and T. Pinch, *The Golem at Large*, Cambridge: Cambridge University Press, 1998.

M. van Creveld, *Technology and War*, London: MacMillan, 1991.

S. Croft, *Strategies of Arm Control*, Manchester: Manchester University Press, 1996.

M. Dando, *The New Biological Weapons*, London: Lynee Rienner, 2001.

C. Dunlop, 'Technology: recomplicating moral life for the nation's defenders', *Parameters*, 1999, Autumn, 24–53.

T. Farrell, *Weapons Without a Cause*, London: Macmillan, 1996.

T. Farrell and T. Teriff (eds), *The Sources of Military Change*, London: Lynne Rienner, 2002.

S. Goose, 'Cluster munitions: towards a global solution', in *Human Rights Watch World Report*, New York: Human Rights Watch, 2004.

C. Gray, *House of Cards: Why Arms Control Must Fail*, Ithaca, NY: Cornell University Press, 1992.

K. Grint and S. Woolgar, *The Machine at Work*, Cambridge: Polity Press, 1999.

J. Guillemin, *Biological Weapons*, London: Columbia Press, 2005.

Handicap International, *Cluster Munitions Systems: Situation and Inventory*, Paris: Handicap International, 2003.

Human Rights Watch, *Fatally Flawed: Cluster Bombs and their Use by the US in Afghanistan*, Washington, DC: Human Rights Watch, 2002.

Human Rights Watch, *Off Target*, New York: Human Rights Watch, 2003.

International Committee of the Red Cross, *Explosive Remnants of War*, Geneva: ICRC, 2003.

D. Jenkins, *The Final Frontier*, London: Verso, 2002.

P. Katzenstein (ed), *The Culture of National Security*, New York: Columbia University Press, 1996.

R. Malcolmson, *Nuclear Fallacies*, Kingston: McGill-Queen's University, 1995.

Mennonite Central Committee, *Drop Today, Kill Tomorrow*, Akron, PA: Mennonite Central Committee, 1997.

J. Miller, S. Engelberg and W. Broad, *Germs*, New York: Simon & Schuster, 2001.

R. Price, *The Chemical Weapons Taboo*, Ithaca, NY: Cornell University Press, 1997.

E. Prokosch, *The Technology of Killing*, London: Zed, 1995.

B. Rappert, *Non-Lethal Weapons as Legitimizing Forces?: Technology, Politics and the Management of Conflict*, London: Frank Cass, 2003.

C. Reus-Smit, 'Imagining society', *British Journal of Politics and International Relations*, 2002, 4, 487–509.

T. Risse, 'Constructivism and international institutions: toward conversations across paradigms', in I. Katznelson and H. Milner (eds), *Political Science: The State of the Discipline*, London: WW Norton & Company, 2002.

V. Rittberger (ed.), *Regime Theory and International Relations*, Oxford: Clarendon Press, 1993.

J. Rotbalt (ed.), *Nuclear Weapons: The Road to Zero*, Basingstoke: Macmillan, 1998.

B. Scharfstein, *The Dilemma of Context*, London: New York University Press, 1989.

T. Smith, 'The new law of war: legitimizing hi-tech and infrastructural violence', *International Studies Quarterly*, 2002, 46, 355–74.

N. Tannenwald, 'The nuclear taboo', *International Organization*, 1999, 53, 433–68.

C. Townshend (ed.), *The Oxford Illustrated History of Modern War*, Oxford: Oxford University Press, 1997.

V. Weibe, 'Footprints of death', *Michigan Journal of International Law*, 2000, 22(1), 85–167.

M. Wheelis and M. Dando, 'Back to bioweapons?', *Bulletin of the Atomic Scientists*, 2003, 59(1), 40–6.

S. Wright (ed.), *Biological Warfare and Disarmament*, London: Rowman & Littlefield, 2001.

J.P. Zanders, 'International norms against chemical and biological warfare', *Journal of Conflict and Security Law*, 2003, 8(2), 391–410.

R. Zilinskas (ed.), *The Microbiologist and Biological Defense Research*, New York: New York Academy of Science, 1992.

Index

abolitionist 20
Afghanistan 28–9, 149
Air Force Magazine (US) 20
al-Qaeda 28, 33
American Society for Microbiology 87
Amnesty International 5–7, 9, 65, 116,
    163–4
anthrax 50, 105
anti-personnel mines 111–12, 130, 143–8,
    169–70, 181–2; definition 144, 146–7;
    relation to anti-tank mines 114; 'smart'
    versus 'dumb' distinction 112
Anti-personnel Mines Convention
    111–12, 130, 139, 143–8, 155,
    170, 181
Army Medical Research Institute of
    Infectious Disease (US) 86
artillery 48
atomic weapons 48

Barnes, B. 62–3
Bauman, Z. 16–17
Berlusconi, S. 37
Billig, M. 52, 77
biodefense 51; distinction from offense
    85–9, 129, 171
Biological and Toxin Weapons Convention
    20–1, 51, 82–8, 91, 181; general
    purpose criterion 85, 128
biological weapons 89, 92–9, 103–4,
    128, 164
Blair, T. 37, 79, 97, 103–4, 107
Bonner, K. 14
British Aerospace 74, 79
Bush, George W. 27–33, 97–8

Carrol, L. 55
categorizing 61–5, 77–9, 111–12,
    125–7, 130

Chemical Warfare Service (US) 47
chemical weapons 46–8, 51–2, 58, 94–5,
    103–4, 112–13, 128, 164
Chemical Weapons Convention 94–5, 128,
    168, 184–5
Cheney, D. 32
Chidgey, D. 8–10
Chomsky, N. 31–3
classification 16–7, 56, 124–5, 175–8
Clausewitz, C. von 45
Clinton, W. 155
cluster munitions (or cluster bombs) 17,
    19–20, 44, 59, 168, 180, 182, 184–96;
    country policies 154–5, 187–8;
    a description of 138–9; design 142,
    145; as mine like 139–43, 153;
    reliability 139, 142, 147–50, 154, 155,
    157–8, 188, 195; technical fixes 139,
    154–5
Cluster Munitions Coalition 19,
    138, 193
CNN 55
Committees on Strategic Export Controls
    (UK House of Commons – also known
    as the Quadripartite Committee) 9–10,
    12, 70–1, 74, 79, 167
Conservative government (UK) 6, 80
Consolidated EU and National Arms
    Export Licensing Criteria 66–7,
    71–3, 166
context 25, 71–3, 78–9, 81, 89–94,
    126–9; of battlefield 110–11;
    documentary method of
    interpretation 99–100; in purpose
    88–90
Convention on Certain Conventional
    Weapons 59–61, 108–9, 111–12, 147,
    152, 156–7, 164–5, 195
CS gas 50